CBW
CHEMICAL AND BIOLOGICAL WARFARE

The London Conference on CBW
held under the auspices of the
J. D. Bernal Peace Library

A

CBW
CHEMICAL AND BIOLOGICAL WARFARE

London Conference on CBW

edited by
STEVEN ROSE

GEORGE G. HARRAP & CO. LTD
London · Toronto · Wellington · Sydney

First published in Great Britain 1968
by GEORGE G. HARRAP & CO. LTD
182 High Holborn, London, W.C.1

SBN 245 59485 X

Composed in Linotype Times and printed at the
St Ann's Press, Altrincham
Made in Great Britain

FOREWORD

This book is based on the collection of papers presented to the Conference on Chemical and Biological Warfare which was held in the Bonnington Hotel, London, on February 22nd and 23rd, 1968. The aim of the Conference was to provide an authentic assessment of the present level of development of chemical and biological weapons, their manner of use in war, and the possibilities of defence against them; to consider the status of such weapons in international law; and to discuss ethical problems, especially the responsibility of the scientist, in relation to their development and use.

The Conference was the first major event to be sponsored by the J. D. Bernal Peace Library, an educational trust set up to collect source material and to provide information of assistance in the struggle for peace and toward ensuring the realization of the fullest potentialities of science in building a world prosperous and without war—aims toward which J. D. Bernal has made a unique contribution.

The Conference took place against a background of the use of defoliants and so-called non-toxic chemical weapons in Vietnam and the reported use of more lethal gases in the Yemen. The discussions at the Conference indicated the practicability of the renunciation of CBW by all the major powers at a time when there is still no major investment of money and personnel in this field. It is in the hope that the spread of factual knowledge about the nature and menace of these weapons will further the campaign for their elimination and for more complete disarmament that these papers are being published.

E. H. S. BURHOP

LONDON
May, 1968

PREFACE

The aim of the Conference whose proceedings form this book was a clear one. While we were concerned to amass as substantial a body of information as possible on current developments in chemical and biological warfare, our object was primarily to help inform opinion and stimulate discussion on the political, military, legal, and moral implications of the research, and on development, stockpiling, and use of chemical and biological weapons in a period of nuclear stalemate when it appears military strategists are placing increasing weight on the potential of these weapons. We attempted —and I have attempted as editor of this book—to separate the presentation of the facts about CBW as a potential and actual war technology, from our assessment of its implications. Such a distinction is of course at best artificial, and its artificiality will be apparent to the reader. It is not really possible to isolate a weapon or a technology from the political or moral climate in which it is made or used. None the less, in military and legal terms, and in the popular imagination, the chemical and biological weapons, like nuclear weapons, have been so isolated, presenting a separate class of problems.

In the Conference, each of these several themes was dealt with in a separate paper, and discussion—often lengthy—followed. In converting the conference texts into book form, I have omitted some few of the papers which seemed to me to be too specialized for a general readership, have slightly edited the individual papers to reduce them in length and to impose a certain uniformity in presentation, and have ruthlessly pruned the discussions which followed the papers, either incorporating points wholesale into the texts, or summarizing the essential themes as they appeared to me at the time or on rereading the transcripts afterwards. All the participants have cheerfully acceded to this procedure, and I must thank them for their participation. I can only hope that the resultant book is readable without losing completely the flavour of a Conference with its implied differences of viewpoint and of personality.

In the task of both planning the Conference and turning its proceedings into a literate and readable text, the Conference committee, chaired by Professor Eric Burhop and including Mr Bill Carritt, Mr Robin Clarke, Dr John Humphrey and Dr Vic Sidel, has provided consistent support; Mr David Pavett has undertaken the major tasks of checking manuscripts and references; and the services provided by Mr Colin Sweet and the Bernal Library have immeasurably lightened the load. I must particularly thank Mr Bert Ede, who recorded our proceedings, and Mrs Margaret Stern, Mrs Anita Taylor, and Mrs Naomi Wolff, who typed and transcribed against an ever-pressing time limit. Mr. Peter Sommer, of Harrap's, has most efficiently handled the task of getting a book which was being almost continuously updated even as it passed through the printer's hands so rapidly into press.

Because of the rapidity with which events have moved even in the few months since the Conference, and the amount of further information that has become available, it has proved possible and necessary to revise some of the papers; statements that were merely guesses in February—particularly about the activities of Porton—can now be documented accurately. This revision has been done where possible without affecting the format of the individual papers by means of editorial insertions. In one or two cases, especially Chapter 9, it has seemed proper to insert substantial additional material. I must take full editorial responsibility for any errors, of fact or interpretation, that these changes may have produced.

STEVEN ROSE

LONDON
August 1968

CONTENTS

PART FIVE: ETHICAL PROBLEMS

ILLUSTRATIONS

between pages 56 *and* 57

CBW Research

The mass-production of anthrax by the batch method at the Microbiological Research Establishment, Porton Down.

The '8-ball' aerosol test sphere.

6,000 sheep accidentally destroyed by nerve gas.
Fort Detrick, Maryland.

Chemical Defence Experimental Establishment, Porton Down.

CBW in Use

Grenade of CS.

Gas-mask

The 'Mighty Mite'

A USAF C-123 *Provider* on a defoliation mission.

TABLES

INTRODUCTION

Lord Ritchie-Calder

It is most appropriate that this Conference should be one of the initial activities of the J. D. Bernal Peace Library. In fact I can say: "This is where I came in . . ."

As my MI5 record shows, over thirty years ago, I was involved with Desmond Bernal and a group of scientists who were exposing the near-cynicism of the Air Raid Precautions. We had managed to get hold of one of the gas-masks which were to be issued in the event of war. I was writing about it, but I was also addressing meetings, tailed by a faithful shadow from the Special Branch. One of the things which I was showing was that the charcoal snout was no protection against arsenical smokes. I stood in front of a screen, had a spotlight thrown on me, and filled my mouth with tobacco smoke and put on the gas-mask. I then breathed out through the canister, and the audience could see the smoke curling up. The then Home Secretary, Sir Samuel Hoare, took a poor view of these activities and he denounced me in the House of Commons. He said arsenical smokes would only make one sick. Whereupon I challenged him to go into a gas-chamber and have the experience of being sick in a gas-mask! But the result was that when the millions of civilian gas-masks were issued on the outbreak of war they all had anti-smoke wafers strapped on to the snouts with sticking-plaster.

That was kindergarten stuff compared with the situation today, but security is still as childish. There has been a conspiracy of silence about these activities which are as fraught with mischief and ultimate peril as the development of nuclear armaments. The Doomsday Bug is under wraps!

The conspiracy is not confined to military security. Some scientists themselves shy away from the implications. One knows of distinguished scientists who can be as forthright as the rest in denouncing nuclear weapons but will avoid the subject of chemical and biological warfare, especially biological warfare. It is quite irrational. Although they may not be dealing with official secrets and their own academic thinking is not classified, they can only guess, with uncomfortable perception, at the military applications. It is a psychological inhibition. They simply do not want to believe that their fundamental work can be perverted.

Perhaps they are preserving their innocence, like the schoolboy who said he was going to be a biologist: "Physics is bombs. Chemistry's insecticides. Biology is about life." Perhaps they do not want to believe it is about death.

This is another crisis of the scientific conscience. Between the Wars Sir Richard Gregory, at the British Association for the Advancement of Science, pointed out that in a chemical dictionary mustard gas and chloroform were on the same page—the malevolent and the benevolent. But the chemist who discovered mustard gas was just as guiltless as the chemist who discovered chloroform; others took the results of science and perverted them. That was relatively true until the nuclear physicists took the initiative over the bomb. It was they—including Einstein, the lifelong pacifist—who impressed upon the policy-makers and the generals the possibilities of turning the laboratory discovery by Hahn and Strassman into a cataclysmic weapon. And the physicists were left with that guilt-sense.

But the same sort of thing was also happening in biology during the War. It has been said that agricultural science has produced an innocent weed-killer which has been transformed into a defoliant. But from my wartime experience I recognized the post-war commercial weed-killer as one of the secret weapons which wartime scientists had dreamed up as anti-crop warfare.

Certainly scientists enlisted for war were not overburdened with scruples. Perhaps the Allied scientists did not lend themselves as the Germans did, to putting people into gas-chambers or using concentration-camp victims for trying out nerve gases and new diseases, but they 'went along' with biological warfare. One of the principals in Canadian Chemical and Biological Warfare revealed in 1949 that "one bacteriological weapon developed late in the second World War could wipe out all human life in a given area within six hours and yet leave the area habitable afterwards. . . . While it kills everybody in six hours, it itself is oxidized in twelve hours, leaving the ground perfectly safe to occupy. . . ."[1]

In fact, it was *botulinus* toxin that was being described. Botulin became part of a double bluff during the War. Supplies existed and might have been used, but only if the Germans had first used something of the same—a principle affirmed by both Churchill and Roosevelt in relation to CBW. So we contrived to 'serve notice' on the Germans. Certain Canadian servicemen were briefed that if taken prisoner they would, in addition to name, rank, and number, reluctantly disclose that they had been vaccinated against botulin. A dicey game of poker! It could have meant (as we intended it to) "Don't do anything rash, chum, or else. . . ." Or it might have provoked a pre-emptive strike, and we would have been in a chemical and biological war.

By that time, we were nervous about CBW. Hitler's major secret weapons—the V1 and V2—had failed, and he was being pushed towards that ultimate culmination in the Berlin bunker. Gas had not been used by either side, but it certainly existed—a fact of which the disaster to the gas-supply ship in Bari was a reminder. Another was when a German shell hit an Allied gas-shell dump in the Anzio bridgehead and the gas started drifting towards the German lines. The Allied commander had to use the hot-line technique to his opposite number saying it was an accident and there was no intention to use gas. We may have had to wait until our scientific search parties went into defeated Germany to discover such refinements as the anti-cholinesterases *sarin, tabun,* and *soman,* but even allowing for any imprecisions of our espionage system, we knew they had them. Why? Because, of course, we had similar chemical weapons. That is how one works in CBW— seeing the other side's potential in the mirror of one's own. What we feared was that Hitler, once he had decided that the German people were not worthy of him, would unleash a CBW *Gotter-damerung.* Then, apart from gas-destruction, we might have had a modern Black Death.

Frederic Joliot-Curie suggested 'The Secret War' over twenty years ago. He extended the example of nuclear security to biological security. Behind the sky-high walls of secrecy the scientists had produced the Bomb. They had condoned the secrecy, so that it became the physicists' Bigger and Better Bomb, without any account being taken of the biological effects of radiation, without any of the premonitions, safeguards, and interdisciplinary reminders that come from free scientific exchanges—and without any sanctions on its use which proper information exerts. One recalls Attlee's statement, as one who had concurred in the dropping of the bomb on Hiroshima: "We knew nothing whatever at that time about the genetic effects of an atomic explosion. I knew nothing at all about fall-out and all the rest that emerged after Hiroshima. As far as I know, President Truman and Winston Churchill knew nothing of these things either, nor did Sir John Anderson who co-ordinated research on our side. Whether the scientists directly concerned knew, or guessed, I do not know. But if they did, then so far as I know they said nothing of it to those who had to make the decision." And in the entire documentation of the British atomic energy effort there was only one brief paper (by the Medical Research Council) on genetic effects, and that apropos not of the bomb but of the use of radioactive elements as a form of biological warfare.[2]

What Joliot-Curie did was to extend the lessons to biology. He pointed out that such a war need never be declared. It could go on for years with only the hidden aggressors knowing what was happening. Then, gradually, successive crop failures, devastation of herds by disease, human epidemics (unexplained because the organisms weren't in the books), and a catastrophic fall in the birthrate, through the sterilization of women by tampering with the water supply, would reveal the truth.

What Joliot-Curie was arguing for was a full scientific disclosure to alert mankind. But in the 'Through-the-looking-glass' world of military expediency the same arguments are used to justify secrecy —Don't put ideas into people's heads!

Thus 'defence' becomes building up stockpiles of chemical and biological weapons. If the Microbiological Research Establishment at Porton is no more than a means of protecting us against threatened diseases, why is it not under the Ministry of Health? If we pursue this further, and we must, we shall find, as the Americans found for their own institutions, that there is a whole network of relationships between Porton and the universities and research institutions, contracts and grants ostensibly for academic research with the right to publish—but not if the Ministry of Defence chooses to classify it! (This prophecy has now proved correct. *Ed*.)

The issues involved are not only the ultimate threat of world war with no holds barred—the ABC war, Atomic, Biological, Chemical—but the corrosion of our attitudes to evil. I return again to the censorship, self-imposed, by the scientists who 'just don't want to think about it.' Many of them, unless they are bereft of imagination, must know that their fundamental work, their 'pure' science, is being corrupted in this way. They knew the implications of DNA, molecular biology, gene manipulation, of their basic chemistry, and they must know also that intensive work on the practical applications of such work is going on in 'defence' establishments. Even if they are not participating, they are accessories before the fact, and they must be frank about this.

But we cannot be too hard on them when those who are concerned with peace and war also duck this issue. One may say "Oh, Lord, I've enough to worry about without *that*!" but while we are wrestling with non-proliferation and nuclear restraints—very important it is true—no systematic work towards CBW control is proceeding. Pious resolutions, yes, but that is where it stops. It belongs to that tomorrow when we shall get agreements on general and complete disarmament.

Meanwhile, as they say in the United States, "C.B.W. ought to have better public relations". What they mean by that is that people should be taught to approve of napalm, defoliation, 'police-gas', and so on. This aims to produce the acquiescence of ignorance, which leads to escalation and the legitimization of the next stage—the point where the military can do what they like. It is an easy progression from justifying the defoliation of jungle so as to deprive guerrillas of cover to 'treating' hundreds of thousands of acres of rice-crops to deprive guerrillas— and the people—of food. And to awarding the highest U.S. civilian medal to a woman scientist who discovered a better riceblast fungus —more effective, that is, than the natural disease which has in the past destroyed Asian rice-crops and killed millions by famine.

We get bland terms like 'humane' and 'anti-bellicose' gases, which include two categories which, in U.S. Army Chemical Corps circles, are jocosely called 'off the rocker' and 'on the floor'—a homely way of describing psychochemicals and paralysers. And if they won't stay on the floor there are the proper lethal gases too.

We have had conventions. At least the Americans are 'legal'; they have not signed the Geneva Protocol. But Britain, Australia, and Canada are signatories, although they exercise the reservation on the right of reciprocity. If one is going to reciprocate one must have something to reciprocate with, and thus one justifies peacetime research and stockpiling. And Britain, Australia, and Canada have a quadripartite agreement with the United States.

But surely the greatest conscience casualty is science itself. While one group of scientists are bending their energies to prevent diseases, another is devising man-made epidemics. While one set is discarding chemicals saying "We dare not use that," another is picking them out of the trash-can and saying "You bet we can!"

This is the Jekyll and Hyde of science.

PART ONE

THE WEAPONS

B

1. Chemical Weapons   J. Perry Robinson

Most of the weapons used today are chemical. The explosion of
TNT is a chemical reaction, so is the combustion of napalm. But
we are concerned here with those weapons which are based on the
toxic properties of chemicals rather than on the energetics of their
interaction. In arming ourselves with them we are following the
lead of the humble ant or snake.

A weapon-system based on toxic chemicals may be looked at
as the sum of four parts: (i) a system to deliver the munitions;
(ii) munitions to disseminate the chemical agent; (iii) the agent
itself; and (iv) the part played by the environment in transporting
the disseminated chemical to each target individual. It must be
stressed that each target is an individual, and that the weapons
we are talking about are purely anti-personnel.

Each of the four parts is dependent to a greater or lesser extent
on the other parts. If an attacker is relying on the atmosphere to
transport the agent to the target individual's lungs, the agent chosen
must be one which can be made airborne in a form which will
penetrate the lungs. If the chosen agent is one which is sensitive
to heat, then the chosen munition must avoid it. This interdepen-
dence must be kept in mind in what follows.

The available chemical agents

In 1956, Edgewood Arsenal, the U.S. chemical warfare research
centre, published a four-volume *Report on Properties of War Gases.*[1]
This report, which presumably corresponds to the 'Red Book' of
the British CW station at Porton, is classified secret, but the
assumption is that it contains collected data on all chemicals likely
to be of any use in chemical warfare. The titles of the volumes are
*G-agents, Blood and Nettle Gases, Vomiting and Choking Gases,
and Lachrymators,* and *Vesicants.*

I shall describe two or three of the chemical agents which can
be assumed to be in each volume, and also mention known agents

which would now be placed in supplementary volumes, notably the V-agents and the incapacitating agents.

VOMITING GASES AND LACHRYMATORS. In the training manuals these are classified as riot-control or harassing agents. They are irritants[2, 3] and are lethal only in very high concentrations. Some are particularly irritating to the eyes (lachrymators), some to the inner surfaces of the nose and upper breathing tubes (sternutators), some to the skin (orticants), and some, if swallowed, to the upper reaches of the alimentary canal (vomiting agents). The body attempts to counter the irritation either by secreting fluids or by initiating reflex actions, for instance, vomiting, or the desire to scratch. It is the incapacitating nature of these responses which gives the agents concerned their harassing effect and their common names. In general any one irritant will provoke all of these responses to a greater or lesser extent.

Nowadays, the principal requirements made of these agents are an immediate action, a lack of persistency in the field, and a brief duration of effect. Those agents which can be disseminated as smokes (inevitably non-persistent) are thus preferred. The principal one is *ortho-chlorobenzalmalononitrile*, known as CS. In order of occurrence its effects are quoted as "extreme burning sensation of the eyes and copious flow of tears; coughing; difficult breathing and chest tightness; involuntary closing of the eyes plus sinus and nasal drip; nausea and vomiting."[4] In the words of the British Government's patent on its use[5], "A concentration of between one part in ten million and one part in a million is enough to drive all but the most determined persons out of it within a few seconds". That is to say, it is instantly effective at field concentrations between 1 and 8 thousandths of a gram per cubic metre.

CS is more effective than the older agent CN (*chloroacetophenone*) in that it supplements the latter's lachrymatory action with a more severe skin irritation, and is more stable on storage. Its effects are shorter lived and quicker starting than those of the other preferred agent, DM or adamsite. The agent known as CNS[6] is a pre-war formulation of CN which has increased persistency in the field. It contains chloroacetophenone and the vomiting agent *chloropicrin* dissolved in chloroform.[7, 8, 9] A lengthy exposure to these agents is exceedingly unpleasant and painful. Soldiers have been driven mad by the pain. Some have tried to kill themselves to avoid it.[10]

CHOKING GASES. The choking gases are those which act by irritating the lower reaches of the breathing apparatus. Far from being merely harassing, their irritancy is sufficient to destroy the more delicate membranes of the lungs or respiratory passages. On the one hand, this may mean that the body's defences against invading micro-organisms are breached; on the other, it may lead to a total blockage of oxygen uptake and hence death either from pneumonia or bronchitis, or from asphyxia. The symptoms are prolonged and excruciating; the final crisis may be delayed for several hours.

The choking gases are the classical agents of chemical warfare. They include *chlorine, phosgene, trichloromethyl chloroformate,* and more recently *disulphur decafluoride.*[11] They are unlikely to be used in a modern chemical war, for their initial irritancy or smell immediately warns of their presence, and gas-masks can be donned before a lethal exposure. In addition, their toxicity is nowadays too low. The lethal exposure to phosgene is around 3200 mg-min/m³[12] (a measure of dose and time of exposure combined; e.g., of 1 mg/m³ for 3200 minutes, or of 3200 mg/m³ for 1 min, or any intermediate combination. *see* Glossary).

NETTLE GASES. The nettle gases are primarily skin irritants, but more painful than those we have already discussed. An exposure to one of them has been compared to being thrown naked into a bed of stinging nettles, hence their name. They were first seriously studied in the 1930's by the Germans, who sometimes referred to them as "Red Cross" agents.

A typical nettle gas is *dichloroformoxime.* The Russians are said to have stockpiled it during World War II.[13] At low concentrations it is a typical skin irritant and lachrymator, but at higher concentrations it blisters the skin and penetrates it to enter the blood circulation. From then on its effects may be lethal; it will reach the lungs and cause pulmonary oedema (swelling due to uptake of water), characteristic of phosgene to which it is chemically related. A 1955 report[14] from Edgewood Arsenal quotes a lethal toxicity in guinea pigs of 25 mg. per kg. body-weight when placed on the skin.[15] Its combination of highly painful skin attack with the possibility of a lingering death by asphyxiation undoubtedly makes it one of the nastiest agents available.

There is probably no tactical need at present for the nettle gases. Lethal agents must nowadays be imperceptible and therefore non-irritating, while riot-control agents must be non-lethal.

BLOOD GASES. Dichloroformoxime can act as a circulatory poison if it enters the bloodstream, and this action is a special characteristic of the blood gases. These are principally intended for inhalation in the field; once inhaled, they are rapidly absorbed into the blood circulation where in very small doses they can completely block oxygen circulation around the body. To quote the long-out-of-print British official Medical Manual of Chemical Warfare,[16] they "may cause death with dramatic rapidity".

The principal blood gases are *hydrogen cyanide* and *cyanogen chloride* which replaced phosgene in certain types of munition in the U.S. arsenals during World War II.[17] The Russians managed to compound hydrogen cyanide into a form which could be successfully sprayed from aircraft, a considerable achievement.[18] The blood gases are not quite as lethal as phosgene, but are far quicker acting and somewhat harder to protect against.[12]

VESICANTS. These agents injure every sort of body tissue with which they come into contact. Their principal targets are the skin and the eyes, which they burn and blister. Because they are not very volatile substances they persist in the field for long periods and can be effective for days or weeks after dissemination. If they are used in sufficiently high concentration lethal doses may be absorbed through the skin. If they can be made sufficiently airborne lethal doses may also be absorbed through the lungs. In fact their inhalation toxicities are generally much higher than those of the other lethal agents which have so far been described.

There are two main classes of vesicant—the *arsenicals* and the *mustards*. The arsenicals, such as *Lewisite* and the other dichloroarsines have sharp, irritating odours and cause immediate eye pains.[19] In contrast the mustards have practically no smell and cause no initial pain or irritation. None the less, their damage is done within a few minutes of exposure, and after three or four hours the victim may be blinded or so blistered as to be incapable of action. Although the arsenicals give enough warning of their presence for protective clothing to be donned in time, the mustards do not, and it is for this reason that they are still in the arsenals fifty years after their introduction.

There are several different mustards, ranging from the comparatively volatile *bis(β-chloroethyl) sulphide* or *tris(β-chloroethyl) amine* to the highly persistent *α,ω-bis(β-chloroethylthio)alkanes*.[20] One of the most dangerous is the agent Q, which will burn or blind at an exposure of less than 50 mg-min/m³, and kill if inhaled (as an aerosol for it is a solid) at dosages of 200 mg-min/m³. Although its tactical use would probably be for skin attack its inhalation toxicity approaches that of the older nerve gases. In the words of an Edgewood Arsenal report[21] its lung action is "a bonus effect".

G-AGENTS. The first nerve gases, or G-agents, were developed in secret by the German chemical industry shortly before and during World War II. They are quick-kill agents of tremendous potency. Some, like *tabun*, are persistent in the field. Others, like *sarin*, are non-persistent. They reduced bomb-loads to one-twentieth or less of what was previously necessary. April, 1942, when tabun first went into large-scale production,[22] was an even more important date in chemical warfare than July, 1917, when mustard shell were first fired. The very largest targets were now vulnerable to chemical attack.

The nerve gases are *anti-cholinesterase* agents, working by blocking the enzyme which the body uses to destroy one of its chemical nerve signal transmitters after it has done its job. This has two effects. One is that control is lost over the affected part of the nervous system. The other is that a large concentration of the chemical transmitter rapidly builds up within the body, and that chemical is itself a powerful poison. The body is first incapacitated, and then forced to poison itself.

The symptoms of nerve-gas poisoning are diverse and spectacular. In a comparatively inactive man an exposure to sarin of 15 mg-min/m^3 dims the vision, the eyes hurt and become hard to focus. This may last for a week or more. At 40 mg-min/m^3, the chest feels tight, breathing is difficult, there is coughing, drooling at the mouth, nausea, heartburn, and a twitching of the muscles. At 55, there is a strangling tightness and aching of the chest, vomiting, cramps, tremors, and involuntary defaecation and urination. At 70, severe convulsions will set in followed closely by collapse, paralysis, and death.[23]

Of the better known G-agents tabun is about half as toxic as sarin, and *soman* about twice as toxic.[24] It is a moot point whether tabun is still considered worth stockpiling. Its toxicity is not as high as the other G-agents, but it has a persistency in the field which may be considered tactically useful, that is to say, midway between sarin and the V-agents, so that it can presumably provide a vapour hazard for some days after dissemination. Again, although it is more quickly destroyed by moisture than are the other G-agents, the resultant hydrolysis product, hydrogen cyanide, is highly poisonous, as is the cyanogen chloride formed when it is treated with decontaminating solutions. In addition, its casualties are rather less amenable to the use of the oxime-type antidotes than those of sarin,[25] but equally there are other G-agents, such as soman[25] and *cyclohexyl methylphosphonofluoridate* (GF)[26] which are even harder to counter.

The Germans stockpiled tabun rather than sarin because they found it easier to make. The final stage in their large-scale process for sarin demanded high fluoride concentrations, and even with elaborate silver-lined apparatus[27] they could not get round the corrosion problems. Although they made some hundreds of tons of its intermediates, they could produce no more than half a ton of sarin itself,[22] as compared with the 12,000 or so tons of tabun.[28] The Americans at least were later able to solve the corrosion problems, and have been making sarin ever since. In 1954 the amount of the substance *phosphoryl chloride,* produced as a by-product, began to prove a severe commercial embarrassment.[29]

NERVE GASES. In some circumstances, lethal doses of G-agents can be absorbed speedily by the skin from airborne field concentrations. Since World War II, new nerve gases have been developed which are absorbed through the skin faster and more reliably than the G-agents.

The new nerve gases are known to the Americans as V-agents. Although they have not yet officially disclosed the chemical structures, it is a reasonable assumption that the V-agents are the *S-dialkylaminoethyl alkyl methylphosphonothiolates.* If this is so then it is interesting to note that the first openly published[30] percutaneous toxicity figures for them were given by Academician M. M. Dubinin, a staff member of the Karpov Institute in Moscow.

The Swedish Ministry of Defence states that between two and ten mg. of F-gas, presumably another name for V-agent, are fatal when placed on a man's skin.[24] Such a dose is so small as to be almost invisible.[31] Their inhalation toxicity is given as about 5 times that of soman.[24] Thus the V-agents are about 2000 times as toxic by skin absorption as mustard gas, and about 300 times as toxic through the lungs.

The V-agents are reputedly a British discovery. Certainly it was ICI who in 1955 applied for a patent[32] to cover the phosphonothiolates mentioned earlier. They thereby prevented Bayer from getting one on their rather later application.[33] One of the inventors named in the Bayer application was the same Gerhard Schrader who was responsible for the nerve gases in the first place.[34]

INCAPACITATING AGENTS. Most people have heard of the 'psycho-gases'; some have seen the film of the cat cowering before a mouse under the influence of one—LSD in that particular film. The idea behind such agents is to put the enemy out of action for several hours without permanently harming him, preferably in such a way that he needs no medical attention. Such agents have long been the ideal of chemical warfare theorists; within a few months of the first German chlorine attack in 1915 the specification for a British patent was filed on the idea.[39] Parts of it read very much like a Chemical Corps press release of the late 1950's. The pharmaceutical industry has indeed produced a great range of compounds which have such effects.[40] But the chemical warfare laboratories demand that they act at very small dosages, exposures of less than 100 mg-min/m^3.[41] If a drug is as powerful as this it will almost certainly be lethal at higher exposures, and no field commander is going to make any great effort to avoid over-hitting a target. Thus it seems most likely that the purely incapacitating agent is more a weapon of public relations than of war.

None the less, the Americans are expending considerable effort in pursuing this particular ideal, both inside the defence laboratories and in those of contractees. Among the earliest of the outside contracts must be that with the Shell Development Company, dating from 1952, which called for an examination of synthetic cannabis derivatives for both incapacitating and lethal properties.[42]

Incapacitation can be brought about by interference with either the mind or the body. Mental incapacitation, particularly by the hallucinogens, has been more in the public eye, so much so that the terms 'incapacitating agent' and 'psychogas' are regarded as synonymous. But for the reasons discussed in the next chapter militarily useful incapacitants are more likely to be found among the body-incapacitating agents—the *paralysants*, for denying movement, the *hypotensives*, for causing fainting, the *emetics*, the *convulsants*, the *laxatives*, and so on, perhaps supplemented by mental derangement. It looks as though the Americans' recently standardized incapacitating agent BZ, upon whose use there are "critical limitations,"[43] falls within this class. Its symptoms include a slowing of mental and physical functions, dizziness, disorientation, and hallucinations, coupled with skin flushing, a speeding up of the heart-beat, urinary retention, and constipation.[43] These seem to be very similar to the effects of certain of the anti-cholinergic drugs,[44] and it may be that BZ came to light during the search for nerve-gas antidotes related to atropine. It may even be such an antidote. How convenient that would be. Guesses at its structure should probably include the *3-quinuclidinyl phenyl glycollates.*

CURRENT DEVELOPMENTS. Before leaving the chemical agents we should indicate one or two lines of research into them which are at present being followed.

One is the use of mixtures of chemical agents with either physiologically active ingredients or inert ones. In the former category come those mixtures in which the toxicity of the main component is increased so that the lethal dose of the mixture is lower than the sum of the lethal doses of the components.[46] This is a well-known technique in the formulation of insecticides. Another possibility is a mixture in which one of the components hampers the medical treatment of the poisoning produced by the other component. Thus Russian workers have found that thiourea considerably slows down the reactivation of acetylcholinesterase inhibited by nerve gas.[47] A third example is the use of adjuvants to promote the penetration of the skin by chemical agents. Thus Canadian workers have shown that in guinea-pigs the lethal dose through the skin of a 50 per cent solution of soman in dimethyl sulphoxide is six times lower than that of pure soman.[48]

In the second category, mixtures containing an inert ingredient, comes the very considerable body of work on the encapsulation of toxic agents, that is the coating of minute particles or droplets of the agents with some other component.[49] There are several reasons for trying to do this, among them the protection of the agent from thermal decomposition during dissemination, or for the sustained release of the agent within a target area so as to maintain active concentrations within it for a predetermined length of time, or to make capsules designed to rupture when trodden on.

Munitions

The job of a chemical munition is to create a toxic environment over as much of the target as is compatible with the toxicity of its charge. It must convert its bulk load either into an even distribution of liquid or solid particles of optimal sizes and velocities, or into a cloud of vapour, or into both. It must do this within a certain time. And for economy it must have a high chemical-to-weight ratio. These are severe demands, and they are made more severe by the diversity of chemical agents now in the stockpiles. Each such agent has a combination of physical characteristics and toxic behaviour which is unique. None the less, all munitions work on the same basic principle. They cause the transfer of energy from a store to the chemical load. Generally the store is either an explosive or pyrotechnic charge or a supply of compressed gas. Its size and mode of transfer depend on the physical characteristics of the chemical agent, its volatility, viscosity, surface tension, as well as the sensitivity of the agent to heat and shock. The simplest chemicals to disperse are the volatile, non-persistent ones such as phosgene. These require little more than a small explosive charge to break open their container. The hardest ones are probably the heat-sensitive solid agents which are intended for lethal effect by inhalation, which we have not in fact described here at all; they include such things as *ricin*, a vegetable protein more toxic than the nerve gases and for which the U.S. Army has developed a cluster-bomb system,[50] and the bacterial toxins and biological agents discussed in Chapter 4. Here, we describe briefly only three known types of modern munition, varying in role and scale.

The nerve-gas artillery shell, such as the American M121 series of 155 mm. projectiles[51] have been in production since the middle 1950's. Each shell is about 2 feet long, weighs about 100 lb. and holds about 6 lb. of chemical. Along the axis is a cylindrical, high-explosive burster tube containing about 3 lb. of the explosive Tetrytol. This is a heavy charge; when detonated for an air-burst (by a proximity or time fuse) the nerve gas is atomized into a cloud of small droplets which hang in the air and, in the case of sarin, quickly vapourize. If a non-volatile nerve gas is used, such as VX, part will remain in aerosol form for lung penetration, and part in droplet or spray form for skin effects. Field trials of sarin-filled shell show that for an air-burst 15 feet above the ground a concentration of 3500 mg-min/m^3 will be set up in under 10 seconds over an area 20 yards in radius. A couple of breaths of this will kill. In about 25 seconds the concentration 50 yards from the burst is about 100 mg/m^3, to which a less than 10-second exposure is likely to be fatal.[24]

The 10-lb. mustard-gas thermogenerator cluster bombs are about 18 inches long and perhaps 3 inches wide.[52] On impact a pyrotechnic charge is ignited in the nose; this sends a stream of hot exhaust gas at high speed out through coarse nozzles in the tail section. The mustard gas, about 2·3 lb, is sucked into this stream and shattered into small droplets and vapour which on mixing with the surrounding air form an aerosol cloud of exceedingly small and penetrating particle size. Within five minutes of the scattering of a 64-bomb cluster of such munitions under suitable atmospheric conditions, the concentration of mustard gas over 8000 square yards would be enough to cause a week-long temporary blindness following a 5-second exposure, or death following the skin absorption of a 2-minute exposure.[52] A B-52 bomber can hold about a hundred such clusters. V-agents can presumably be substituted for the mustard gas if necessary.

As a final example, there are chemical warheads for the larger missiles. Chemical warheads are made for, amongst others, the U.S. Sergeant missile, which has a range of about 100 miles, but the actual details of the warheads are classified.[53] What is known is that the Americans have standardized a number of different types of bomblet for clustering within such warheads. Shortly before the missile reaches the target, the warhead breaks open to scatter these bomblets. There may be several hundred per missile. In appearance, the various types of bomblet look alike; they are spherical, and their surface is vaned to impart rotation during descent, the rotation being used both for flight stabilization and to activate the fuses. Various dissemination mechanisms are used: high explosive burst, gas propellant and nozzles on the American's E120 BW bomblet,[54] and so on. One type which would be particularly well suited to such labile substances as the botulinal toxins consists of two halves held together by a spring-biassed bellows. As the bomblet falls the bellows expand under the influence of increasing atmospheric pressure until, at a pre-determined height, the two halves fly apart.[55] The load of micro-encapsulated powdered agent falls slowly to the ground as a fine cloud.

Delivery Systems

One of the assets of chemical warfare is that it does not depend on extraordinary delivery systems. Chemical munitions may be adapted for delivery by almost any means—grenade-throwers, artillery, aircraft, missiles, and so on. Indeed, in some cases the delivery system may be the environment itself—the chlorine cylinders of World War I for instance, or the flow of conditioned air or drinking water in a modern building. An example of one of the few modern delivery systems designed specifically for chemical munitions is the U.S. Army's M55 truck-mounted rocket launcher which launches salvoes of up to 45 small rockets in a space of 30 seconds.[56]

Missiles are well suited to chemical payloads. A warhead which distributes its load widely tends to counter the inherent inaccuracy. Whether missiles are in fact preferable to artillery or aerial bombing from a cost-effectiveness point of view is another matter.

THE METEOROLOGICAL PROBLEM. Once a chemical munition has been set off its user has no further control over it. This is of course true for any other munition, but whereas the effects of, say, high explosive, follow within a fraction of a second of detonation, those of a chemical may be delayed for minutes, hours, or even days. In this lies both the strength and the weakness of chemical warfare. On the one hand a toxic atmosphere may be set up which will envelop the whole target area, seeping into tunnels and bunkers, and permeating buildings. On the other hand, the entire load may be blown uselessly away by a sudden wind, or become so diluted by it as to be impotent.

A chemical weapon system must take these problems into account. By and large a random scatter of small munitions over the target area will be preferred to the delivery onto it of a single large munition, for not only is the former easier to achieve, it will also tend to be self-compensating in an adverse environment.

It must be emphasized that, however well-designed the weapon system is, its effectiveness will still depend critically on the prevailing weather conditions. Thus a 1944 report from the Dugway Proving Ground in America[57] indicates that to produce lethal effects in unmasked personnel over a third of a square mile with 1000-lb. M79 phosgene bombs between 17 and 192 bombs may be required, depending on conditions. On a calm, clear night, using M79's, about 3 tons of phosgene would be needed, but during a breezy, sunny day, upwards of 35 tons—the difference between $\frac{1}{4}$ of a B-52 bomb load and $2\frac{1}{2}$ such loads. Not that phosgene would be used nowadays, of course, nor that a single bomber could produce the necessary spread.

All this implies that previous knowledge of target conditions is essential to a chemical attack. An unexpected wind profile or temperature gradient over the target could easily render the whole attack useless. Modern chemical troops are therefore equipped with meteorological apparatus, and a great deal of the research carried out at chemical warfare laboratories is concerned with improving that apparatus and extending its successfulness. Certainly the Chemical Defence Experimental Establishment (CDEE) at Porton maintains close ties with the Meteorological Office. It was not for nothing that the 12th Earl of Dundonald consulted that Office in 1914 before revealing to Lord Kitchener his grandfather's plans for chemical warfare.[58]

Defence

It could be that the introduction of the V-agents and mixed systems goes a long way towards restoring chemical weapons to that position of strategic capability which they lost when the first gasmasks were supplied to counter chlorine in 1915. We said earlier that with the introduction of tabun the very largest targets became vulnerable to chemical attack. With the introduction of the V-agents those targets can no longer be adequately defended, at any rate not without extraordinary and debilitating effort. One should therefore consider briefly what are the available defences against a chemical attack.

Broadly speaking, there are three methods of defence—physical, chemical, and medical.

PHYSICAL. The physical defence is the oldest. It involves putting up physical barriers against the entry of toxic agents into the body. For the individual, it means a gas-mask to protect the eyes and lungs, and chemically impermeable clothing to protect the skin. For collective protection, it means air-conditioned shelters. Over the past fifty years the necessary equipment has in fact been developed to a high degree of efficiency.

CHEMICAL. In chemical defence, the toxic agent is chemically decomposed before it can enter the body. For the individual, this means ointments containing reactive chemicals for smearing over the skin before an attack, or powders for dusting onto contaminated skin after an attack. Or it means clothing impregnated with reactive chemicals. For collective protection, it means the equipment of anti-gas squads with chemicals and spraying apparatus for destroying toxic agents deposited on the terrain. Or it means the chemical purification of contaminated food or drinking water. The reactive chemicals used are generally alkalis or chlorine-liberating substances,[35] as in general the biochemical mechanisms whereby toxic agents exert their effects mean that the toxic agents react with these substances. The chemical purification of contaminated air is less easy, but suitable decontaminants are becoming available, for example aqueous solutions of compounds of *iodine monochloride* with *polyvinyl pyrrolidone*[36] for spraying into mustard-gassed air.

MEDICAL. Medical defence (or prophylaxis) involves the destruction of the toxic agent *within* the body before it can exert its toxic effect, or the reversal of its biochemical effect, or the biochemical protection of susceptible sites within the body. All these require the presence within the body before an attack of the appropriate drug at the appropriate site. With one notable exception, *British Anti-Lewisite*,[37] this is almost impossible to achieve satisfactorily. But a fourth, less difficult, possibility exists, namely the application of drugs which will poison the body in the *reverse* direction to the toxic agent. Thus, part of the normal treatment of nerve-gas poisoning which results in an accumulation of the chemical transmitted, acetylcholine, is to block those sites which are attacked by the accumulating chemical transmitter, using as a blocking agent the drug *atropine*, the active ingredient of deadly nightshade. Obviously the application of antidotes which are themselves poisons poses severe problems, which when coupled with the speed of action of modern chemical warfare agents greatly weakens the potential of medical defences.

I think it is true to say that the only reliable defences are the physical ones. But these have the drawback that they are only effective if they can be adopted *before* an attack takes place. They cannot protect an individual once he is poisoned. And while in the past the smell or initial irritancy of chemicals gave enough warning, chemical agents have now been developed specifically to deny such warning even at lethal concentrations. This means that it is possible for a lethal concentration to be set up over a target without its occupants being aware until too late. If those occupants are to be immune, they must either wear all-enveloping, nerve-gas impermeable clothing and gas-masks, and wear them all the time, or they must be warned by sensitive and automatic chemical alarms to so protect themselves. Alarm systems being studied range from the adaptation of the laser to long-path infra-red spectroscopy to the training of animals. Dogs have been taught to bark at sarin concentrations of about 1 mg/m^3, but BZ apparently defeats them.[45] There can be no doubt whatever that any man not so protected would be beyond help before medical aid could reach him.

Certainly it is true that the necessary impermeable clothing has been developed and indeed supplied to troops as standard equipment. It is true also that gas alarms are available, but even the best of them give no more than a few seconds warning. During the pre-war rearmament period the British Government did of course provide everyone in the country with a civilian-type gas-mask. The cost of this ran into tens of millions of pounds.[38] In view of today's extra requirements of impermeable clothing and alarms, not to mention defences against nuclear attack, is it likely that any government, British or otherwise, would still be able to foot the bill?

TABLE 1 Principal Agents of Chemical Warfare

	US Army Code	Trivial Name	Chemical Structure	Normal Physical State	Smell	Disseminated Form	Symptoms of Intoxication
LETHAL AGENTS	CG	phosgene	$Cl_2C=O$	colourless gas	new-mown hay; imparts metallic taste to tobacco smoke	gas	lethal coughing, retching, frothing a mouth, cyanosis, asphyxia; pneumor
	AC	prussic acid	HCN	colourless liquid	bitter almonds	vapour	lethal giddiness, convulsions, uncons ciousness, asphyxia
	HD	distilled mustard	$S(CH_2CH_2Cl)_2$	colourless to amber oily liquid	faint garlic	vapour liquid	harassing eyes : inflammation photophobia, ulceration, blindne
	T		$O(CH_2CH_2SCH_2CH_2Cl)_2$	oily liquid	none	liquid aerosol	skin : redness, irritation, blisters
	Q	sesqui-mustard	$CH_2SCH_2CH_2Cl$ | $CH_2SCH_2CH_2Cl$	solid	none	aerosol	lethal resembles C in its action on lun other systemic effe
	HN3	nitrogen mustard	$N(CH_2CH_2Cl)_2$	colourless to amber, oily liquid	faint geranium smell	vapour liquid aerosol	
NERVE GASES	GA	tabun	$(CH_3)_2N-\overset{O}{\underset{CN}{P}}-OCH_2CH_3$	colourless to dark brown liquid	none to fruity	vapour liquid aerosol	harassing eyes: pupils constri vision blurs and dir eyeballs hurt
	GB	sarin	$CH_3-\overset{O}{\underset{F}{P}}-OC\overset{CH_3}{\underset{CH_3}{H}}$	colourless liquid	almost none	vapour liquid	respiration: chest tightness, difficulty in breathi
	GD	soman	$CH_3-\overset{O}{\underset{F}{P}}-OC\overset{CH_3}{H}C\overset{CH_3}{\underset{CH_3}{H}}$	liquid	slightly fruity to camphor-like	vapour liquid aerosol	lethal drooling, sweating, nausea, vomiting, involuntary defaeca tion or urination, twitching, jerking, staggering, headach confusion, drowsin coma, convulsions, asphyxia
	GE			liquid		vapour liquid aerosol	
	GF	CMPF	$CH_3-\overset{O}{\underset{F}{P}}-OCH\overset{CH_2CH_2}{\underset{CH_2CH_2}{<\quad>}}$	liquid		liquid vapour aerosol	
	VE		$CH_3-\overset{O}{\underset{OR}{P}}-SCH_2CH_2NR_2 \quad (R=alkyl)$	liquid		liquid aerosol	
	VX			liquid		liquid aerosol	
HARASSING AGENTS	CA	BBC Camite	benzene–$CH(Br)CN$	pinkish to brown oily liquid	soured fruit	vapour aerosol	harassing burning feeling in mucous membranes, severe irritation and lachrymation, heada
	CN	CAP	benzene–$CO·CH_2Cl$	white crystals	apple blossom	aerosol	harassing burning feeling on moist sk copious lachrymati
	DM	adamsite	$AsCl$ (dibenzazine with NH)	canary yellow to brownish-green crystals	almost none	aerosol	harassing headach sneezing, coughing chest pains, nausea vomiting
	CS	OCBM	benzene(Cl)–$CH=C(CN)_2$	white crystals	peppery	aerosol	harassing stinging burning feeling on s coughing, tears, ch tightness, nausea
Incapacitating Agent	BZ		benzene–$\overset{OH}{\underset{R}{C}}-COO$–pyridine	solid		aerosol	slowing of physical mental activity, giddiness, disorien tion, hallucination occasional maniacal behaviour

PRINCIPAL PROPERTIES of the major known chemical weapons are out-lined in the table above. Smell and normal physical states vary greatly with the purity of the agent, and lethal and incapacitating concentrations depend

Time of Onset of Symptoms	LD_{50} * Percutaneous Absorption (mg per man)	LCt_{50} * Inhalation (mg-min/m³)	LCt_{50} * Percutaneous Absorption (mg-min/m³)	Incapacitating Dosage (mg-min/m³)	First Use or Country of First Development	Remarks
generally delayed for several hrs.		3200			Germans 1915	produced 80% of WW1 gas fatalities; extensively stockpiled in WW2
immediate		5000	200,000-1,000,000		France, about 1865 ; French, 1916	stockpiled by U.S.A. from 1942 on
delayed 1-48 hours	(blisters : 0.032)	1000	>10,000	7-day blindness: 200 2-week skin burns : 1000	Germans, 1917	most widely stockpiled agent of WW2
delayed	(blisters : 0.004)	about 400			UK, USA pre-WW2	used mixed with mustard; their production methods yield such mixtures ; the British stockpiled 60/40 HT during WW2
delayed	(blisters : 0.0003)	about 300			UK, USA, Germany, pre-WW2	
delayed	(blisters : about 0.06)	1000		7-day blindness: 200 2-week skin burns : 1000	UK, USA Germany, pre-WW2	less smell than HD, so even more insidious
up to 10 min following inhalation, or up to half an hr. following percutaneous absorption	1500 (30 'drops')	150		20 (unmasked)	Germany, 1937	standard German tabun contained 20% chlorobenzene ; to be aerosol dispersed
	2000 (40 'drops')	70	15,000	>20 (unmasked)	Germany, 1938	Germans stockpiled large quantities of its intermediates but could make only ⅓ ton
	about 1250	about 70			Germany, 1944	highly resistant to oxime therapy
					UK, USA Canada late 1940's or early 1950's	harder to treat than GB
	small					
	small					
immediate		3500		30	French 1918	useful as a persistent harassing agent
immediate		8500		80	USA 1918	
up to 3 minutes		30,000		20	UK, USA 1918	
immediate		very large		10	UK early 1950's	
					USA, middle 1950's	only standardized incapacitating agent by 1963

on the rate of breathing and the size of the aerosol particles; figures given are for a breathing rate of 15 litres/min (typical of mild activity). Optimum aerosol size, for maximum lung penetration is 0.5 to 3 microns. * defined in glossary

C

Performance and Evaluation

We have quoted figures to illustrate the performance of certain munitions, and also for the same munition under different weather conditions. The great divergence that these show should indicate just how difficult it is to prepare in advance to launch a chemical attack. And the meteorological factor is by no means the only performance variable. Chemical weapons are purely anti-personnel weapons, so a commander must know just how mobile his target is, how well-protected and disciplined it is, not to mention where it is. He must know the type of ground which it occupies, whether it is open or wooded, dry or damp.

Although it is very probable that a Sergeant or a Scud* tactical missile loaded with nerve gas can produce 30 per cent casualties among a fully deployed battle group of 1400 men, and within seconds and under almost any conditions, there is doubt. Performance figures for chemical weapons such as those which suggest 30 per cent casualties over 100 square miles per B-52 bomb-load, are, although often quoted, in fact based on nothing more than an assumption.[59]

If an adequate prediction of a weapon system's performance under all likely conditions cannot be made, then, however potent that system may be, a commander will be reluctant to employ it, for long term planning will be logistically impossible. It is this fact more than any other which is likely to keep toxic chemicals off future battlefields.

One way to evaluate a chemical system is to carry out small-scale field trials and to blow them up to life-size with all the modern techniques of operational research—sensitivity analysis, war gaming, and so on. But this is not enough; there are too many imponderables, at any rate for today's techniques. The only reasonably certain way is by large-scale field trials carried out under all foreseeable types of condition. This would be a huge operation. Fortunately the political pressures against it are equally huge.

---

* The Russian equivalent of the Sergeant—*see* p. 131. *Ed.*

2. Psychedelics   C. R. B. Joyce

There are at least two conflicting reasons for giving an early place
to psychedelic drugs in a catalogue of potential agents of chemical
and biological warfare: that they are useless; or that they are non-
lethal and therefore in certain circumstances ideal. Here, we will
briefly examine both these claims.

The first is easy to support or refute at the semantic level. The
term 'psychedelic' is the result of an attempt to coin a word for
what some regard as a characteristic effect of this kind of drug—
its power to "expand consciousness". A psychedelic compound was
first defined as "one, like LSD or mescaline, which enriches the mind
and enlarges the vision."[1] But the word seems always to have been
used since as a qualifier or as a collective term ('psychedelics' or
'psychedelia') for the chemicals or physical objects that are employed to produce the experience. It thus contains a rather sad
implication that man cannot attain such a desirable state, an aspect
of which is detachment from material preoccupations without
material assistance.

However, if for the moment we accept this definition for lack
of a better, it is clear that any psychedelic drug is one that enlarges the vision. A sufficiently enlarged enemy vision will contain
all other points of view. Since one of these will be the objective, as
far as the enemy is concerned, of any political commander, a psychedelic drug should be an ideal chemical warfare agent for major
strategic use.

At a lower strategic level, the techniques of what is inelegantly
called brain-washing usually have a similar end in view for an
individual or small group. Thus, whatever the possibilities may be
for successful widespread use of these substances, it would be surprising if some have not already been tried out in face-to-face
interrogations of prisoners, the obvious test situation before wider
use is contemplated at all. Although we have no evidence that
psychedelics have been used in this way, hypnotics certainly have.
The parallel with psychotherapy is obvious, and LSD has been

extensively used as an aid to psychotherapy. For the most part, the results have been as deeply equivocal as their interpretation has been partisan.

On the other hand it can also be maintained, at least for the sake of argument, that psychedelics would be worse than useless in warfare because the possessor of a truly enlarged vision would realize that the standpoints of both sides are equally absurd. The major use in wartime for a true psychedelic would be its impartial application to both sides by a disinterested third party. If a recent news report has any foundation, cannabis at least is not such a substance: or alternatively, such drugs are not always the pacifiers their civilian users claim. According to this report at least 75 per cent of NLF (Vietcong) and American Forces are regular users. Psychedelics are more commonly known as psychotomimetics or hallucinogens, although in fact drug-induced psychoses can be distinguished from naturally occurring ones by outside observers, although not so easily as by those experiencing them, and even at the height of their experiences most drug-users are aware that these have no external reality, and so are illusory rather than hallucinatory. The three terms will be used henceforth interchangeably.

Mind-enrichment is not experienced by everyone who takes LSD, and it may be that there is no such universal psychedelic. Short of death or of some major toxic effect which untreated would be fatal, there is no drug which is absolutely consistent in the type of its effects from one individual to another, or even reliable from one occasion to another in the same individual. One well-known hallucinogen, *trimethoxyamphetamine* (TMA) was found by one group, contrary to the experience of others, to cause "unexpectedly anti-social responses" such that "provocation would have precipitated homicidal violence,"[2] an unsatisfactory characteristic for a drug intended to reduce the will of the adversary to resist. Not only do people have different thresholds, but these are affected by experience, by expectations, and by previous exposure to the same drug. The development of tolerance to LSD itself, for example, is extraordinarily rapid—a highly significant degree is induced by a single dose. The subsequent loss of tolerance also occurs rapidly, and is complete in two to four days. Together, these phenomena mean that LSD cannot be taken effectively more frequently than once every three days or so: within that time a second attack with the substance after a first had failed would itself be bound to fail.

In discussions of this problem it often seems to be assumed, at least by those not privy to official secrets, that an effective 'psychochemical' must be of the lysergic acid diethylamide (LSD) type. This is not necessarily true. There are many other candidates for the job. A recent dictionary of psychotropic drugs[3] contains the formulae of "all compounds which have been reported to have any psychotropic activity", of three specified kinds: tranquillizing, energizing, and hallucinogenic. It excludes only certain large but well-established categories, such as the opiates and barbiturates, that have by now rather well-defined properties. Of 690 compounds in this collection no fewer than 90, or 13 per cent, are reported to have hallucinogenic activity. The name of at least one manufac-turer is given for about half of these; the proprietors of the others are anonymous, but one or two manufacturers' names, such as Sandoz, Lakeside, Penick and Dow (who are also large-scale manu-facturers of napalm[4] and of at least one chemical—which has found use among American 'hippies/the notorious DOM, or STP) appear relatively frequently among those which are named. Some 15 of the 370 companies listed as supplying at least one psychotropic drug are responsible for at least one hallucinogen each.

Although certain chemical groupings, such as the indoles, are closely associated with hallucinogenic activity, there is no single structural feature that is common to all reported hallucinogens: even nitrogen is not essential, as the cannabis derivatives demon-strate. On the contrary, of the major groups of psychotropic drugs there is not one that lacks a hallucinogenic member. Of 140 relatives of phenothiazine, for example, two are said to be hallucinogenic; of 66 phenylethylamines, 13, while 11 out of 17 LSD derivates are hallucinogenic. Hallucinogenic properties are therefore widespread. Even the anti-depressive *imipramine* is said to have caused hal-lucinations at doses of over 300 mg,[5] an amount not infrequently given to depressed psychiatric patients. Just as there often appears to be a dose of any so-called sedative that is excitatory, it may be that a further increase in dosage of most drugs active on the central nervous system will produce the kind of disruption known as psychedelic. If this is so the effect of changes in chemical structure will be shown upon such features as potency, or the ease with which the agent reaches its site of action, rather than upon the behaviour elicited.

Several well-known examples are shown in Table 2. It is very important that many of them are known to be lethal. If the claim often made for riot-control or disabling substances—that their effects are entirely reversible—is to be taken seriously, the organic fluorophosphonates are not eligible as 'off the rocker' agents— those under discussion. On the other hand, their effects resemble those reported for the American gas BZ[7, 8] more closely than do those of most other contenders (Table 3), (See also Chapter 1). One additional comment may also be made about BZ. When the drug known as STP, originally a Dow product, began to circulate among the 'hippie' communities in California there was some suggestion that it might be, at least tentatively, identified with BZ. But this perhaps is no more than an indication of the difficulty of this area —for instance at one point the U.S. Food and Drug Administration also identified BZ as the herb drill, an innocuous enough substance. But it is very difficult to be sure how many substances, or synonyms for the same substance are used; it may be that the real BZ is a mixture of a number of the compounds described in Chapter 1.

Even those indoles previously thought to be virtually non-lethal are now believed to be responsible, albeit indirectly, not only for deaths by suicide or under psychotic delusion, but to have delayed effects extending through the machinery of chromosomal damage to the offspring of those exposed.[9, 10] This may prove to be a general effect of psychedelics; work is in hand at the moment to examine the possibility. It cannot be too often repeated that there is, in any case, no such thing as a safe chemical. Even water can kill.

Table 2 also makes it clear that the range of doses of different substances which may be given for their hallucinogenic effects is about a million. This is a thousand times larger than that for their duration. The two aspects are not correlated. There is a wide range of extremely potent substances available—at least one is more potent than LSD[11]—some short- and some relatively long-acting. Potency alone is unlikely to be a major consideration in the development of new psychedelic agents. One bomber or rocket with a ten-ton payload can deliver thirty-three effective doses of LSD, or one effective dose of atropine, for every present inhabitant of the earth. However, such a delivery would only effectively saturate a much smaller area: perhaps some 400 square miles, which is enough for many purposes. On the other hand, more potent agents do have the advantage that they take up less storage space and hence are also less easily discovered, whether at their site of manufacture or in transit.

The other properties listed in Table 2 for the relatively non-lethal substances—their speed of onset and the time for which their actions last—are of more interest in determining the circumstances under which they could be used. In general, these factors are directly related: the faster the onset, the faster the recovery. The route by which the drugs are administered is also relevant, as in most pharmacological situations, but substances with powerful effects on the brain are in general readily absorbed, whether given by mouth or by injection, and they are of course particularly well absorbed from gases or aerosols. Only the skin unmarked by lesions may be an effective barrier, and then not to all—not, for example, to the mustards and the phosphonates.

Some ingenuity is probably being shown, and not only by the writers of thrillers, in developing selective delivery systems for drugs with psychedelic properties. Contamination of a major water supply has often been discussed, and dismissed as too crude, too unpredictable in its effects because of the variable affinity for water of different human beings—especially, perhaps, the decision-makers who are the major targets. Air-conditioning systems, pepper-pots, a prepared cigarette are progressively more selective and hence more suitable for use in small groups, particularly when these contain certain members of both the attacking and the attacked communities. A microphone prepared to deliver an aerosol could help to discredit a politician in the eyes of his own community without any of his adversaries being present. At times one is inclined to imagine that some technique of this kind has already reached a considerable degree of sophistication. But if so it is disappointing that the method does not seem to work better. However, according to the U.S. Field Training Manual[7] the information available about BZ shows that the means for delivering and dispensing it are intended for non-selective use on a medium but indiscriminate scale.

The psychological objectives of theoretically reversible chemical warfare agents are summarized in Table 4. In the absence of hard scientific evidence it can be no more than a personal opinion, but it seems that the objectives, which may be worthwhile and easily attainable by pharmacological means, are not to be achieved with psychedelic drugs. They seem at the moment to be a side issue if not a side-effect, more attractive for propaganda purposes because of the fantasies about mind-control that they may arouse in the minds of the opposition, than for the military or political usefulness of the actual experiences the engender. Since, however, it is relatively easy to produce new compounds with activity on the central nervous system and it is not very difficult to synthesize many of them in quantities that would make their large-scale employment feasible, a measure of effective political support or of successful 'selling' by scientists involved in their production may well be enough to guarantee their continued research and development.

This chapter has been obliged to concentrate upon the little that is known about American experience with military psychedelics. Next to nothing is known about experience in other countries. An important review of the properties of psychotomimetic compounds by a former member of the CDEE at Porton, subsequently on the staff of the DRS at the British Embassy in Washington, contained no reference to the uses of such substances for defence or attack.[12] Such silence, at the time as well as subsequently, can be constructed in any way one wishes. It is impossible, therefore, to be sure how chemicals with these actions are seen militarily and politically.

To discuss the other major problems of protection, treatment, detection of use, detection of manufacture, and international control of manufacture would be to pile fantasy upon a foundation that is already far too speculative. A form of protection might be chronic medication with the agent expected to be used, or one similar to it, in order to achieve a degree of tolerance or cross-tolerance, but the consequences might be dangerous.

The best treatment of non-fatal poisoning is inactivity. No drug can restore uncomplicated normal function faster than healthy inactivation and excretion. To attempt to hurry it on with analeptics, even after an overdose of morphine or of barbiturate, is often misguided. There is some suggestion that to treat methoxyamphetamine poisoning with a tranquillizer—the approved way to abort a 'bad trip' on LSD—may deepen the intoxication.

To detect in use such drugs as these, which have their characteristic effects upon behaviour, is particularly difficult. For the most part they are tasteless, odourless, and colourless, and active in minute quantities. Sensitive animal indicators (the analogue of the miner's canary and fire-damp), such as the Siamese fighting-fish which responds characteristically to LSD, do exist. It is said that dogs have already been trained to detect the smell of cannabis. But a general detector based on physical techniques, for the presence of bacteria and vesicants as well as psychedelics seems more useful.

The question of international control is a depressing one: at least some of the substances discussed are still prepared, when required on an appreciable scale, from natural sources—cactus, mushroom, tree-bark, or fungus. But they are synthesizable; most have been synthesized; and the syntheses are continually becoming simpler. Although illicit LSD manufacture can sometimes be detected, prohibition of manufacture is another matter. Meanwhile there are additional risks: supplies of psychedelics, like poison gases, can leak. Whether they leak or not, they have an equally disastrous history, present, and future.

TABLE 2 Some Properties of Selected Psychedelic Substances

Class	Example	Human Ed$_{50}$*	Onset hr	Termination hr.	Lethality	Antidote
ANTI-SEROTONINS Indoles [12,13]	LSD	50 μg	0.5–3	6–24	Indirect; delayed	Tranquillizers
	DMT	50 mg	0.1	1–4		
ANTI-CHOLINERGICS Piperidyl benzilates [14]	Benactyzine	100 mg	0.1–0.5	6–24	Small	Prob. unnecessary
Tropine derivatives [13]	Atropine	10 mg	1.0–6	12–72	Appreciable	
ANTI-CHOLINESTERASES Organic phosphonates [11,13]	DFP	10 mg	0.5	120+	High	Oximes
G-V-agents [11]	Tabun (GA)					
ANTIMONOAMINE OXIDASES Phenylethylamines [3]	TMA	200 mg	0.5	12	?	Tranquillizers
	DOM (STP)	5 mg?	0.5?	?	? Indirect	? Unknown
CANNABIS DERIVATIVES [14]	Δ^1—THC	5 mg	0.1	5	? None	Hypnotics Tranquillizers
ANTIMITOTICS [15,11]	Dimethylacetamide	100 g	72+	100+	High	?
	BZ	10 μg?	0.1?	250?	?	?

* Dose effective in 50 per cent of population.

TABLE 3 Identification of BZ by Comparison of Activity Profiles

SIGNS

	Hallucinations or Illusions	Paralysis	Hypothermia	Mental Slowing	Vertigo	Hypotension	Headache	Lacrimation Salivation Sweating	Diarrhoea Vomiting
BZ [7,8,17]	+	+	+	+	+	+	+	?	?
LSD [13,16]	+	−	?	+	?	?	−	−	−
Anticholinergics [13,16]	+	−	+	?	?	−	−	−	−
Anticholinesterases [11,13]	+	+	+	+	+	+	+	+	+
Cyanogens [8,11,13]	?	?	?	−	+	+	+	+	?
Arsenicals [8,13]	+	−	−	?	+	+	+	+	+
Benzothiazoles [11]	?	+	?	?	?	?	?	?	?

TABLE 4 Some Objectives of Reversible CW Agents

Time-Scale	Technique	Agent	Objective	Behaviour-type disorders
1. LONGTERM	Conversion Brain-washing, psychotherapy	Conflict resolution——→ Psychological Warfare——→	Enlightenment Acceptance	Motivational
	Starvation, chronic cytotoxic anoxia	Defoliants————→	Apathy Aging, mutations	Somatic
2. INTERMEDIATE	'Psychedelic' experience	Indoles	Disengagement (hallucinations, illusions, derealization, amnesia)	Cognitive
	Intoxication	Anticholinesterases Piperidyl benzilates		
3. BRIEF	Skeleto-motor paralysis Autonomic crisis	Nerve gases Hypotensives Laxatives	Immobilization	Motor

3. Napalm   V. W. Sidel

There are two reasons for a brief discussion of napalm. First, circumstances in Vietnam have led to an association of napalm with chemical weapons. But it is important in developing control measures that the issues in dealing with incendiary weapons, such as napalm, be separated from the problem of dealing with chemical weapons, for different issues are involved in the control of the development, production, or use of the two different types of weapons, and confusion of the two may lead only to weakening controls against either. Second, one of the major issues in the development of chemical and biological weapons is the role of secret weapons research in universities. The development of napalm is a fascinating case study of applied weapons research by a university chemist on a well-known university campus.*

The Weapon

Napalm is gelled petrol or, in the American terminology, gelled gasoline. Originally, the term 'napalm' denoted the thickener that produced a gel when added to petrol; later it was broadened by usage to denote the incendiary gel itself. The name is derived from the first syllables of *naphthenate* and *palmitate,* two fatty acids first thought to be the active principles of the thickener. However, the material used in the original synthesis was mislabelled, and actually contained the soaps of all the fatty acids of coconut oil. These other acids, especially *lauric acid,* were found to be essential to the gel. Although literally a misnomer, the name napalm has been retained as a generic one for weapons of this type.[2, 3] Recently the term has also been applied to a gel consisting of petrol, benzene, and polystyrene which is also called 'incenderjell' or Napalm-B.[4]

When mixed with thickener petrol changes from a thin volatile

* Much of this material has been gathered in co-operation with Dr Peter Reich; some of it has previously appeared in the *New England Journal of Medicine.*

liquid into a tough, stable, sticky gel. Raw petrol is useless as an incendiary weapon; napalm is ideally suited for this purpose. In contrast to many modern weapons, napalm is produced from cheap common ingredients and can be delivered in simple devices.[5]

Incendiary techniques and the development of napalm

Incendiary weapons have a long history in warfare, references to the use of fire in war going back to 2400 B.C. Although the introduction of explosives in the fourteenth century temporarily eclipsed the use of incendiaries, the advantages of fire over blast were well known to military strategists. Blast is self-limiting; incendiary agents are self-propagating, have a prolonged duration of action, and are capable of producing far more disruption and terror than an equal weight of explosives. But it was not until the advent of aerial warfare and the development of efficient incendiary substances, notably napalm, that fire reclaimed its role in war.

Incendiary agents were used in World War I, and an attempt was made by both the German and the Allied Forces to use petrol in flame-throwers.[6] This was hazardous and unsuccessful, but it led to a recognition of the potential danger of incendiary warfare. The treaties of Saint-Germain-en-Laye in 1919 and Trianon in 1920 prohibited the use and manufacture of the flame-throwers along with that of chemical agents. Several provisions against the use and manufacture of flame-throwers and chemical weapons were included in the separate peace treaties negotiated by the United States with the Central Powers. However, it is of interest that the Geneva Protocol of 1925 which prohibited the use of poison gases and bacteriological warfare did not deal with the use of incendiary weapons.[7]

At the time of the outbreak of World War II, the United States Army Chemical Warfare Service was interested in developing an improved incendiary mixture. They enlisted the aid of Professor Louis Fieser of Harvard University, a distinguished organic chemist. He first supplied the Chemical Warfare Service with a formula for a petrol gel using raw rubber as a thickener. This was a moderately effective agent, but the Japanese invasion of the East Indies cut off the supplies of natural rubber and necessitated the development of a synthetic thickener. The research programme that followed, conducted at Harvard University, was presented subsequently in great detail in Fieser's book, *The Scientific Method*,[3] and Fieser has never expressed concern for his part in its development. The first successful napalm detonations were conducted on a Harvard University games field and behind the football stadium. It is thus an excellent example of applied weapons research in the universities.

The napalm gel proved far superior to the original rubber-based gel, and napalm was used extensively by the United States in incendiary raids on Japan during World War II.[8] Napalm was also used in Korea, where it was called the United States' "best all around weapon,"[9] and it has been used extensively in Vietnam.[10]

Effect of napalm

Napalm casualties are caused primarily by heat and by carbon monoxide poisoning.[11] The adhesiveness, prolonged burning time and high burning temperature of napalm favour third-degree burns, and such burns are likely to be deep and extensive, often resulting in severe scarring and deformities, especially when they occur under conditions making early skin-grafting difficult. Kidney failure may be another serious complication. The igniting agent in napalm weapons, white phosphorus, may become embedded in the tissues and continue smouldering and re-igniting long after the initial trauma. It was reported in Korea that panic is more likely to be observed among napalm victims than among those wounded by other agents.[5] The weapon caused far more deaths in Japan than were caused by the atomic attacks on Hiroshima and Nagasaki.[8]

Conclusion

Although certain incendiary weapons such as flame-throwers were coupled with chemical weapons when mentioned in peace treaties after World War I and although napalm has, due to circumstances in Vietnam, been coupled with chemical weapons in recent years, the most important control document on chemical and biological weapons, the Geneva Protocol of 1925, does not link the two. Control would be strengthened by clearly maintaining the separation of the two types of weapons—that is, chemical and biological on the one hand and incendiary on the other—in measures for control and disarmament. Although explosives are also chemicals there has been no attempt to link them with 'chemical weapons' in arms control documents (see Chapter 1). Perhaps control would be most facilitated by recognizing both the nature of the weapon and the modality by which it has its effect. Thus explosives and incendiaries are 'physical' weapons, producing their effects by blast and heat. Chemical weapons and biological weapons have special toxic modes of action which are not mediated through such 'physical' effects. Although the distinction is a scientifically inexact one, it may be useful in developing controls: the special quality of nuclear weapons—their radiation effects—has proved useful in control efforts. I believe the special toxic quality of chemical and biological weapons which may permit their definition and control should not be blurred by coupling them with incendiaries.

4. Biological Weapons I. Màlek

In this chapter I wish to deal with the most important and most dangerous types of biological weapons—those that use micro-organisms (e.g., bacteria, bacilli, viruses, rickettsias, and fungi). This should be more accurately termed microbiological than biological warfare, as some biological agents can doubtless be devised that do not fall into these categories. I will indicate the scope of the potential weapons and the possible defences against them. Lastly, I will consider possible means of controlling the use of such weapons.

The extent of the threat

There are two extreme points of view on biological weapons. One view underestimates them and regards them as weapons whose effects and potential danger to humanity cannot be compared with those of nuclear weapons. The other stresses not only their danger, but their relative ease of production and use (compared to nuclear weapons), especially in local wars. Such a view also stresses the difficulty of controlling the production and use of biological weapons, thus enhancing their potential danger.

This second view is strengthened by the knowledge that some countries are spending enormous sums on the research and development of biological weapons with huge research institutes, often with better facilities than microbiological institutes, studying the peaceful utilization of micro-organisms. As Elinor Langer points out in Chapter 10, even if these sums seem small in comparison with annual expenditure on research and development of nuclear weapons and rockets, when one examines the scale to which biologists are accustomed in conducting their research they are substantial.

The reality of the threat is sharpened by the persistent memory of the terrible plagues which in the course of history have taken a far greater toll of human lives than war itself. The Spanish influenza epidemic after World War I is still relatively recent, and people are regularly reminded of it by the after-effects of similar epidemics which, though less dangerous, occur even today. In addition, contemporary techniques make it relatively easy to produce infectious aerosols and to disperse them over wide areas. Much research effort has been devoted to a study of exactly how such an aerosol cloud spreads, how long it remains in the atmosphere in an active state, and what is its most effective means of dispersal. Certainly, much of the work at Porton and Detrick is directed to this end.

Without overdramatically raising apocalyptic visions of the effectiveness of biological weapons, it must be apparent that I, as a microbiologist, believe that there is a greater danger from underestimating biological weapons than from overestimating them. After all, these are potential weapons which can easily affect the balance of forces in any conflict, especially in those cases where the control of epidemics is difficult, whether in territories with poorly developed health services or a terrain that has not yet been sufficiently investigated epidemiologically, or when the normal life and physical resistance of the people have been severely damaged by nuclear attack. I do not wish at this point to go into the technical details of the conditions under which biological weapons can be used. We can be sure however that in the research on biological weapons, on which the military spend such enormous sums, attention is being paid to these questions of strategy. That is why I cannot side with the fatalistic view that in a situation where the effective restriction of the use of biological weapons is difficult we must be content to rely on effects of public opinion and the fact that as yet the agents may not be sufficiently controllable to make them as reliable as chemical weapons.

The scope of the weapons

The idea of using microbiological weapons goes back to the experience with infections and epidemics, which have been a serious military problem throughout the history of wars. Despite the development of vaccines, sera, and antibiotics, they remain, even without artificial introduction and dispersion, an important and difficult military problem. There are in fact several examples of the use, or alleged use, of micro-organisms against populations even in the pre-microbiological era; for example, the introduction of smallpox to the American Indians by the early settlers who gave or sold them infected blankets or trinkets. Allegations of 'the poisoning of wells' form a similar class.

D

ADVANTAGES AND DISADVANTAGES OF BIOLOGICAL WEAPONS. The most powerful argument in favour of the use of microbiological techniques in warfare aimed at population destruction is the relatively great *variety* of possible agents, often with completely different routes of infection, ways of spreading, incubation periods, and very limited possibilities of prevention, defence, and cure.

Some of the infectious agents enter the human body most effectively by way of the respiratory tract, and these can be either bacteria (e.g., plague, *tularaemia*), spores of *bacilli* (e.g., anthrax), *rickettsiae* Q-fever, viruses (e.g., *influenza, psittacosis,* different types of *encephalitis*), or even fungi (e.g., *coccidiomycosis, histoplasmosis*). Naturally each of these infections needs a completely different diagnostic approach and demands a different cure. Specific prevention, where this is possible, varies from case to case. Such infections can, in principle, be very easily spread under favourable meteorological conditions over vast areas by the use of aerosols.

Other infective or toxic agents can penetrate the human body directly through mucous membranes, such as the eye or nose. Among these are several viruses and some bacteria (e.g., those causing tularaemia, *brucellosis, rickettsias,* and *botulism*). Some others are most effectively absorbed orally with food or contaminated water (e.g., *salmonellosis, dysentery,* and *cholera*). And to make the situation still more complicated, these agents can be used in mixtures, thus causing extremely complex diagnostic problems for those attempting to identify and combat the disease.

All this, together with the minute dimensions of the organisms— of the order of one micron in diameter (a micron is 0·001 mm)— and the often complicated and slow methods of detection and identification, means that a population subjected to a microbiological attack would probably not be able to identify its cause before the infection had become widespread.

The second important quality of these microbiological agents is that they are alive and can reproduce. Thus a chain of infection from one infected person to others can easily occur. This is especially dangerous with respiratory infections, where the time of greatest infectivity often begins in the incubation period when the symptoms are very slight and non-specific, and when infection spreads through minute exhaled droplets to all persons in the vicinity of the infected persons. Even in communities not unbalanced by war conditions such spreading of infection can be very hard to control. Experiences with the recent foot-and-mouth disease in cattle in Great Britain, with smallpox epidemics introduced from countries where it is not adequately controlled, or with myxomatosis—originally introduced artificially to limit the rabbit population and afterwards spreading uncontrollably—are examples of this problem even in highly organized societies. All these problems can be still more severe in countries with insufficiently developed medical and public health services or, of course, under war conditions.

A further advantage of the biological agents as weapons is that some are very resistant to external conditions and can remain latent but potentially infective for many years. An example is the anthrax bacillus, whose spores may remain infective for a hundred years or more—as evidenced by the case of the Scottish island, Gruinard, discussed by Robin Clarke in Chapter 9. With other organisms, conditions can be created to make them sufficiently resistant to survive in the form of aerosols for long periods of time.

Because of the minute dimensions of micro-organisms, they can be easily dispersed in the form of aerosol clouds of great dimensions which can move for very long distances. Field tests have been carried out in the United States, using either fluorescent particles or non-pathogenic bacterial spores of bacilli, showing that such aerosol clouds generated by spraying from a ship along a 150-mile stretch of coast, spread out over 55,000 square miles of land, over which a minimum dose of 15 particles and a maximum dose of 15,000 particles were inhaled by members of the affected population. In spite of the rather unfavourable conditions during this experiment, the cloud could be followed about twenty-three miles in the direction of the wind with viable cell densities corresponding to sufficiently high infective doses, even inside buildings. To achieve this it was sufficient to spray some 500 litres of a suspension of a harmless bacteria (*bacillus subtilis*).[1] The infectious effectiveness of such aerosols depends greatly on the size of the dispersed particles or droplets: the smaller the particles, the more effective they are. With the techniques available today it is easy to produce highly effective aerosols with relatively small devices—perhaps small enough to make possible individual sabotage without real danger for the saboteur, particularly as the incubation period for the disease would give him time to disappear from the scene before the first symptoms were noticed. Similarly it would be much easier to carry massive amounts of such infective agents in aeroplanes than, say, bombs. It can be objected that these are mostly hypotheses made on the basis of experiments with animals and with experience gained in the laboratory. But even these results show that the danger caused by infectious aerosols, especially with some micro-organisms where the inhalation route is not the natural one, could be greater than supposed.

The infectious or toxic dose of some micro-organisms or their toxin (*i.e.*, the poison they produce) can be very small, so a very small amount of dispersed material could infect or intoxicate large numbers of people. Thus the aerosol doses of *Pasteurella tularaemis* on humans was experimentally evaluated at about 25 to 50 cells; in the case of Q-fever, only one micro-organism (*Coxiella burneti*) might be sufficient to cause infection, so that in one gram of dispersed material many million infectious doses can be present. Drinking 100 ml. of water from a reservoir of some 5 million litres capacity would cause serious infection or intoxication if as little as half a kilogram of Salmonella, 5 kg. of *botulinum* toxin, or 7 kg. of *staphylococcal enterotoxin* had been introduced.[1] Of course, these are only illustrative data upon which it would be possible to enlarge further by considering other infections and other conditions of dispersal.

There is also the possibility of the spread of infection by use of living vectors, such as insects, ticks, or lice, thus forming persistent foci of infection under favourable conditions. Very much is now known about the ecology of such vectors and the way in which they participate in the dissemination of infection. Allegations about the use of germ warfare by the United States in Korea claimed that animal carriers had been used in this way.[5]

A minor but important potential advantage of biological agents is that they do not require large, expensive, and complicated equipment for their use, especially in comparison with equipment necessary for nuclear weapons. Any well-equipped microbiological laboratory with normally skilled technical personnel can readily produce large quantities of the agents if infectious strains of micro-organisms are available.

In the case of intended microbiological attack it is possible to prepare one's own personnel, for instance by vaccination against selected micro-organisms, so that they would not be seriously endangered when entering the infected area.

The possibility of clandestine use of the agents must also be raised, for identification of the artificially introduced infection is often not easy and can take a long time, while allegations of their use are not easily proved or disproved—witness the allegations about Korea[5]—especially where the epidemiological background of the country is not sufficiently known and its medical services are not fully competent.

And one final advantage: biological weapons are directed against a population (human or animal). They cannot cause any material damage; they lead only to great human losses and produce profound effects on morale, and cause panic. This alone could make the microbiological weapons attractive to a potential aggressor.

These then are the main reasons which make the weapons extremely dangerous and could make them attractive to an attacking force under some special conditions. Bearing these in mind why then have biological weapons not been already used, since nuclear and even chemical ones have been? The answer lies in the fact that these weapons also have their disadvantages, particularly, perhaps, in comparison with chemical weapons. The most important of these is that their effectiveness depends on not only the agent itself, but also on ecological and meteorological conditions, over which the aggressor has no control. In addition the relatively slow development of most infections diminishes their short-term tactical value to a commander concerned with immediate advantage. The effect of biological agents lies in the strategic dimension only.

But I believe that it is not merely because of these disadvantages nor of insufficient knowledge that the weapons have not been used. I am convinced that those huge installations and organizations which study their potential with such efficiency have been able to gather sufficient technological experience to be able to use these weapons on a large scale, fully corresponding to the level of highly sophisticated contemporary military techniques.

Defence against biological warfare

Over the past hundred years a number of techniques for controlling the spread of infectious diseases have been evolved. Among the major achievements have been the ability to isolate and identify a great many infectious agents, the discovery of how these agents behave, how they are able to enter the human body, and the mechanism of their pathogenic activity. This knowledge has created the possibility of a variety of epidemiological measures, notably isolation, disinfection and sterilization, and most important, immunization and vaccination. These last depend on the introduction either of mitigated or dead infectious agents or of specific antimicrobial agents such as chemotherapeutics or antibiotics. All these possibilities are naturally also at our disposal for use against microorganisms disseminated as weapons. But there are difficulties which make all this highly elaborate system less effective in the case of massive artificial infection with microbial weapons.

Firstly, despite the great success in controlling infectious diseases, there still exist dangerous infections where control is not yet very efficient, either because of the difficulty of diagnosis, as is the case with some virus diseases, or because we do not have sufficiently efficient preventive vaccination or therapeutic measures of chemotherapy or antibiotics. It must be assumed that precisely these microbial agents will find favour in a potential attack.

Secondly, even where epidemiological knowledge is sufficient, in the case of massive dispersion of agents, any counter measures will inevitably lag behind the speed of the outbreak. It will be possible to identify the infection only after the appearance of clear clinical symptoms, and this is usually too late, as the greatest infectivity often occurs during the later stages of the incubation period and before the clinical symptoms have become clear. If one adds the time necessary for exact laboratory identification it is obvious how difficult it will prove to cope sufficiently with the speed of an induced epidemic.

This is still more true of any attempt at preventive immunization. It is hard to imagine that all the population at risk by exposure to microbial attack could be vaccinated against *all* possible agents. And if the vaccination is begun after attack with an identified agent it would take days or even weeks before sufficient immunity could be achieved.

Another difficulty is connected with the fact that nearly all the dangerous micro-organisms likely to be used as biological weapons can exist in *mutant* forms for which further preventive measures would be necessary. Mutant forms can develop naturally, as in the ominous case of penicillin-resistant organisms, but it is also possible to create them artificially by means of exposure to radiation or toxic chemicals.

And the last difficulty results from the fact that immunity— be it natural or artificially induced by vaccination—can readily be destroyed by exposure to radiation. Thus all the advantages of prior vaccination would be lost and all the induced infection would occur in much more dangerous forms in the case of nuclear attack. Thus the greatest danger of the possible use of microbial weapons is in conjunction with the dropping of nuclear bombs.

That is why, in spite of the fact that suitable strains are available for use as vaccines or in the production of antigens, which could be used for immunization against many potential biological agents, a full immunization programme will probably never become a general prophylactic measure.[1]

Thus it becomes necessary when thinking about defence to seek ways which would enable us to make it more efficient and which would diminish these gaps. The most important would be the development of methods to make the detection of possible microbial attack more efficient. Hedén[1] subdivides detection into three stages, those of warning, sampling, and identification. All of these must be accomplished so as to shorten the time necessary for active defensive steps. Modern microbiological methods and knowledge offer several possibilities which have probably already been explored in the existing special military institutes. An important step towards international confidence in this area would be to distribute this information as widely as possible. There are available, for instance, devices for sampling of air probes with a very high capacity, which can gather some 10 cubic metres of air per minute into a liquid flow of 10 ml., making rapid warning of the presence of infective aerosol clouds possible and effective.[1] Or a method using fluorescent labelled anti-bodies (substances which would bind onto specific microbiological strains) could be used for rapid identification of the agents present in such a cloud. Other possible protective systems are of the mechanical variety—efficient, positive pressure shelters, or disinfection procedures and, in the case of suspected insect vector attack, repellents and so forth. But these must inevitably have a limited role in any protection of the population at large.

Thus biological weapons provide, by comparison with chemical ones, a much greater diversity of agents and methods of induction, they can only be identified with much greater delay, and in spite of considerable knowledge about the agents and the possible defence against them in principle, in practice they are much more difficult to control. They could probably cause much greater disaster among people for a smaller expenditure of effort. On the other hand the chemical weapons are much better defined, more easily manageable, and their effect more immediate. Thus they have a potential *tactical* significance which the biological weapons lack.

One of the characteristic features of biological weapons is that it is difficult to distinguish work done purely for defensive ends from that which is mainly offensive. Furthermore, if defence is to be effective and prepared in time it must be based on knowledge that can easily be transferred to offensive uses. That is why military establishments working on the development of these weapons do it mostly under the label of defence. Biological weapons, therefore, can be used as an excuse for not reaching agreement on general disarmament, especially in the absence of an early and thorough study of the problems involved, to enable the arguments on the impossibilities of disarmament and inspection to be refuted (see Chapter 13).[3, 6, 7]

Such considerations have led to the establishment of a study group attached to the international scientists' Pugwash Movement, with the objects of (a) identifying the questions that had to be solved; (b) contributing to their solution on a contemporary scientific level; (c) helping spread knowledge of the actual danger of biological weapons and the struggle against the secrecy of their preparation and production; and, (d) seeking ways and means of speeding the banning of biological weapons and disarmament.[3, 6, 7]

The work of the Pugwash study group was directed also towards three questions: new methods for the quick detection of any biological weapon attack; the possibility of control and inspection of institutes in countries voluntarily giving up any activity which could be misused for the development of biological weapons; and, finally, the general tactics of a campaign leading to complete biological disarmament.

Interesting experimental results were obtained on the second question. By trial inspections of four microbiological institutes in different countries that volunteered (Sweden, Denmark, Czechoslovakia, Austria), relatively effective methods of inspection were worked out. The conditions were also defined under which such a voluntary ban on work on biological weapons and control of such a ban would be effective, while insuring protection against their use by another party. At the same time, it was estimated to what extent the experience of the International Atomic Energy Agency in Vienna, in the control of the peaceful uses of nuclear energy, could be used for a similar system of control of means of biological warfare and the use of micro-organisms for peaceful purposes.

Finally, a significant contribution was made when the Stockholm Peace Research Institute (SIPRI), founded and financed by the Swedish Government, chose as one of its research projects the problem of biological weapons.* It has started work on the legal implications of biological weapons and their ban. Rapid detection

* Representatives of SIPRI were present at the Conference, including Dr Bjornerstedt and Dr Nemec, and were able to give a preliminary account of this study, which, however, has not been included as such in this text. Ed.

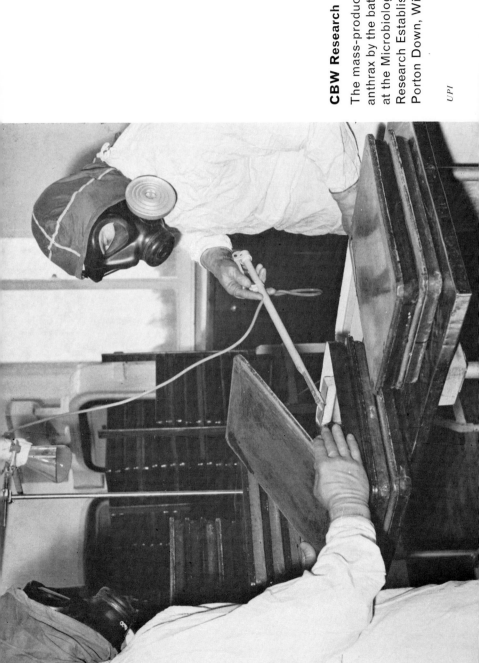

CBW Research

The mass-production of
anthrax by the batch method
at the Microbiological
Research Establishment,
Porton Down, Wilts.

UPI

CBW Research

U.S. Army

The dispersal capabilities of bomblets are tested inside this vast aerosol test sphere nicknamed 'the 8-ball'

CBW Research

Science

During recent tests of a new nozzle for the dissemination of nerve gas 6000 sheep were accidentally destroyed on lands adjacent to the Dugway proving ground. This communal grave holds 1200 pregnant ewes

CBW Research

A portion of Fort Detrick, Maryland

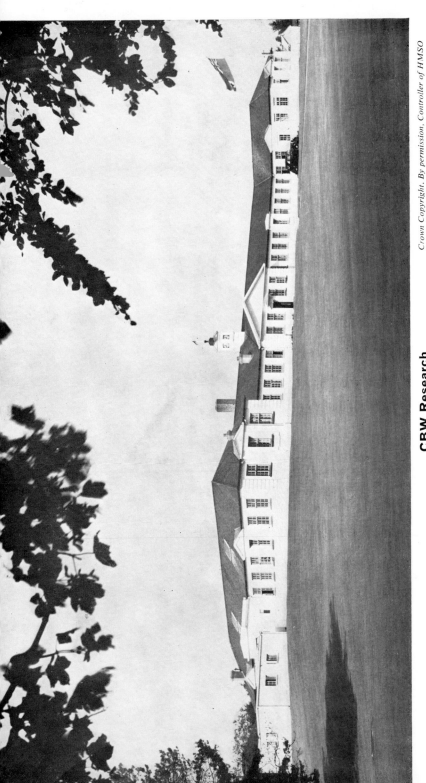

CBW Research

Crown Copyright. By permission, Controller of HMSO

Headquarters Building, Chemical Defence Experimental Establishment, Porton Down, Wilts.

CBW in Use

Above
Grenade of CS
gas as used in
Vietnam

Right
Gas-mask
approved for use
in Vietnam

U.S. Army

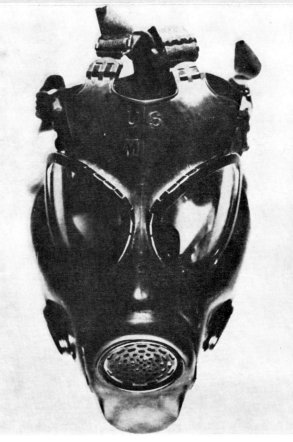

CBW in Use

The 'Mighty Mite' is in effect a fan which can blow gases (*e.g.* CS, or in this case DDT) in a concentrated stream

U.S. Army

CBW in Use

A U.S. Air Force
C-123 *Provider*
sweeps low along a
road in mountainous
central Vietnam on a
defoliation mission.

USAF

methods and the possibilities and forms of inspection have also been studied, but the findings are so far only in a preliminary stage. These are the main tactics of real defence against biological warfare. In my comments on the limitations of conventional defence against these weapons, I tried to make clear that a consistent and co-ordinated international effort leading towards the complete ban of these weapons is the only truly efficient way of defence of mankind against a disaster which will bring it back to medieval times where pestilence can decimate populations.

DISCUSSION

The major issues of the discussion were whether the state of biological weapons research had indeed reached the point where the weapons were technically feasible, and whether inspection techniques of the sort outlined by Academician Malek were likely to prove effective.

Dr Humphrey, while not denying that biological weapons could be developed to a stage where they could be useful strategically or tactically on a large scale, queried whether the difficulties which face their use had been solved for the simple reason that it is extremely difficult to try them out on man. All biologists are aware that one cannot argue from another species like guineapig or pig to man.

In the case of chemical weapons, we have fairly precise data on their properties and behaviour, but biological weapons are considerably less predictable. From the point of view of the field commander biological weapons fall into two categories: the first are those which carry a high rate of infectivity but which would not then normally develop, passing from person to person; and the second, those which rely for their effect on spreading, plague-like, through the population. An example of the former is the incapacitating Dengue fever which produces severe symptoms two or three days after infection, knocking out the fighting potential of the victims. Dengue fever would not, however, spread from person to person as it is a systemic disease, does not produce sputum, and is normally carried by an insect, the sandfly. In the absence of sandflies, therefore, the effects of the use of the weapon die out within a few days. This is one sort of weapon that has achieved a degree of popularity in certain circles on the grounds that it is a humane, non-killing weapon, but it is hard to put this theory to the test without involving a large number of people.

The other sort of biological weapon, analagous to the plague, is even more difficult to test. It is clear, however, that such weapons would have no military value until they had achieved epidemic proportions. In addition it would be necessary for the military commander to ensure that his own troops were specifically immunized.

Professor Meselson pointed out that if biological weapons do become militarily significant one would see it developing because the tests required would have to be under combat conditions. The chance of having an effective biological weapon developed secretly is very remote. The only way one can do the kinds of tests that would develop a predictable weapon would be under wartime conditions, and if that went on one would surely know it. Even development is a fairly conspicuous process, whereas simple manufacture of an already perfected weapon might be more easily concealable (the very conspicuousness of the process made it amenable to inspection techniques such as that pioneered by SIPRI).

But as both Dr Humphrey and Professor M. Pollock pointed out, one still knows very little about the real problems involved in dissemination, in maintenance of biological agents (other than anthrax spores) in a stable form, and so on. The problems are similar, but still more complex than those, outlined by Mr Perry Robinson, for chemical weapons, with the additional complication that the biological systems are self-reproducing ones. To Professor Pollock this lack of knowledge that anyone had of the possible spread and mutation of such infective agents would be enough to make any country think twice about their use, in case they rebounded. Dr Viney, by contrast, raised the spectre of the potential use of biological warfare agents against comparatively isolated targets—garrison islands or ships at sea—which could presumably be attacked with a fair degree of optimism that the attack would not rebound onto the attacking side.

A second point raised by Professor Pollock was whether it was really possible to distinguish between offensive and defensive research on biological weapons. Such a distinction seemed tenuous to him. It does not, for instance, seem possible to devise a maximally efficient defence against bacteriological agents without studying in detail the particular agents a potential aggressor might use. But, as Dr Viney pointed out, offensive research does not necessarily imply an offensive capacity; this might still not be necessary and provide a point at which control could be exercised.

The final issue concerned the feasibility of actually detecting the use of biological weapons. Professor Pollock thought the problem a greater one than Academician Malek had perhaps allowed. With the case of Korea in mind, unless one actually has the opportunity of finding evidence, for instance an aeroplane shot down filled with infected flies or a bacterial bomb clearly marked with its label of origin, would it not be extremely difficult to know definitely whether in fact biological weapons had been used?

But, as Dr Viney said, despite the difficulties of such an international inspectorate, it must not be dismissed even by the sceptics and hard-headed, because the real function of such a body would be quite as much to disprove allegations as to prove them. From the point of view of persuading politicians who are not likely to believe that a committee, in actual war circumstances, could do scientific work on the spot fast enough for it to matter (especially as it is quite likely that biological attack would come after a nuclear attack or after a conventional attack, so that the questions might have rapidly become irrelevant), it would still be very useful for such a body to exist for the purpose of disproving panic allegations or even malicious allegations. Hence the value of the SIPRI studies.

TABLE 5 Principal Agents of Biological Warfare

DISEASE	ORGANISM	INFECTIVITY	EFFECTS	SURVIVAL	TRANSMISS[I]
BACTERIAL DISEASES					
anthrax	Bacillus anthracis	20,000 organisms of $<2u$ inhaled	respiratory form normally fatal if untreated	spore forming highly stable	inhalation (also from anim[] skin infection
brucellosis	Brucella melitensis	high 1300 organisms ?	long lasting recurrent severe fever; rarely fatal	stabilized with dextrin and protein products	inhalation ingestion (also from anim[]
cholera	Vibrio cholerae	low by ingestion	severe intestinal infection; sometimes fatal		ingestion (also from anim[]
glanders	Malleomyces mallei	high 3200 organisms inhaled	in acute form, severe fever often fatal		inhalation ingestion (also from anim[]
melioidosis	Whitmorella pseudomallei	high	normally fatal fever, producing mania and delirium		inhalation ingestion (also from anim[]
plague	Pasteurella pestis	high 3000 organisms	very severe; often fatal		inhalation ingestion injection by flea[]
tularaemia	Pasteurella tularensis	very high <50 organisms inhaled ?	severe fever; 5-8% fatal	unstable	inhalation ingestion injection by ins[e]
VIRAL DISEASES					
breakbone fever	dengue viruses	high single mosquito bite 2 organisms inhaled ?	most incapacitating fever known; very rarely fatal	high	injection by mos[] inhalation
mumps		high	incapacitating but not severe		inhalation
poliomyelitis		low	severe, permanent disability; sometimes lethal	85% survive 23h at 21-24°C as aerosol	ingestion inhalation of moist air
psittacosis		high	mild to severe fever; sometimes fatal		inhalation ingestion injection by ins[e]
smallpox	Poxvirus variolae	high a 'few' organisms	severe; often fatal		inhalation ingestion
yellow fever		high single mosquito bite	Jaundice type fever; 30% mortality		injection by mos[] inhalation
RICKETTSIAL DISEASES					
Q-fever	Coxiella burnetii	very high I organism inhaled ? 10^{-6}g infected tissue	fever for 1 week; 1% mortality	stable	inhalation ingestion injection by tick
epidemic typhus	Rickettsia prowazeki	high	severe; often fatal	poor	injection by lous[] inhalation ? ingestion ?
FUNGAL DISEASE					
coccidioido-mycosis	Coccidioides immitis	1350 spores	mild to severe fever; rarely fatal	spore forming highly stable	inhalation
TOXIN					
botulism	Clostridium botulinum	toxic dose $0\cdot12ug$?	severe poisoning; 60-70% mortality	decomposes in 12h in air	inhalation ingestion

CHARACTERISTIC PROPERTIES of some biological agents are shown in the table above. The properties are those of the naturally occurring strains which can, of course, be altered; a highly infective strain of poliomyelitis, for instance, has been produced. Relatively few of the properties of the organisms causing diseases such as tularaemia and yellow fever, for instance, would have to be changed whereas those of epidemic typhus are almost

CCINES	THERAPY	STORAGE	EXTENT OF IMMUNITY	EPIDEMICITY	REMARKS
ble	antibiotics	as spores	limited ?	low	one of the most stable agents
ble in	antibiotics	several months	?	low	affects both man and domestic animals
ne reduces ity and ence	difficult		present to unknown extent	high	unlikely to be effective via water systems
isfactory	antibiotics		limited	low	affects both man and domestic animals
isfactory	difficult		?	low	very rare and little known disease
ble	antibiotics		present to unknown extent	high	only pneumonic (respiratory) plague likely to be of BW use
ble	antibiotics		present	none	good BW agents apart from doubts concerning stability
ble	difficult	stable eight years at 41°F	present	low	might be useful as an incapacitating agent
produced	difficult		widespread	high	little use as BW agent because of widespread immunity
produced	difficult		widespread	low	limited by low infectivity and widespread immunity
isfactory	antibiotics		present to unknown extent	high	birds act as reservoir of disease; immunity may be fairly widespread
produced	difficult	stable when freeze dried	widespread—on decline in Europe and N. America ?	high	generally immunity too widespread
produced	difficult	stable at 0-4°C	present	none	naturally a sub-tropical disease ; a strain which could survive in temperate climate might be dangerous
able	antibiotics	stable	present	none	very high infectivity
produced	antibiotics	difficult	present	high but cannot spread man-to-man	unlikely BW agent ; poor stability
isfactory	antibiotics?	as spores	present	low	highly stable ; suitable agent if a vaccine were produced
able as id	difficult	bacteria as spores or toxin in airtight container	none	none	acts more quickly than any other BW agent ; troops could invade after 24 h

entirely unsuitable. Agents against which vaccines are in mass production are not likely to be used in BW; on the other hand, an agent would not be used in BW unless a vaccine were *available*. The psittacosis organism is no longer technically classed as a virus, but is included under that heading for convenience. Mumps is unlikely to be used in BW but is included for comparison.

5. Defoliants*   A. W. Galston

The programme

Chemicals are being used against forested and agricultural lands in Vietnam as part of United States military strategy and tactics. This is the first time that chemicals designed to damage or kill plants have been used in war. To damage or kill a plant may appear so small a thing in comparison to the human slaughter every war entails as to be of little concern. But when we intervene in the ecology of a region on a massive scale we may set in motion an irreversible chain of events which could continue to affect both the agriculture and the wildlife of the area—and therefore the people—long after the war is over.

The purpose of using herbicides, as stated by a U.S. Government spokesman, is twofold:

> Chemical herbicides are being used in Vietnam to clear jungle growth and to reduce the hazards of ambush by Viet Cong forces. . . .
> Destruction of food is undertaken only in remote and thinly populated areas under Viet Cong control and where significant denial of food supplies can be effected by such destruction. . . .[1] †

A precedent is being set which is important for two reasons:

In the first place once chemicals become accepted weapons in the arsenals of nations, it may be difficult to draw the line between one chemical and another; between one use of chemicals and another. Secondly, the widespread aerial spraying of herbicides can affect the land, water, and living things which must support the people in peace or in war, in independence or under foreign domination, and whatever their form of government. It is this aspect of herbicide use which concerns us here.

Assistant Secretary of State Dixon Donnelly, the U.S. Government

---

* The basic data in this chapter first appeared in *Scientist and Citizen*, August–September, 1967. Used by permission.
† But *see* pp. 152–53.

spokesman quoted above, also said that the chemicals in use in Vietnam are "used extensively in most countries of both the Free World and the Communist Bloc for selective control of undesirable vegetation. They are not harmful to people, animals, soil or water." The implication of the word 'selective' is that these herbicides are also not harmful to plants other than the target species.

Less reassuring were the words of the twelve plant physiologists who wrote to President Johnson that the massive use of chemical herbicides could upset the ecology of an entire region. In the absence of more definite information than we now have about the effects of such use, they suggested that such an upset could be catastrophic.[2]

With two such diametrically opposite interpretations before us, an examination of what is known and what is unknown about these chemicals is in order.

American biologists who visited Vietnam in 1966 observed damage to a variety of plants.[3] This ranged from serious damage to fruit trees and other commercial plants in rural areas not deliberately sprayed to effects on various species in and around Saigon. Without a controlled study it is difficult to relate plant damage to source; in some cases other agents, such as jet-plane exhausts, may be partly responsible for the effects. There has also been some spraying with malathion for mosquito control. Species affected are listed in Table 6.

It is important to note that spraying is being done quite close to Saigon, and that plants are being affected within a range of about thirty miles from the target areas. The information contained in the Table comes from informal observations by scientists who have been in Vietnam. There appears to be no formal study of the effects of the spray programme on the many interconnected plant and animal species of Vietnam.

The fact is that even in limited and controlled conditions we do not fully understand the basis for the altered behaviour of a plant when we apply various chemicals from outside the plant. To add to the uncertainty, only a few species have been investigated intensively, and as we shall see shortly, species differ greatly in their response to synthetic growth regulators. As a result, when we spray a synthetic chemical from an aeroplane over a mixed population of exotic plants growing under uninvestigated climatic conditions—as in Vietnam—we are performing the most empirical of operations. We learn what the effects are only after we perform the experiment, and if these effects are larger, more complex, or otherwise different from what we expected there is no way of restoring the original conditions.

The scale

The 12th Air Commando Squadron, in the first nine months of 1966 alone, defoliated a Vietnamese area of 1000 square miles, equivalent to the size of the entire State of Rhode Island in the United States, Derbyshire in Great Britain, or the entire state of Luxembourg.[4] Included in this area were about 70,000 acres of crops, mostly rice. The acreage of cropland rendered unproductive by sprays had risen to more than 150,000[5] by the beginning of 1967. In the early part of 1967 the special Spray Flight of the 309th Aerial Commando Squadron expanded operations to include the so-called demilitarized zone separating North and South Vietnam, as well as war zones C and D and areas adjacent to Laos and Cambodia, and during 1967 a total area of 965,000 acres was sprayed. This is expected to rise to 2 million acres in 1968.

The spraying programme, named 'Operation Ranch Hand', started in 1961 with two C123 transport planes, and has gradually grown to this much larger programme. The chemical most used is a mixture of esters of *2, 4-D* and *2, 4, 5-T*[6] released from high pressure nozzles beneath the wings and just under the upswept tail of the planes. Each plane carries about 1000 gallons of spray and approximately 3 gallons are released per acre, usually in the early morning, when the air is calmest and the danger of drifting is least. Within twenty-four hours the foliage begins to wither and turn brown. By the end of six weeks the leaves fall off the trees. For defoliation, reapplication is usually necessary at the beginning of each new growing season.[7]

In 1961 sixty spray sorties were flown; 1962 saw the number increased to 107, which included defoliation along canals and rivers in a large part of the heavily populated Mekong delta and a mountain pass near Qui Nhon, the port city north of Saigon. In 1966 combined defoliation and crop-spraying operations had increased to the point where approximately 1,324,430 gallons of herbicides were sprayed over more than half a million acres of land, and plans were to triple the programme.[6]

During 1967, 965,000 acres of land were affected, perhaps 450,000 acres of this being cropland. This would be about five per cent of South Vietnam's eight million acres under cultivation, and the programme has continued unabated into 1968.

The amount of herbicides being used is suggested by a *Business*

TABLE 6　Plants Damaged Outside Sprayed Areas (Vietnam)

FOOD CROPS AND COMMERCIAL PLANTS

Common Name	Genus (and Species when known)
Rubber-trees	Ficus elastica
Cassava	Manihot esculenta
Breadfruit	Artocarpus integrifolius
Papaya	Carica papaya
Starapple	Chrysophyllum cainito
Figs	Ficus
Sweet Potato	Ipomoea batatas
Beefwood, or South Sea Ironwood, cultivated for lumber	Casuarina
Mango	Limnanthes mangifera

PLANTS IN THE VICINITY OF SAIGON
(perhaps thirty miles from the nearest sprayed area)

Common name	Family	Genus (and Species when known)
Sweet cassava	Euphorbiaceae	Jatropha
Cassava	Euphorbiaceae	Manihot esculenta
Starapple	Sapotaceae	Chrysophyllum cainito
Piney tree	Guttiferae	Calophyllum
Willow	Salicaceae	Salix
Beefwood	Casuarinaceae	Casuarina equisetifolia
Papaya	Caricaceae	Carica papaya
Hibiscus	Malvaceae	Hibiscus
Flowering maple	Malvaceae	Abutilon indicum
Tropical or Indian almond	Combretaceae	Terminalia catappa
Petarboom	Leguminosae	Peltrophorum ferrugineum
Royal Poinciana (peacock flower)	Leguminosae	Poinciana regia
Silk Cotton Tree	Bombacaceae	Eriodendrum anfractuosum
Dogbane	Apocynaceae	
Sweet potato	Convolvulaceae	Ipomoea
Breadfruit	Moraceae	Artocarpus integrifolius
Figs	Moraceae	Ficus

E

Week item announcing the disappearance from the U.S. domestic market (except in small packages for home owners) of 2, 4-D and 2, 4, 5-T. The military demand is said to be four times present U.S. capacity.[8] Total production in 1965 of 2, 4-D and 2, 4, 5-T was close to seventy-seven million pounds.[9]

It was announced on July 11th, 1967, that contracts for $57,690,000 worth of chemicals for defoliation and crop destruction have been awarded by the Defense Supply Agency. The quantity of chemicals being purchased was not announced, but even allowing for some price increase the amount in dollars suggests a purchase of between six and seven million gallons. (The Air Force budget for the fiscal year that ended June 30th, 1967, provided $39,500,000 for about five million gallons. If prices remained the same the new contracts would be for more than seven million gallons,[10] according to official Pentagon figures.) Meanwhile the value of British exports of herbicides and associated substances to the United States has risen from $730,986 in 1964 to $2,739,949 in 1967.

Targets are selected by U.S. or Vietnamese officers and must be approved by a province chief, the Vietnamese Army general staff, the U.S. Military Assistance Command, and finally the American Ambassador.

Effects of defoliation

There are reports[6, 11] that *cacodylic acid,* an organic arsenic-containing compound, is being used against elephant grass and rice; both of these are the narrow-leaved type of plant which would be expected to be fairly resistant to the usual formulations of the 2, 4-D type of herbicide.

Of the three herbicides mentioned above cacodylic acid is probably the most toxic to man. According to the authoritative Merck index[12] it is *dimethylarsenic acid,* contains 54.29 per cent arsenic, and is extremely poisonous. The lethal subcutaneous dose in dogs is one gram per kilogram body-weight. (Other sources suggest that cacodylic acid may be even more poisonous with an LD_{50} of 184 mg/kg —*Ed.*)[14]* If the same toxicity held for man about seventy grams, or slightly over two ounces, would kill the average 150-pound man if administered subcutaneously.

Smaller doses could result in nausea, diarrhoea, headache, muscular pains, weak pulse, and coma. All these symptoms flow from

* *See* glossary.

the paralysis of capillaries and degeneration of the lining of the intestinal tract known to be induced by arsenic. In view of the persistence of this material and the cumulative nature of arsenic toxicity, its wide use certainly may pose dangers for the civilian population of Vietnam. And indeed, eye-witness reports from individuals in the sprayed areas have apparently described such symptoms (see Chapter 7). The additional danger that arsenic may be accumulated by plants which would be eaten by man must also be investigated, since such an effect would greatly magnify possible toxity. It has already been reported[13] that injection of cacodylic acid into trees can kill the bark beetle, *Dendroctonus*, infecting the trees.

Official statements have referred usually only to the less toxic 2, 4-D and 2, 4, 5-T, but Assistant Secretary of Defense, Cyrus Vance, when asked in 1965 whether arsenic and cyanide compounds were being sprayed over the rice fields of South Vietnam, replied, "We are making limited use of them in the southern part of Vietnam but not yet in the north."[14] It is hard to escape the conclusion that aerial spraying of cacodylic acid produces some harm to the human and animal life below.

The basic formulation for 2,4-D and related herbicides varies with the region, the climate, and the target plant. For example, the Dow Chemical Company product called Esteron R 245 O.S. designed "for the control of trees, bush, and broadleaved weeds" contains 67·7 per cent of 2,4,5-T. This material is usually mixed with either diesel oil, No. 1 or No. 2 fuel oil, or kerosene before spray application, although water sprays are sometimes recommended. About one gallon of Esteron per one hundred gallons of water is a usual mixture. If applied by aeroplane, the practice in Vietnam, about one to four pints of Esteron per acre is the recommended amount.

The label on this Dow preparation carries a "WARNING" on which the following statements are found:

Do not contaminate irrigation ditches or water used for domestic purposes.
Caution. May cause skin irritation. Avoid contact with eyes, skin, and clothing. Keep out of reach of children.

Another Dow product, called Formula 40 R, which contains alkanolamine salts of 2,4-D and is designed "for the selective control of many broad-leaved weeds in noncrop areas and in certain crops" carries a more definitive statement:

Causes irritation of skin and eyes . . . In case of contact, flush eyes with plenty of water for at least 15 minutes and get medical attention; wash skin with soap and plenty of water. Remove and wash contaminated clothing before re-use. Do not wear contaminated shoes.

Herbicides have not been successfully designed to act against only a single plant or group of plants. If carried by wind, drift, or even vaporization they can destroy neighbouring plots of useful plants. The warning on Esteron states:

Do not apply Esteron 245 O.S. directly to, or otherwise permit it to come into direct contact with . . . desirable plants which are sensitive to 2, 4, 5-T, and do not permit spray mists to drift onto them, since even minute quantities of the spray may cause severe injury during both growing and dormant periods. . . . Applications by airplane, ground rigs and hand dispensers should be carried out only when there is no hazard from drift. Do not apply by airplane in the vicinity of cotton, grapes or other 2, 4, 5-T susceptible vegetation. At higher temperatures, vaporization may cause injury to susceptible plants growing nearby. Do not graze to dairy animals within seven days after treatment (to avoid contamination of milk).

Effects on birds and animals were noted in a Reuter dispatch from Saigon which said that "Chemical sprays have played havoc with bird life, destroying vegetation and the insects on which birds feed. Monkeys and deer have also been affected."[15]

The extent of the damage that may be caused by the widespread and indiscriminate use of herbicides can only be approximated because of the paucity of direct experimental data. The reassuring statements about the innocuous nature of the herbicides in use in Vietnam are based on laboratory and field tests in the U.S.A. These have shown the selective nature of these chemicals—their effectiveness against one kind of plant, while leaving some other kinds unharmed. (Although, as noted above, there are limitations to this selectivity.) These tests have also demonstrated that 2,4-D and 2,4,5-T do not persist for a long time in the soil. A serious ecological upset is nevertheless possible.

The main points of concern are as follows:
The mechanism of action of the defoliants is imperfectly understood. We are therefore setting in motion on a large scale a biological process whose action and consequences we cannot altogether foresee or control.

Most experience with these herbicides has been in environments very different from that in which they are now being used. Their effect on individual plants indigenous to that part of the world has not been studied nor have we information about their movement through the food chains in that area.

While experiments performed in Great Britain and the United States indicate that numerous species and strains of common soil micro-organisms are effective in breaking down these compounds, in this process they are transformed into new compounds which may, under some circumstances, have deleterious consequences.

Let us look at each of these problems in more detail.

Mechanism of action

Defoliation with herbicides mimics the natural seasonal defoliation. Leaves of deciduous plants are attached to the stem by a narrow stalk called the petiole. Through this petiole runs vascular tissue which conducts water and nutritive materials into the leaf and organic matter out of the leaf. As long as the leaf-blade produces the hormone *auxin* in moderate concentrations the leaf remains on the plant. In normal concentrations auxin plays a useful role in various aspects of plant growth. If, for natural reasons, such as the shortening days of autumn, or for artificial reasons, such as injury to the leaf blade, the production of auxin in the leaf-blade ceases or slows down measurably, then a layer of large, weak, thin-walled cells which are easily ruptured is formed at the petiole and results in leaf fall. (This is called the abscission layer.)

The knowledge that lowered auxin levels in the leaf-blade result in leaf fall suggested to chemical plant physiologists that the deliberate application of auxin 'antagonists' or compounds which lowered auxin levels in the leaf could furnish a means of controlling leaf fall. This suggestion was put to work in agricultural practice many years ago when defoliants were applied to cotton plants several days in advance of harvest of the bolls, so that the mechanical cotton-picker would not be clogged by the undesirable leaves. The reverse practice, that of prolonging the retention of leaves and fruits on trees to promote better growth and ripening, can be accomplished by spraying with carefully controlled concentrations of substances with auxin activity. The concentration must be carefully controlled, because if it becomes too high undesirable side effects are produced which may even kill the plant. We will deal with these later.

There are still many gaps in our knowledge of the control of leaf fall. (For example, there are three other classes of hormones (*abscissins, gibberellins,* and *cytokinins*) in addition to the auxins, which play a role—as yet unknown—in leaf fall.

Recent investigations[16] have revealed that high, toxic levels of auxins, which kill some plants and alter growth patterns in others, probably work through the control of the synthesis of still another plant hormone, *ethylene.* This substance, which can cause leaf fall, abnormal flowering, and altered growth patterns in various plants, has long been used to ripen fruits artificially by causing the sharp increase in respiration (the climacteric) which normally precedes ripening. Ethylene is normally absent, or present in very small quantities, in growing plants. The application of abnormally high auxin levels or some appropriate stimulus from the outside world can cause its production in the plant. Application of chemicals with high auxin activity, such as 2,4-D and 2,4,5-T, might have this result.

Ethylene is volatile and effective in several parts per thousand million of air; it can readily migrate from plant to plant and cause growth aberrations. The old observation that one rotten apple in a barrel causes them all to spoil is based on the fact that ethylene is produced in greater quantities in infected and injured fruit tissues; once produced it can induce adjacent fruits to ripen and spoil prematurely. Thus, however carefully a herbicide might be applied to a restricted area, if it gave rise to significant quantities of ethylene the results in neighbouring crops could be catastrophic.

Effect in the South-east Asian environment

2, 4-D and 2, 4, 5-T are especially effective against broad-leaved plants. In fact, this selectivity is so marked that 2,4-D is sold for application to grass lawns, where appropriate concentrations will kill dandelions, plantains, and other common lawn weeds without affecting the growth of the grass. Of course, as many home gardeners have discovered to their sorrow, raising the 2,4-D concentration somewhat can result in greatly inhibited grass growth. Thus, the same 2,4-D and 2,4,5-T which are being used extensively as tree defoliants may be used, with somewhat different, stronger formulation, for the purpose of killing or rendering unproductive various food crops, including rice. Unless carefully controlled, both as to area and concentrations sprayed, the jungle defoliation aspect of the herbicide programme in Vietnam can kill crops in areas where such an outcome is *not* intended.

In addition to the observations cited earlier, there is other evidence that aerial sprays have done considerable unwanted damage as a result of drifting and volatization of sprayed materials. For example, it is widely known that rubber-trees at a Michelin plantation were inadvertently killed by drifting spray. The United States has compensated the French owners at about $87 per tree.[17]

On December 13th, 1965, three aircraft flew over Thoi An Dong, a village of the Phong Phu district, spraying defoliant extensively. Watermelon only 20 days from full maturity were seriously damaged, as were rice, vegetables, and fruits. Crops in the adjacent villages of Phuce Thoi and Tong Tuyen were also heavily damaged. The entire area was supposed to be 'secure' from the United States point of view, and thus should not have been sprayed at all. Con Son, an island half a kilometer from Can Tho, was subjected to defoliation treatment six times between June and December, 1965. Papaya, jack fruit, milk fruit, coconut, watermelon, mustard cabbage, and beans were adversely affected. At An Nghiep hamlet, beans, cabbage, and tomato were adversely affected. The damage ranged from 40 to 100 per cent, rendering the crops unprofitable for harvest. Some farmers also decided not to replant, thus amplifying the economic loss.[18]

Another problem is that herbicides may affect a susceptible link in an important food chain. For example, fish are an important element in the Vietnamese diet and are frequently bred in rice paddies.[19] Herbicides may not be directly toxic to fish, yet may affect them indirectly if they prove toxic to the micro-organisms on which the fish feed. The appearance of chlorophenols (derived from 2,4-D and 2,4,5-T) in a water supply, at concentrations as low as one part per thousand million renders the water unpalatable, and possibly harmful.[20]

The toxic levels of sixteen aquatic herbicides for the micro-crustacean *Daphnia,* which is a fish food and thus an important elementary link in the food chain of streams, lakes, ponds, and rivers, have recently been measured.[21] Among the more important conclusions are the following: (i) While herbicides are in general less toxic than insecticides, the high concentrations required for effective action suggest that several (not including 2,4-D) could be dangerous to *Daphnia* under field conditions. (ii) Lethal action may be delayed until long after the test compound has been removed. This suggests that previously determined inhibitory levels may be seriously in error. (iii) Mammals (such as laboratory rodents) cannot be used to estimate damage on *Daphnia,* and vice versa. (iv) ". . . even brief exposure of *Daphnia* to certain compounds intentionally released in the environment may lead to more far-reaching effects on populations of these important animals than might be anticipated from data on acute toxicity."

Similar ecological investigations on other important organisms in the zone being sprayed might well reveal a multiplicity of such effects. Even slight differential toxicities to two different competitor organisms could thus have serious ecological consequences.

Transformation in the soil

There are not to our knowledge any data pertinent to the action of these herbicides on the soils of Vietnam, but the class of chemicals to which 2,4-D and 2,4,5-T belong, the chlorinated phenoxy acids, usually take from two to fifteen weeks to disappear from the soil in temperate climates after a single application. Some of them, such as *2-chlorophenoxyacetic acid*, may linger for more than a year, and *3,4-dichlorophenoxyacetic acid* does not disappear at all.[22]

The rate at which applied herbicides disappear from soil depends on the content of water, the amount of organic matter, and the temperature. In addition, the structure of the compound greatly influences its stability; of the commonly employed herbicides, 2,4,5-T is many times more persistent in soil than is 2,4-D.

The micro-organisms in the soil break down these chemical compounds, changing their structure. The end products are not known with certainty, but among them must be included the pheno-substances which result from the loss of the two carbon atoms of the side chains of these molecules (*2,4-dichlorophenol* and *2,4,5-trichlorophenol*). The significance of these phenolic substances may be that they promote destruction of natural auxins within a plant, even when fed from without. Although the original herbicide has disappeared, it may have been replaced by another substance which is also toxic to plants.

These phenolic substances may also affect the growth of the soil micro-organisms themselves, and since, especially in tropical soils, the activity of such organisms is essential to preservation of soil structure, the build-up of such materials in the soil may have serious ecological consequences. An inhibited soil microflora, especially during torrential downpours, could facilitate soil erosion and produce a radically altered ecology. This makes all the more serious the recent announcement by the Secretary of Defense, Mr R. McNamara, that the United States plans to "poison the soil" so as to denude completely the vegetation from a strip of land going entirely across Vietnam from east to west. Specifically mentioned were two agents: *chlorophenyl-dimethylurea* and *dichlorophenyl-dimethylurea*.[23] These agents kill plants within days after sprouting, rather than affecting them much later in their life cycle, as the defoliants do.

Reaction of the United States scientific community

In fact we are still too ignorant of the interplay of forces in ecological problems to know how far reaching and how lasting will be the changes in ecology brought about by the widespread spraying of herbicides in Vietnam, and the American scientific community has begun to react to this danger. Thus, following the petition by twelve plant physiologists to President Johnson in September, 1966, and the reply by Assistant Secretary of State, Dixon Donnelly, already mentioned, action was initiated to attempt to persuade one American scientific organization, the American Association for the Advancement of Science (AAAS) to interest itself in the problem. Dr E. W. Pfeiffer,* of the Department of Zoology at the University of Montana, authored a resolution urging the AAAS Council to set up a committee to investigate the ecological consequences of the widespread use of chemical and biological agents. On December 30th 1966, the AAAS Council passed a modified version of his proposal and set up a committee, chaired by Professor René Dubos of the Rockefeller University to study the problem.

The only significant action taken by the committee during its year of life was to call the attention of Secretary of Defense McNamara to the problem. The Department of Defense (D.O.D.) responded by authorizing a literature study and report by the independent Midwest Research Institute (MRI) to be presented by the following December to the AAAS. In the meantime, in a letter to Don K. Price, AAAS president, the D.O.D.'s director of defence research and engineering, John S. Foster, said that "qualified scientists, both inside and outside our government, and in the governments of other nations, have judged that seriously adverse consequences will not occur. Unless we had confidence in these judgements, we would not continue to employ these materials."

By the time of the December, 1967, meeting of the AAAS the report was not ready for study. But a new AAAS Committee on

---

* Dr Pfeiffer was present at the conference to discuss these activities of the AAAS.

Environmental Alteration, under the chairmanship of David R. Goddard, was set up to examine both the MRI report and an analysis of it to be prepared by the National Academy of Sciences. Before either document could be examined the Pentagon released its own summary of the report, and through its director of plant science research at Fort Detrick, Dr C. E. Minarik, minimized the ecological impact of herbicides and defoliants used in Vietnam. Two articles quoting extensively from Dr Minarik appeared in articles written by Walter Sullivan in the *New York Times* of January 4th and 7th; Dr Minarik was also heard over CBS news, repeating the same message. Clearly, the Pentagon felt some need to respond to the challenge.

The Pentagon's *Summary Digest of the MRI Report* did reveal that relevant scientific studies in the ecological area are very scanty and that practically no scientific reports dealing with the Vietnamese area's response to applied herbicides are available. They also admitted to the use of another compound, *picloram*, a derivative of *picolinic acid*, which the Dow Chemical Company's own house organ *Down to Earth* reveals is remarkably long-lived in the soil. In one study, less than 5 per cent of the picolinic acid derivatives had disappeared from soil in well over a year. The D.O.D.'s comment on this is "Picloram . . . is persistent in soils but will tend to leach to depths of two to four feet under average rainfall and soil conditions." In commenting on the danger that humus removal from tropical soils may reduce the soil to an impervious rock (an almost irreversible process known as laterization, and a risk of the defoliation campaign which had been expressed by several scientists), the summary says: "No evidence has been obtained that such irreversible changes have resulted in areas in Vietnam subject to defoliation. Observers in Vietnam have indicated that the vegetational succession following defoliation in tropical forests is one in which grasses rapidly cover the ground in dense stands followed by rank growth of weeds and vines which are effective in minimizing soil change." If this is true, soil laterization is probably not a danger . . . but, then, the entire purpose of the defoliation operation is vitiated by an even denser ground cover than existed before.

The National Academy of Sciences assigned the report to Dr A. Geoffrey Norman, head of the Division of Agriculture of its affiliate, the National Research Council. Dr Norman, himself former head of plant research at Fort Detrick, in turn appointed a committee composed of four academic people, one U.S. Department of

Agriculture researcher, and the director of plant science research at Dow Chemical Company to advise him. Their report, forwarded to the D.O.D. on January 31st, 1968, was called "only a first step in investigating further the ecological effects of intensive use of herbicides" by Frederick Seitz, president of the National Academy of Sciences. In the *New York Times* of February 13th, 1968, Walter Sullivan again wrote an article under the headline "Defoliation Study Casts Doubt on Long-Term Damage in Vietnam" indicating that: "There are no clear indications that widespread aerial spraying to strip Vietnamese war zones of foliage will do long-term damage." He admitted that too little is known to have confidence in these conclusions and that all data were gathered from literature review and interviews, rather than on-the-spot experience. Quite a different picture was painted by Thomas O'Toole of the *Washington Post* who wrote on February 20th, 1968, under the headline "Report paints grim picture of Defoliation in Vietnam": "The chemical defoliation of Vietnam's jungles and forests may be doing permanent damage to its wildlife, soils and streams, a Pentagon-commissioned report acknowledges. At a minimum, two rare species of monkeys and four other animals are in danger of extinction because of the spray programme. The danger of soil laterization is present, and damage to water resources cannot be excluded." These contrary views of the same report summary indicate the need for continued study of this complex situation.

As of now, we await the AAAS evaluation of the full report. But whatever the outcome, the decision, it is clear, will be based on insufficient data. To quote the report, "The extent and pattern of herbicide treatment in Vietnam have no precedent. Therefore, it is difficult to predict the effects with any accuracy."

6. Starvation as a Weapon*   Jean Mayer

A United States Government spokesman explains that food is as important to the Viet Cong as weapons, and that herbicides are used "where significant denial of food supplies can be effected by such destruction."[1, 2]

There is as yet little direct evidence from Vietnam of the effects of crop destruction on the NLF, no data on starvation of persons who can be categorically defined as 'Viet Cong', no reports that NLF prisoners have been found to be physically incapacitated by malnutrition, no clear evidence of a lessening of the NLF's will to fight. Yet it is clear that malnutrition is common among Vietnamese civilians, whether due to diet deficiences unrelated to the war, to food problems resulting from other war conditions, military and economic, to the conscious efforts of denying food to the NLF, or to a combination of all three.

Information justifying the programme has never been released by military or other U.S. Government sources. In the absence of such data we must turn to other, less direct information and to historical inferences. In spite of the paucity of information from Vietnam, the effects of food denial as a weapon are no mystery. We can turn to well-documented sources for answers to the questions: How does a food shortage affect a population? Which elements of the population are most affected? Is starvation an effective strategic weapon? The answers to these questions can then be related to the situation in Vietnam.

The effects of starvation on the human body are well known and were described in detail in a number of populations immediately following World War II. Famine affects different elements of the population in different ways and to different degrees; this has been observed in famines occurring in peace-time as well as in war. The author has personally observed famines on three continents, one of them Asia.

* The basic data in this chapter first appeared in *Scientist and Citizen*, August–September, 1967. Used by permission.

Finally, although herbicides have not been used in previous wars, the creation of famine through blockade has been frequently used, and there is historical evidence of its effects.

Effects of Starvation

The first and most obvious effect of starvation on the human body is the wasting of its fat deposits. A nutrition survey of South Vietnam in 1959 found that the average weight of civilian males was 105 pounds,[4] suggesting that such body-fat deposits would generally be meagre in Vietnamese to start with. The stomach and intestines, heart and lungs are affected next; the size of the liver is drastically diminished. The intestinal lining becomes thin and smooth, thereby losing some of its absorptive capacity, and diarrhoea results. Thus starvation is a self-accelerating process, particularly in children; because of intestinal damage, the food that is available is poorly absorbed, undernourishment increases correspondingly. The damaged lining of the stomach fails to secrete hydrochloric acid, which is important for digestion. Both blood pressure and pulse rate fall.

Early effects of starvation are cessation of menstruation in women and impotence and loss of libido in men. Hair is dull and bristling, and in children abnormal hair grows on the forearms and back. The skin acquires the consistency of paper and not infrequently shows the irreversible dusty brown splotches which are permanent marks of starvation. In extreme cases, particularly among children, the lips and parts of the cheeks are destroyed. The body becomes susceptible to infection and disease. The psychologic state deteriorates rapidly; the individual becomes obsessed with food, mentally restless, apathetic, and self-centred.

A recent paper prepared by U.S. Physicians for Social Responsibility, for Senate hearings on the refugee problem, summarized the medical problems in South Vietnam.[5] It pointed out that malnutrition is widespread among South Vietnamese civilians; beri-beri, night blindness, and anaemia are found frequently; Kwashiorkor, a form of protein malnutrition, occurs and is a major component of the problems of wound-healing and resistance to infections; infant and child mortality is high. Kwashiorkor is a deadly disease affecting children after weaning. It causes degeneration of the liver, pancreas, and intestines, oedema, and eventually death. Diseases associated with malnutrition, such as tuberculosis, are rampant. Although it is impossible to know to what extent these problems stem from the crop-destruction programme, there can be no doubt that if the programme is continued these problems will grow.

In many parts of South-east Asia, there are food shortages in the best of times, and any strain on the food supply, whether from political factors or natural disasters, may result in famine. A general consequence of famine is the social disruption, including panic, which accompanies it. Starving people attempt to journey to other areas where they hope to find food, and chaos increases. Weakened by lack of food they are susceptible to disease, and these factors interact with one another; disease adds to social disorganization which in turn makes disease more difficult to combat.

In Vietnam, migration has been set in motion by military attacks, or fear of such attacks, on villages or towns, and by the destruction of agricultural lands. At Senate hearings on refugee problems in South Vietnam and Laos, Frank H. Weitzel, Acting Comptroller General of the United States, gave the number of refugees in South Vietnam in the fiscal year 1965 as 600,000, six times what had been expected.[9] In November an additional statement from Mr Weitzel gave a total of 719,000, but said 258,000 were classified as resettled. At the end of 1966, the *New York Times* put the figure at a million, growing at a rate of about 70,000 a month.[10] A news item on July 3rd, 1967, states that almost two million refugees were now in government resettlement camps—one in every seven South Vietnamese.[11]* These recently uprooted people are a different population from the 1955 refugees from North Vietnam who, according to the South Vietnamese Government, are now resettled. In 1965 refugees were almost 100 per cent women, children, and older men.[12]

Twenty-six years of almost uninterrupted war have placed strains on the food supply, especially severe in the last two years. South Vietnam, which exported 49,000 metric tons of rice in 1964,[13] must now import it. Figures for 1966 are not yet available, but 240,000 tons were imported in 1965.[14] At the time of writing infant mortality is estimated at 25 to 30 per cent, more than ten times that of the United States or Britain. Maternal death rate is twenty-five times that of the United States. Life expectancy at birth is about thirty-five years. In an environment where sanitation is primitive and medical facilities are in short supply, a great additional hazard is the risk of epidemics which can grow like wildfire in a weakened, starving, and migrating population.

---

* More recent figures do not appear to be available; but the aftermath of the Tet offensive must have greatly increased them.

Bubonic plague is endemic, and although only eight cases were reported in 1961, the number is said to have risen to 4500 in 1965.[5] Malaria is also endemic, and the appearance of a form of the disease which does not respond to traditionally effective drugs is a matter of grave concern. Cholera and smallpox have been habitual fellow-travellers of Asian famine with influenza and relapsing fever also frequent. In 1965 the number of cases of cholera in Vietnam increased by 25,000 according to the World Health Organization.[15] In that same year Dr Howard Rusk reported that among refugees "tuberculosis is highly prevalent, as are skin infections, intestinal parasites, trachoma, and other diseases of the eyes, typhoid, and leprosy."[16]

A study of three examples from wars fought within the past hundred years goes a long way towards indicating the effect of food denial as a weapon.

THE SIEGE OF PARIS. Paris was under siege by the Germans for 129 days in 1870–71, during the Franco-Prussian War. One of the reasons given by the Government for surrender was the lack of food within the city. However there was a desperate military situation in the rest of the country. Prior to the siege one of the main French forces was defeated at Sedan; during the siege the other was defeated at Metz. Thirty-six new divisions were organized and equipped from Tours, but a number of them were driven into Switzerland, where they were disarmed and interned.

According to Baldick,[17] the total number of deaths in Paris rose from 3680 in the first week to 4465 in the third—and presumably rose higher as the siege dragged on for eighteen weeks. The winter was severe and people suffered from cold as well as hunger; epidemics swept the city, with smallpox the biggest killer.

Melvin Kranzberg describes the effect of the food shortage on the people of Paris: "With the exception of the dent made in their pocket-books the rich did not suffer from famine during the siege. . . . As for the poor, the men were not badly off, but the women and children suffered. The men could get enough to eat and perhaps too much to drink merely by enlisting in the National Guard."[18]

BLOCKADE OF THE CENTRAL POWERS. In the early days of World War I, the Western Allies were optimistic that the hunger engendered by the blockade of the Central Powers—Germany, Austria-Hungary, and the smaller countries allied with them—would help win the War quickly. After the War, the importance of the Blockade may have been exaggerated by German historians in order to play down military defeats; it may have been underestimated by British, French, and American historians. The fact remains that it took four years of the combination of blockade and military action to defeat the Central Powers.

Famine oedema, a relative increase in the water content of the body, was observed in civilians in Hamburg in the winter of 1916–17, in Berlin in January, 1917, and in Vienna and the Rhineland later the same year. In 1918 it became common throughout Central Europe. Tuberculosis, which is closely related to malnutrition, began to rise in 1914 and continued to rise throughout the War. In Vienna, the mortality rate from tuberculosis rose almost 100 per cent; in Germany, 44 per cent.[19] The excess of deaths in the civilian population during each of the War years over the number of deaths for the year 1913 totalled 762,796 (see Table 7).

These figures represent the number of deaths which under 'normal circumstances' presumably would not have happened. They were probably due to a combination of food shortage with other factors. Medical care of civilians suffered because of the army's drain on medical personnel and facilities. There was a shortage of fuel because importation of coal was reduced by the Blockade and internal distribution was disrupted by the War. Although most of the War was fought on French and Russian soil, the Austro-Hungarian Empire was invaded, with some if its villages and countryside becoming a battleground.

If the figures below are compared with deaths in the army it can be seen that civilian deaths in excess of normal may have been about half as great as the army losses. However, it must also be said that the very war conditions which cause excess civilian deaths make reliable statistics difficult to assemble.

George A. Schreiner, an Associated Press correspondent, spent the first three years of the War in Germany and the nations allied with it, including considerable time with the armies on both Eastern and Western fronts. He states that many men in the army received better food than they had as pre-war civilians. He says that the army "came first in all things", and that when it became necessary to reduce the bread ration, this was made good by increasing the meat and fat ration.[20] Schreiner quotes a "food dictator" as saying that thousands of the poor aged were going to a premature death.

THE SIEGE OF LENINGRAD. The most recent, the most lethal, and yet the most completely ineffective use of starvation as a strategic

TABLE 7[29] Deaths during Blockade of the Central Powers
(1914-18)

	Deaths in the Army		Excess deaths in the Civil Population
	On the battlefield and through wounds	Through sickness	Due to the Blockade (presumably)
1st War Year	451,506	24,394	88,235
2nd War Year	330,332	30,329	121,174
3rd War Year	294,743	30,190	259,627
4th War Year	317,954	38,167	293,760*
Post-war due to the war	62,417	10,902	
Total	1,456,952	133,982	762,796

* To end of 1918.

weapon of war was the siege of Leningrad by the Nazis in World
War II. It closed around the three million people of the city on
September 8th, 1941. For four months only 45,000 tons of food
were brought in by water, air, and finally by the road across the
ice of Lake Ladoga, and this was expected to sustain the military
as well as the civilian population. Late in January, 1942, a corridor
was opened which permitted both the importation of food and the
evacuation of large numbers of people, but the siege was not completely lifted until two years later. By this time almost a million
people—about a third of the city's population—were dead from
hunger, cold, and their attendant diseases, and from the bombing
and shelling of the city.

As in the previous cases, the soldiers defending the city had better
rations than the civilians, although their rations, too, had to be cut
in November, 1941, when things were at their worst.[21] Hospital
records for the starvation period show some of the effects on infants
and pregnant mothers: an increase in stillbirth and premature birth
and a rise in neo-natal mortality.[22]

The early and worst parts of the siege were accompanied by
German victories elsewhere in the nation; German armies came
within a few miles of Leningrad homes and factories where people

F

continued to live and work. Nevertheless, the troops, besieged along with the city, defended it successfully and eventually broke the blockade.

While historians differ in assigning significance to these blockades as effective military techniques, it is clear from all three of these examples that food denial in war affects the fighting man least and last, if at all, and is therefore unsuccessful unless accompanied by military victories by the blockaders. It is hardest on civilians, particularly children and the elderly; where economic class divisions are sharp, it is particularly hard on the poor.

Destroying food in Vietnam

The increasing use of herbicides in Vietnam referred to in the previous chapter suggests that the U.S. Military plans to enlarge the area where food crops will be destroyed.

News stories have reported other methods being used in the food-denial campaign. In areas under the political control of the NLF, U.S. and South Vietnamese troops may establish temporary military control long enough for a 'harvest protection' operation. This is carried out by entering the area at harvest time, holding off NLF rice-collectors, while peasants are required to sell their surpluses to the government or to the commercial market, and then withdrawing.[23]

The agricultural area in the demilitarized zone and just to the south of it has been rendered completely unproductive, as have special areas in the immediate proximity of Saigon (Operations Junction City and Cedar Falls in the 'iron triangle'). As many as 600,000 Vietnamese have been removed from agricultural productive labour and at the time of writing are residing in camps.[24]

Rice that has already been harvested may be destroyed. Sometimes it is dumped into large pits and covered with shark repellent or other obnoxious compounds; attempts have been made to burn or scatter it. Captured rice has been dumped into the Rachbenggo River by U.S. troops.

According to General William W. Berg, U.S. Air Force Deputy Assistant Secretary of Defense, "Our combat units are well aware of the food shortages in South Vietnam and are not wantonly destroying captured rice whenever it can be salvaged and put to local use. However, in a fluid combat situation, available time, manpower, and transportation will not always permit removal of captured goods to a safe area."[25]

Charles Mohr has reported in the *New York Times* that the

troops have found rice to be "one of the most maddeningly indes-
tructible substances on earth. Even with thermite molten-metal
grenades, it virtually will not burn. The scattering of rice does not
prevent its collection by patient men."[23]

These practical difficulties suggest one reason for the use of
chemical sprays. Another, and perhaps the most important reason,
is that it entails a more efficient use of personnel.

"What's the difference between denying the Viet Cong rice by
destroying it from the air or by sending in large numbers of ground
forces to prevent the enemy from getting it?" a Pentagon spokesman asked. "The end result's the same; only the first method takes
far less men."[26]

Whatever method is used, the examination of past wars and
famines makes it clear that the food shortage will strike first and
hardest at children, the elderly, and pregnant and lactating women;
last and least at adult males, and least of all at soldiers.

That these conclusions have applied to Vietnam as well is suggested by the Vietnamese nutrition study, carried out in 1959 by
Americans and South Vietnamese under the latter's Committee on
Nutrition for National Defence, in which an equal number of army
and civilian Vietnamese were compared.[27]

"In the general sense, the nutritional status of the military is
superior to that of the civilian population, without appreciable
differences between Army, Navy, and Air Force," says the study.
While the average civilian male weighs 104·3 pounds, his counter-
part in the military weighs 113·0 pounds. And, for those who might
suppose the difference results from military selection procedures
favouring bigger men from the general population, the study
reports:

> Inductees (Quang Trung) weighed 107 pounds on the average,
> the lowest weight among any of the military. A group of similar
> men completing their basic training (Quang Trung) has an average
> weight of 114 pounds, suggesting that the change from a civilian
> to a military diet resulted in a prompt weight gain, in spite of
> the strenuous activity of basic training. Considering the combined
> military services, continuation of such weight gain during the
> first year of military life was further evidenced by the weight
> gain from an average 107 pounds for those in the service less
> than three months to an average of 118 pounds for those with
> six months to one year of service.

South Vietnamese army medical care was also superior to that
available to civilians, as Dr John Reed of the U.S. Public Health
Service testified on his return from working with Vietnam refugees:

". . . there are only about 800 qualified physicians in the Republic of South Vietnam. Of this 800, 500 are in the military service. Of the remaining 300, approximately half, or 150, are in private practice in Saigon, so this leaves only about 150 doctors for the entire rural population in South Vietnam."[28]

This refers to the South Vietnamese government side, but on the other side, NLF soldiers were likewise expected to get the fighter's share of whatever food there was. Whether extra rations were enforced by an organized government structure or confiscated by armed bands of guerillas, the end result was the same. Unless direct evidence to the contrary from U.S. observations in Vietnam is forthcoming, this conclusion seems unavoidable: from a military viewpoint, the attempt to starve an enemy can be expected to have little or no effect. What it can be expected to do is to add to the flow of refugees already far beyond the capacity of the programme designed to care for them.

The history of modern war has been one of increasing involvement of civilians. Starvation as a weapon is an aspect of such involvement, one which has the peculiar property of inflicting suffering on civilians while doing little damage to the military. To destroy crops—with herbicides or in any other way—is therefore to employ a weapon whose target is the weakest element of the civilian population.

I would strongly suggest that the proscription of famine as a weapon, whether by chemicals, through food destruction, fire, or mechanical methods, or through food denial by blockade, seizure of foodstuffs, or imposed excessive rationing, be the subject of a separate international convention. The manner in which food is destroyed or denied is less important than the final result. Abandonment of this method of waging war should be all the easier in that it is cruel while at the same time of no definite military value.

DISCUSSION

In the discussion to this Session, Dr Lindop suggested that international scientific pressure, such as through a group of scientific assessors, from the International Confederation of Scientific Unions (ICSU), the major international scientific body, could report on the defoliated areas and predict the possible damage produced. Dr Galston agreed that this would be desirable, and that the more pressure that was put on the Pentagon in particular, the more the chances that some teams of inspectors would be sent out there. There had been a few visiting scientists sponsored by the Department of Defense to survey the effects of drifting chemicals and to take a look at possible upsets in the ecology and disappearance of certain rare species. The argument that was used by the Department of Defense against the journey to Vietnam of experts who might like to take a look for themselves is that a great many of these operations had been carried out in areas controlled by the NLF, and that the U.S. Army could not then in good conscience release a group of people into an area over which they had no control militarily. Dr Lindop pointed out, however, that International Red Cross inspection teams were sent into combatant areas without guarantee of safety. The influence of an international team would be immense.

PART TWO

CBW IN USE

7. Vietnam   M. F. Kahn

Sources

In this report I shall deal mostly with practical aspects of the use of CBW in Vietnam. I will also report on my personal experience as an investigator for the International War Crimes Tribunal (IWCT) set up by Bertrand Russell, and also as a member of the Scientific Commission of the Tribunal.

I would like first to describe the methods used by the Tribunal investigators and also the sources of the information made available to us.

Our sources were as follows: (i) Reprints or photostats of the main U.S. reports and papers, appearing in both the general and technical American press, dealing with CBW in Vietnam. (ii) Texts of all the dispatches issued by American war correspondents in Vietnam, including those which were not (for whatever reason) published by the news agencies. (iii) Official reports of the Commission of Enquiry on the American War Crimes in Vietnam, a body set up by the Democratic Republic of Vietnam (DRV) (North Vietnam) with a technical appendix of material evidence and numerous pictures. (iv) Official reports of the Committee for the Denunciation of War Crimes Perpetrated by the U.S. Imperialists and their Puppets in South Vietnam, an organ of the NLF of South Vietnam with technical appendix of material evidence and pictures. (v) Reports of the investigation teams, sent by the IWCT to both the DRV- and NLF-controlled areas of South Vietnam. (vi) Reports of the members of the Scientific Commission of the IWCT, including a technical appendix and results of chemical analyses and of animal experiments.

I shall add to this documentation data collected through my personal experience as a member of both investigation teams in the DRV and South Vietnam (NLF-controlled areas) and as a member of the scientific commission.

Comment on the use of Napalm and Phosphorus

Although napalm and phosphorus are not in the strict sense chemical or biological weapons (see chapter 3) since they are mainly incendiary weapons, it is worth pointing out that this classification is somewhat arbitrary.

As far as napalm is concerned, numerous reports show that this compound, when burning, gives rise to large amounts of carbon monoxide. This happens mostly when napalm is burning indoors, when its combustion is incomplete. Thus there are reports of Japanese soldiers killed during World War II by napalm without any visible burns. While in South Vietnam, I had the opportunity to observe the following case: M. Nguyen Van Ba, male, 36 years old, had received a small amount of napalm while trying to protect himself in a shelter during a U.S. Air Force attack over the village of Ta-Bang (Province of Tay-Ninh) in 1966. He had felt a burning on his hand, and then became comatose for several hours. When he awoke, according to the people who discovered him, he was in a bad state of complete disorientation and had hallucinations. Since then he had had a tremor with hypertonia, exaggeration of postural reflexes, and complained of significant loss of vision. On examination I found a very large concentric narrowing of his eye field on both sides; these symptoms are suggestive of the results of intoxication, similar to domestic gas poisoning. The burning scar was very tiny, and the effects induced by this burning were obviously not sufficient to explain his state; other people with him in the shelter were found dead.

It is worth pointing out that carbon monoxide intoxication greatly increases the lethality of napalm since it prevents the victim from escaping the fire.

As far as phosphorus is concerned, as well as horrible burning this compound causes a severe intoxication and hepato-nephritis (liver and kidney poisoning), which in most cases is fatal, even when the burning appears superficial. In fact, phosphorus penetrates deeply into the skin and the subcutaneous tissues, since it produces phosphoric acids which are very acidic, and spreads all over the body.

In addition to these toxic effects on man one has to consider the effects on cattle, poultry, and fish. Fish forms the bulk of the protein intake of the Vietnamese peasant, and poisoning results when a phosphorus bomb or shell falls into any lake or area of water used for breeding fish.

Defoliants and Herbicides

Chapters 5 and 6 have already discussed these compounds and their use in Vietnam. I shall mention only some particular aspects of their use which I noted during my investigations in South Vietnam.

TARGETS. The province of Tay-Ninh, where I stayed mostly, had been heavily attacked by defoliants. I saw large areas of rice fields and of jungle which had previously received amounts of defoliant. Over the jungle the results of the attack were hardly noticeable. I never saw the cover provided by the leaves completely destroyed. However I did see in some places an abnormal amount of freshly fallen leaves on the earth and occasionally some more heavily damaged trees, proving that the defoliants had been used. Most of the places attacked in the jungle areas were in fact on the edge of the jungle close to the rice fields. On the other hand, I saw heavy damage caused by defoliant on plantations including trees and papayas. Dessicated leaves, swollen, cracked, and fissured stems, and stunted fruits unfit for eating were evident. The witnesses who testified to our Commission were unanimous in their accounts of the spraying of chemicals and the resultant damage to crops. As far as the rice fields were concerned, our evaluation was less precise as the results of the chemical spraying were mixed with the results of neglect caused by the non-stop land and air bombardment in the 'free-killing zones', but here, too, the testimony of the Vietnamese peasants was unanimous concerning the damage caused to the rice by the chemicals.

Thus, for the investigation team on the spot it was beyond doubt that concentrated attacks on the food supplies of the Vietnamese people was the main target of the so-called defoliants in Vietnam. The obvious ineffectiveness of the chemicals on the declared target —the jungle—contrasts sharply with the relative efficiency against crops and food and trees.

TOXICITY OF THE DEFOLIANTS FOR HUMANS AND ANIMALS. Assistant Secretary of State, Dixon Donelly, quoted by Galston in Chapter 5, said that the chemicals in use in Vietnam ". . . are not harmful for people, animals, soil or water". Despite this, several dozen witnesses heard by our Commission in South Vietnam told us of the physiological troubles they underwent following the spraying of chemicals. In most of the cases it is true that these troubles were relatively mild or transitory in adults. But we were told about lethal cases occurring among children. In fact adults take care, being informed by the medical services of the NLF, to avoid eating fruits and herbs after chemical spraying. But children do, on occasion, eat fruit coated with chemicals. Miss Thuy-Ba, M.D., chief of the medical staff of a provincial NLF hospital, described to us a lethal case she observed. A five-year-old boy was brought to the hospital after he had eaten contaminated fruit. He had severe abdominal pain, vomiting, then diaorrhea with blood in his stools, followed by collapse and death. On pathological examination, the post mortem revealed disseminated necrosis of the intestinal mucosa.

We collected numerous reports of the heavy losses inflicted on cattle and poultry by the chemicals. Buffaloes, pigs, hens, and ducks died by the dozen after spraying. These animals—like the children —were not reluctant to eat foodstuffs, even heavily coated by chemicals.

The Commission of Inquiry of the DRV has carried out experiments to test the animal toxicity of these compounds, and in a first set of experiments the animal tested was the duck. The chemical was DNOC (Dinitro-ortho-cresol). Each animal weighing 0·75 to 1·0 kg. received either 20 or 100 mg. of the substance. Death subsequently occurred from 5 minutes (120 mg.) to 14 minutes (20 mg.). Pathological findings in these animals revealed extensive damage to the digestive tract with haemorrhages. One has to bear in mind that an amount of 20 to 100 mg. may easily* be ingested by animals feeding in a chemical-coated area.

Thus localized vitamin deficiencies were sometimes associated with these symptoms, and one has also to consider the possible, yet unpredictable, delayed consequences not only for the exposed people, but also for their descendants.

Gases in use in Vietnam

THEIR NATURE AND DISSEMINATION METHODS IN USE. Despite the first official denials concerning the use of gases in Vietnam, the use of CN (chloroacetophenone); DM (adamsite), an arsenical compound; and CS (ortho-chlorobenzalmalononitrile) has now been admitted by the Americans, and there is a persistent report that the

---

* Some of the conference participants were less certain that it would be easy to build up an intake of quite so large a dose as this. However there now exists, in the French literature, a case of the near fatality of a small French girl and the death of her dog following the use of 2, 4,-D as a herbicide near Lille, France.[14] *Ed.*

hallucinogen, BZ, was used on at least one occasion, in Bong-san, in March 1966. The method of dissemination of these gases calls for further comment.

It has been reported that the chemicals are used mostly in the form of aerosols.[11] In fact, at least for CS on which I was able to collect precise data and material evidence, the methods of dissemination involve the dispersion of solid particles which undergo direct sublimation from solid to gas. They are not dispensed as droplets, or true solution dispersed with an aqueous phase, which is the definition of a true aerosol. In the projectiles, such as hand grenades of either cylindrical or spherical form, CS is present as a powder which is disseminated in small particles by the explosion of a standard detonator. This detonator is the same as the detonator of the explosive hand grenade. The heat caused by the explosion helps the sublimation of the solid compound. This factor is important when attempting to calculate the concentration obtained by the use of these projectiles in an enclosed space.

Another way of dissemination which is especially adapted to a closed area is the dispersion of the powder by means of a high velocity wind machine, nicknamed 'Mighty Mite' by the Americans. This machine provides a very powerful air stream, and can very easily build up high concentrations of gases in caves and shelters.

In some cases gases are used in the open air, thrown in cluster canisters for example, or in numerous small projectiles dispersed by a special type of multi-barrelled portable mortar. One of these was shown to the IWCT in Roskilde by the North Vietnamese delegation. But reports from the American side acknowledge the fact that this kind of use was rather ineffective because of the quick dispersion of the gas in the atmosphere and the fact that Vietnamese troops were able to protect themselves with gas-masks.

But it is the alternative use of the gases which is more disturbing —their injection into shelters and caves to force out people from their safe underground protection. In fact, as many reports have confirmed, virtually the whole population (both soldiers and civilians) is obliged to take protection in caves or underground shelters to escape shells, bombs, and the less conventional weapons such as cluster-bomb units, napalm, and phosphorus.

When gases are thrown into such shelters a condition is obtained which differs completely from that following use in the open air. All the data available for CN, DM, and CS are calculated for low concentrations obtained by dispersion in the open air. But it must be emphasized that when powder is thrown into a closed area much higher concentrations build up. In fact, these concentrations cannot actually be calculated by the users of the gas. For a given dose the concentration of gas in the air depends on temperature, humidity, and above all, the volume of air into which the gas is dispersed, and it is obvious that this volume cannot be either calculated or even estimated by troops using the gas.

When applying the gases soldiers inevitably pump in the maximum amount they feel possible. Such machines as 'Mighty Mite' provide the possibility of blowing in more than 22 lb. of CS into one shelter. A very high concentration of this compound within the shelter can easily build up.

ARE THE GASES 'HARASSING' OR LETHAL? This point has been discussed, particularly by the Americans themselves, in the context of the fact that 'riot-control' and tear gases are not prohibited by the Geneva Convention. However, some semi-official U.S. sources acknowledge that even if a gas is formally labelled as 'harassing', death may sometimes result from their use. Thus in his book *Tomorrow's Weapons*[1] Rothschild states that CS has a *low* lethality potential. For CN, DM, and CS, toxicity figures indicate a lethal concentration of 100 to 300 mg/m^3 of air.*

For DM, which has been reported in use over the South Vietnam town of Hue in February, 1968, it is stated that this compound . . . "is not approved for use in . . . any operation where deaths are not acceptable" (e.g., riot control). However the field manual of the U.S. Army reports that it may be used combined with CN in munitions and in "military or paramilitary operations, in counterinsurgency operations, or in limited or general war . . . where *possible deaths are acceptable*" [my italics]. One has to remember that the gases used in World War I, in 1915, and now prohibited by international law were not, by far, 100 per cent lethal gases; mortality was only about 10 per cent of those affected.[2]

THE FACTUAL REPORTS. The first information appeared in March, 1965 in the *New York Times*[3] when George Reedy of the Presidential Press Office stated, "The gases are rather standard types of riot-control agent".

On the same day Secretary of State Robert McNamara stated that these gases "could be obtained through commercial channels." He

---

* Mr Robinson has also pointed out that toxicity data on CS is also to be found in the open literature[12, 13]. The use of DM as a harassing agent by British forces has been ruled out on the legal grounds that its use contravenes the General Protocol, 1925, according to Porton Technical Paper No. 651, declassified in June 1968. *Ed.*

displayed an illustrated catalogue issued by one manufacturer, and it was stated that "Mr McNamara is understood to have tried the effectiveness of CS gas personally to compare it with types used in World War II."[3] He added that: "Rather than use firepower, thereby jeopardising the lives of non-combatants, to drive the Vietcong out of the area the South Vietnamese troops dispensed riot-control agent". Dean Rusk, quoted by the *New York Times*, stated that, "It wasn't very effective. When the wind blew it away, it was dissipated, it did not achieve the purpose", and he concluded, "the anticipation is, of course, that these weapons be used only in those situations involving riot control or situations analogous to riot control".

As it can be seen from these declarations, the use of these gases in shelters or caves was not under consideration, officially at least, in March 1965.

The following month, *Time* magazine stated: "Compared with napalm bombs that incinerate whole villages, or a white phosphorus shell that burns a man to the bone, the temporarily disabling gases used in Vietnam seem more humane than horrible".[4] There followed many reports from Trung Lap[5, 6] describing how the gases were injected into tunnels and shelters, including those where civilians were hiding.

Then came the story about Robert Bowtell, given as follows in the *New York Times*: "Non toxic (sic) gas and smoke being used against Vietcong guerillas, in tunnels north-west of Saigon, have killed one Australian soldier and sent six others to hospital, officials said today. Cpl. Robert Bowtell, 21, of Sydney, died of asphyxiation although he was wearing a gas mask".[7] This information was confirmed from different sources.* It was the first official admission of the possible lethality of the so-called tear gases.

As a matter of fact, dispatches from Vietnamese sources alleged that in Han Nghia (Long Hu province) troops belonging to the 173rd U.S. Brigade together with Australian and New Zealand troops had used gases extensively against the civilian population hidden in shelters. From January 8th to 15th, 1966, more than one hundred people were killed by the gases in the shelters.

It can be seen that the two reports fit completely, and provide

---

* Since the conference my attention has been drawn to a rather more detailed account in the *Courier Mail* (Australia), January 13th, 1966. The report suggests that a build-up of carbon monoxide in the tunnel may have been a contributory factor in Bowtell's death. The involvement of CS, though, is not disputed. *Ed.*

TABLE 8

FRONT NATIONAL DE LIBERATION DU SUD VIET NAM

Comité pour la dénonciation des crimes de guerre commis par les impérialistes US et leurs valets au Sud Viet Nam

EPANDAGE DE GAZ TOXIQUE

N.5

Date	Faits et localité	Dommages
28 janvier	- Plusieurs bombes à gaz toxique larguées sur le hameau de Phu Lac, village de Hoa Hiep, district de Duy Hoa (province de Phu Yên)	- 100 habitants morts, plusieurs autres intoxiqués
27 février 1965	- Plusieurs ballons à gaz toxique largués sur les villages de Binh Hoa, Thanh Phuong (province de Kiên Tuong)	- Plusieurs enfants ayant ramassé ces ballons ont été gravement intoxiqués
Février 1965	- Epandage de gaz toxique sur la localité de Bông Son (province de Binh Dinh)	- Plusieurs habitants intoxiqués
9 mars 1965	- Epandage de gaz toxique sur les habitants de la localité de Tân Uyên (province de Biên Hoa)	- Plusieurs habitants morts
Fin Mars 1965	- Epandage de gaz toxique sur la localité de Boi Loi (province de Tây Ninh)	- Des centaines d'habitants intoxiqués dont plusieurs femmes et enfants morts dans la suite.
3 avril 1965	- 4 bombes à gaz toxique larguées sur le village de Phuoc Tân, district de Tiên Phuoc (province de Quang Nam)	- Presque tous les habitants du village gravement intoxiqués.
9 avril 1965	- Des bombes à gaz toxique larguées sur le village de Phuoc Son (district de Thang Binh) province de Quang Nam.	- 72 habitants intoxiqués.
13 mai 1965	- Dans une opération de ratissage, épandage de gaz toxique, à Vinh Chau (province de Soc Trang)	- Des centaines d'habitants intoxiqués dont 30 morts dans la suite.

- 3 -

Date	Faits et localité	Dommage
De 8 août janvier 1966	- Les GI's de la 173ème brigade et les mercenaires néo-zélandais ... retissage à Hâu Nghia (province de Long An) ont insufflé dans les abris de la population des gaz toxiques à forte dose.	- Plus d'une centaine d'habitants dont la plupart des femmes et des enfants. Au cours de cette même opération le sergent américain Robert Bowtell mourut lui-même d'intoxication, 6 soldats australiens intoxiqués ont dû être transportés à l'hôpital.
9 - 14 janvier 1966	- Ratissage à Cu Chi (province de Gia Dinh) insuf...	- Plus d'une centaine d'habitants morts, des cen...

- 2 -

Date	Faits et localité	Dommages
26 août 1965	- Insufflation de gaz toxique par 4 pulvérisateurs sur la population groupée au canal de Rach relevant du village de Long An (province de Long An)	- 146 habitants intoxiqués, 30 morts
5 septembre 1965	- Dans une opération de retissage au hameau de Vinh Quang, village de Phuoc Son, district de Tuy Phuoc (province de Binh Dinh) insufflation de "az CN" par 37 pulvérisateurs dans les abris de la population.	- Plus de 100 habitants intoxiqués dont 24 enfants de moins de 10 ans, 26 femmes, 16 vieillards gravement atteints, 35 morts, 7 ont les yeux crevés.
3 septembre 1965	- Ratissage, lancement de plusieurs grenades à gaz toxique dans la localité de Ba Lang An (province de Quang Ngai)	- 78 habitants morts dont presque tous sont des vieillards, des femmes et des enfants.
6 octobre 1965	- Insufflation de gaz toxique sur la population de la localité de Tân Cat sud (province de Binh Duong)	- Plusieurs habitants intoxiqués, 3 morts.
24, 25 Novembre 1965	- Bombes et grenades à gaz toxique larguées sur la localité de Thach Tru, district de Lo Duc (province de Quang Ngai)	- Plusieurs habitants intoxiqués et atteints des maladies graves.
2 janvier 1966	- Ratissage à Bau Trai (province de Long An) insufflation par slightly mile de gaz toxique parmi la population	- Des centaines d'habitants intoxiqués, plusieurs morts dans la suite.
2 janvier 1966	- Ratissage à Duc Hoa, Duc Hue (province de Long An) lancement de grenades à gaz toxique dans des abris de la population.	- Des centaines de femmes, d'enfants et de vieillards intoxiqués faisant plusieurs morts.

Date	Faits et localité	Dommage
20, 28 février 1966	- GI's et mercenaires Sud ... dans le district de Binh Dinh ... grenades gaz toxique sur la population, ont chargé les gens de la bar, ... dans des masons qu'ils incendièrent par la suite	- 280 habitants morts dont la presque totalité est constituée de femmes, de vieillards et d'enfants (13 femmes, 6 vieillards, 6 enfants)
21 février 1966	- A Bông Son nord (province de Binh Dinh) ...	- ...sieurs habitants in-

Date	Faits et localité	Dommage
27, 30 janvier 1966	Mon (province de Binh Dinh). Les GI's et mercenaires Sud Coréens ont lancé des grenades à gaz toxique dans les abris où ils ont parqué des femmes vieillards et enfants.	
	Des ballons de gaz toxique ont été largués sur les villages de Khanh Hung, Trấn Hoi, Khanh Binh (province de Bac Liêu)	Plus de 1.000 habitants intoxiqués dont plusieurs enfants; à petit ... perdu la faculté de parler.
1 février 1966	Insufflation de gaz toxique dans des abris de la population du village de Ky Anh, district de Tam Ky (province de Quang Nam)	14 enfants morts, plusieurs personnes intoxiquées.
14 février 1966	Au cours d'une opération de ratissage à Dong Son (Binh Dinh) où étaient engagés 20.000 GI's et mercenaires, des hélicoptères de la division de cavalerie mobile US n°1 ont lancé 600 grenades à gaz toxique sur les différents hameaux du district.	Des centaines d'habitants intoxiqués.
13 avril 1966	... la population civile de ... 3.000 grenades à gaz toxiques. A Dâu Tiêng (province Binh Duong) lance ... de 10 grenades à gaz toxiques en répression d'	
30 avril 1966	Au village de Hoa Hiệp district de Châu Thanh (province de Tây Ninh) lancement de nombreuses fois de poudre toxiques	Nombreux habitants intoxiqués, nombreux animaux domestiques ...
Première semaine de mai 1966	Lancement de 15 tonnes de poudres toxiques dans le Nord-Ouest de Tây Ninh au cours de l'opération "Birmingham"	
Juin	Epandage de poudres toxiques sur les villages de Ham Cuong, Ham Liêm, Ham Phu, Ham Ninh, Ham My (district de Ham Thuân), Tân Hiệp (district de Hàm Tân) province de Binh Thuân.	Des certaines d'habitants intoxiqués
5 juillet 1966	Epandage de toxiques en poudre sur la localité de Da Bao (Tây Ninh)	Nombreux habitants intoxiqués, mort.

- 5 -

Sud Viet Nam, le 1er octobre 1967
Le Secrétaire général
Signé : Ung Ngoc Ky

Pour traduction conforme :
P. Le Chef de la délégation permanente
du FNL du Sud Viet Nam ... Nord Viet Nam et P.O
Le ...

G

official evidence of the lethality of the gases used in the tunnels and shelters. From Vietnamese sources, more data was obtained which indicated an extensive use of gases, and numerous deaths. The NLF in South Vietnam prepared a detailed report, parts of which are reproduced on pp. 94–95. In fact, the NLF claim that there have been a minimum of thirty well-authenticated cases of the lethal use of gas prior to December, 1967. Deaths must run into several hundreds and those less affected into many thousands. These are inevitably minimum figures. One may recall that the mortality rate from gas in World War I was only about one in ten, yet the post-war records of those in France and Britain who did not die from gas at the time made it clear that the after-effects may persist, and many deaths attributable to the gas may occur years after the gas attack itself. For instance, any kind of bronchial irritation may increase the rate of lung cancer incidence in the affected population.

During our inquiry in Vietnam in Tay Ninh Province, peasants told us that they found big barrels that the local officers had identified as probable gases. We went to see these barrels and found a large, heavy container, easily identified, since the contents were clearly labelled. Each barrel was said to contain eighty lb. of CS. It is noteworthy that the label put on these barrels read "RIOT CONTROL". I remember our thoughts when looking at these words; they were obviously misleading, since it is difficult to imagine how the average policeman could handle an 80-lb barrel in an attempt to control any kind of riot. It is possible that this barrel was intended to feed a 'Mighty Mite'—which is not intended for use against riots. We made a small hole in the barrel and took away a sample of grey powder. Very soon we became severely ill with tearing coughs, agonizing abdominal pains, vomiting, and headaches. This happened despite the fact that we were in the open air, had protected our faces with a kind of mask made of plastic, and were well aware of the toxicity of the compound. We were sick for several hours.

The samples we took back to France were formally identified by Professor Lederer's laboratory in Paris and were used for the experiments described in the following section.

Experiments done with the gases used by the United States in Vietnam[8]

As has been said, it appears that the gases used by the United States in Vietnam were not simple harassing agents, owing to the way in which they were used in confined and closed areas where the concentration becomes high. The potential lethality of these gases is, as we have shown, recognized by the United States (reluctantly and indirectly) and by the Vietnamese. To further elucidate this point, experiments were carried out on animals.

The first set of experiments were carried out at Hanoi, by the members of the Vietnamese Commission on the U.S. War Crimes. Dr Vigier of France attended the experiments.[9] All these experiments were filmed and the film was shown in Copenhagen for the Tribunal.

The experiments were as follows: DM was tested on a monkey at a concentration of 15,000 mg/m³. The monkey showed severe respiratory seizures within 20 minutes and died within 45 minutes. Pathological findings included severe liver damage. CS was tested first on a cat, at 15,000 mg/m³. The animal died within 30 minutes. Pathological findings included severe lesions, mainly of liver, brain, and kidneys. The same compound was tested on a monkey at a concentration of only 5000 mg/m³. Death occurred in 25 minutes, with severe lesions similar to those seen in cats.

The second set of experiments were carried out in France by Professor Roussel in his laboratory devoted to industrial and environmental toxicology. He made a precise study of the toxicity of CS on mice, and found that at a concentration of CS powder of 200 to 2,500 mg/m³ of air, two-thirds of the exposed mice died in 10 hours. The pathological findings included severe lesions in kidney, liver, and respiratory tract.

Conclusions

It is not possible at the time of writing to assess whether other gases or toxic agents have been used by the United States in Vietnam. Many reports have referred to the possibility of use of compounds such as LSD as a weapon in Vietnam, and it must be emphasized that if any such experiment has been carried out by the United States in Vietnam it would be difficult to collect sufficiently precise data to present reliable evidence here.

Moreover, American statements on the use of these weapons have been consistent only in their evasiveness. Thus even when they were trying to make the world believe that they were using only "tear gas" in Vietnam, it was revealed that DM was prohibited even in the open air for riot control, because it was known that fatal casualties could result from its use. In the *New England Journal of Medicine*, Sidel and Goldwyn have stated:

Even if a "humane weapon" is developed, its humanity will require the delivery, as in the laboratory, of a precisely measured dose to a standard victim. Both these requisites have thus far been impossible to obtain in the field. Chemical and biological weapons are notoriously uneven in their dispersal and therefore in the amount absorbed by each recipient; to ensure that every person receives an incapacitating dose, some will have to receive an overdose. Furthermore, the young, the elderly and the infirm will be the particularly susceptible victims.[10]

There is little to change in this statement. Only a word. Instead of "will be", we have to put "are".

ADDENDUM

The following information has since come to my notice. M.F.K.

Recent scientific reports have shown that defoliants like 2, 4-D do not need to be ingested in order to be toxic; they are able to penetrate the skin so that mere contact is sufficient. (LACOMBE, A., *Revue Française de pédiatrie*, 1967, III, 207. *See also* NEILSEN, K., Fatal poisoning in man by 2, 4-D. *Acta Pharmacol.*, 1965. 22. 224–234.)

A first-hand testimony of the lethality of the so-called riot-control gases was made available to me by Dr Alje Vennema. While serving in Quang Ngai Provincial Hospital he saw many cases of fatalities following exposure to the gases. The principal cause of death was respiratory. See *New York Review of Books*, May 9th 1968.

8. The Yemen   M. Meselson

The History

Since 1963 there have been sporadic reports of the use of poison gas in the Yemeni civil war. It has been alleged that the gas was being used by the Egyptians on behalf of their allies, the Yemeni Republicans. The charges have come from the Yemeni Royalists, their supporters the Saudi Arabians, from various journalists, and, most authoritatively, from the International Red Cross.

So far as the outside world is concerned suggestions of the use of gas in the Yemen began on July 8th, 1963, with an article in the London *Daily Telegraph* by Richard Beeston stating that there had been a gas attack on the village of Al Kanma. Following this story, U Thant initiated an inquiry "to determine whether poison gas has been used in the fighting in the Yemen." A United Nations observation team in the Yemen produced a preliminary report stating they had no evidence that gas had been used but that inquiries were continuing. No definite conclusion was ever announced by the U.N.

I find no further reference in the press to the use of gas in the Yemen until November, 1966, when Wilfred Thesiger, a British archeologist and explorer who had spent some time with the Royalists, stated that he had come into a village shortly after a gas attack. Thesiger reported seeing twenty victims of what he termed "blinding gas" and said that he treated a boy suffering from "blister gas" that might have been a form of mustard.

The first alleged use of nerve gas took place on January 5th, 1967, on the village of Kitaf, the military headquarters of the Yemeni Royalists. This would be the first use in any war of nerve gas, a class of compounds far more deadly than any other known war gases. Judith Listowel, writing in the *Statist*, reports an interview with the survivors and states that 155 persons were killed and 200 more severely poisoned. There happened to be a Red Cross team in the vicinity of Kitaf at the time, and they are alleged to have sent a cable to their superiors reporting the gas attack and requesting gas-masks. The Red Cross did not officially acknowledge the telegram, but the Red Cross Director in Geneva stated that all parties had been appealed to not to use illegal weapons. On January 24th, Jordan threatened to withdraw recognition of the Yemeni Republican government unless the use of gas was stopped.

On January 31st, the United Arab Republic Minister of National Guidance, Mohammed Fayek, denied that the U.A.R. had ever used gas and furthermore said that Egypt would welcome a United Nations fact-finding commission to investigate the charges.

Over the next three months, the Saudi Arabian ambassador to the U.N. urged U Thant to speak out against the use of gas in the Yemen apparently not wishing to place the matter before the U.N. himself. The Saudi Arabians did however produce several pages of medical and chemical evidence purporting to show that nerve gas had been used at Kitaf. The evidence includes measurements of the phosphate content of the blood of human and animal casualties, supposedly an indication of the use of nerve gas. However, some of the figures seemed far too high to be reasonable.

On May 10th, 1967, according to a report published in the *New York Times* and attributed to the International Red Cross, there was an attack using gas on two Yemeni villages, Gadafa and Gahar. On the following day the International Red Cross team in Jidda, Saudi Arabia, received an urgent request for help. They arrived in Gahar on May 15th after being attacked on the road by military aircraft. The team conducted an autopsy and examined several survivors. Their report claims that 75 people were killed by the attack and 273 more by attacks on other villages later in May. The autopsy results were sent to the Faculty of Forensic Medicine at the University of Berne for evaluation, where it was concluded that the victims described had indeed been killed by poison gas, the most likely agent being mustard. Although these details have never been officially acknowledged by the Red Cross, on June 2nd, 1967, it issued a statement saying:

> The International Committee of the Red Cross has again received, from delegates in the Yemen, reports of bombing by toxic gas. A medical team led by the head of the R.C. Mission in the Yemen went on May 15 and 16 to a village in the northern part of the country to attempt to give aid to the victims of bombing which had taken place some days previously and as a result of which, according to the survivors, many inhabitants had died of asphyxiation. Delayed by air raids to which the convoy was victim, I.C.R.C. doctors on arrival at the site immediately

gave treatment to some of the wounded and collected various indications pointing to the use of poison gas. Extremely disturbed and concerned by these methods of warfare, which are absolutely forbidden by codified international and customary law, the International Committee of the Red Cross at once communicated its delegates' reports to all authorities concerned in the Yemen conflict requesting them to undertake a solemn engagement not to resort in any circumstances whatever to the use of asphyxiating gases or any other similar toxic substances.

The salient points in this record are that poison gas has been used in violation of the Geneva Protocol, that it has been used against civilians, and that nerve gas may have been employed in some of the attacks. The evidence indicates that Egypt is responsible, but Egyptian officials have denied the charge and have asked for an international investigation.

There have been no reports of gas warfare in the Yemen since the Arab-Israeli war of last year. However, it was not until about that time, with the first official Red Cross confirmation that gas had been used, that world reaction began to assume serious proportions. This, together with a variety of political reasons, may explain the failure of the world community to take more decisive steps to enforce the 1925 Geneva prohibition against gas warfare.

The Yemeni events and the United Kingdom   D. E. Viney

The first official British comment on the accumulating evidence of the use of toxic gas in the Yemen came on January 31st, 1967, when the Prime Minister agreed in the House that "such evidence as I have suggests pretty strongly that poison gas may have been used". It was immediately after this that Egyptian papers invited the U.N. to investigate, and the U.A.R. National Assembly was told by its Arab Affairs Committee (February 6th) that the allegations were a defamatory invention put out by Jordan and Saudi Arabia.

After unauthorized versions of the International Red Cross team's report had reached the press, and interest in the subject had been enhanced by Israeli apprehensions during the Middle East conflict in June, the Government was again pressed for comment. Minister of State, George Thompson, stated on July 3rd: "We have received well substantiated reports that gas was used several times. Both a mustard type and a choking type have been used on different occasions."

When the possibility of a British initiative was raised Foreign Secretary, George Brown, reiterated that "we condemn the use of gas in the Yemen," but argued that it would be most appropriate for some Arab country, such as Saudi Arabia, to take action in the first place. That was on July 6th. Later in the month over two hundred Members of Parliament nevertheless signed a letter requesting that the Government should do something, and Mr Brown told an all-party delegation of three that the United Kingdom would consult with other powers as to "the best means of putting a stop to this clear breach of generally accepted rules of conduct".

Immediately after this Parliament went into recess. When it met again the Egyptians were pulling out of the Yemen; the British Government made it clear that none of the other powers consulted was interested in initiating further action and that it considered in any case that such an initiative might now exacerbate the situation in the Yemen rather than assist a settlement. It was of course widely assumed that a desire to avoid further unpopularity with the Arab world in the wake of the Middle East war played a major role in setting this attitude, and the West would no doubt have found itself isolated if it had impugned Egypt. The Soviet Union, Czechoslovakia, and other countries who had taken up a strongly pro-Arab line could not have been expected to lend any diplomatic aid for such a purpose, even though they were better placed to exert persuasion on Arab countries than the British were. If they made private representations in Cairo on the undesirability of flouting the Geneva Protocol—and it cannot be excluded that they did so—they evidently had little success.

Since the expert evidence of the use of lethal gases in the Yemen was not made public, no-one without special access to the facts can point the finger dogmatically at Egypt. However, the evidence was apparently found persuasive by British Ministers who had every political reason not to inflate the issue. The reasons why no international action was in the end taken are understandable enough. But the net result is that the Geneva Protocol, that lone achievement in the history of attempts to proscribe particular classes of weapons, is seen to have been flouted with impunity in the very kind of military confrontation where, because of the extreme inequality of strength and the impossibility of deterrence or reprisal in kind, respect for law is almost the only motive for restraint; and indeed to have been flouted (it seems) by a state which signed the original Protocol in 1925, reaffirmed its adhesion on becoming a Republic in 1953, and joined in the general acclamation of the ban on lethal chemical weapons during the United Nations debate in 1966.

PART THREE
RESEARCH POLICY

9. United Kingdom

Robin Clarke and
J. Perry Robinson

The organizers of this conference felt it important that representatives from the Ministry of Defence or its chemical and biological research centres at Porton Down, Wiltshire, should be asked to attend the conference and give papers on official United Kingdom policy. In consequence, representatives of both the Chemical Defence Experimental Establishment and the Microbiological Defence Establishment at Porton, as well as the Director of Chemical and Biological Defence, were invited to deliver papers on research policy and on matters of defence.

Unhappily, all three were unable to get permission to do so, although there have been television appearances both before and since.[1] What follows, therefore, is an attempt by two outsiders interested in the problem to summarize the results of some fairly extensive detective work and present what little is known about the British Chemical and Biological Warfare effort and the policies that lie behind it. Later, we shall indulge in a little speculation, but first we shall list what little is already public knowledge.

The research establishments

CHEMICAL DEFENCE EXPERIMENTAL ESTABLISHMENT. Much the oldest is the Chemical Defence Experimental Establishment (CDEE), as it is now called, which began on its present site in Wiltshire in 1916[2]—shortly after the first chemical weapons were used in World War I. As its name implies, it was from the first designed to be a defensive organization for all three military services. It now comes within the compass of the Ministry of Defence. Its budget is not publicly known and nor is the size of its staff. According to a press release[2] which was prepared in 1964 on the occasion of a press visit to Porton, much of its work is devoted to the solving of peace-time problems in civilian life; for example, it gives advice on the design of respirators for protection against industrial dusts and poisonous vapours and gives assistance in the treatment of poisoning from accidents in the use of agricultural chemicals.

However, undoubtedly one of the main contributions of the CDEE has been the improvements made by it in the respirator. From the respirators used in the last war, the CDEE developed a number of new models, of which the Light Respirator Mark 7 was in service in the early 1960's and which has now been replaced by the S6. A third type was developed at the CDEE for civilian use, and others have been developed for special service requirements, such as those of air crew. But the respirator is likely to be insufficient protection in time of chemical attack. The CDEE has also produced air filtration units for use where respirators may not be practicable, and these units are already installed in certain buildings and ships. One of these units, built entirely from non-magnetic material, has been designed for use on mine-sweepers.

The CB suit, which is said to be impervious to radioactive dust and to all chemical and biological weapons, was also developed at the CDEE. It is a remarkable advance on other protective CB suits in that it is very light and porous to allow passage of both air and moisture. Various other types of protective overclothing have also been developed there, sometimes as a result of close collaboration with the American, Canadian, and Australian establishments.[3] Alarm equipment to go with these protective devices has also been produced. It includes alarms said to give virtually instantaneous warning of the presence of nerve gases in either liquid or vapour form, another device for indicating when it is safe to remove the respirator, as well as detective pads which will indicate the presence of liquid chemicals by changing colour.

The CDEE has also been at the forefront in the therapy of nerve-gas poisoning.[4] Like the Swedish and the American establishments, it has developed devices[5] for the automatic injection of a standard dose of atropine into the bloodstream through the thigh. The injector is claimed to be superior to either of the other two models available in that the needle is pressure-sensitive. One of the first drawbacks of such injectors was the danger of the needle striking the bone with consequent medical complications. The British injector is designed so that pressure on the needle of the kind likely to be caused by contact with the bone causes the needle to halt its advance. A pill to be taken at the same time as the injection has also been developed. It contains the oxime known as P2S and has also found uses in treating cases of agricultural poisoning from phosphorus-containing insecticides.[2]

This side of the CDEE's activities, at least, is publicly known and is, indeed, described extensively in its scientific literature. Development work of this kind is also backed up by a pure research programme into the classical subjects of chemical and biological research centres—the physics of aerosols and sprays, micrometeorology, measurement of the size of particles and their concentration in the atmosphere, etc. Perhaps the only other publicly known fact—and certainly the only publicly known fact of offensive relevance—is that the riot-control agent CS was developed in the 1950's at the CDEE.[6] [The information that has become available about CS since the conference is quite extensive and is summarized in an addendum to this paper. Ed.]

MICROBIOLOGICAL RESEARCH ESTABLISHMENT. The other main unit at Porton, the Microbiological Research Establishment (MRE), is much more recent in date and probably better known if not to the public then at least to civilian scientists. In 1945, some forty-five people[7] were employed there, of whom fifteen were scientists, but the laboratory facilities were at that time far from ideal. The laboratories were therefore expanded, a job which was completed in June 1951,[8] and which was apparently carried out so that microbiologists, which the defence effort needed, could be attracted. This move was clearly successful, and the scientific work of the establishment gained rapid recognition. Clearly the MRE also grew in size, and though its exact complement of scientific staff is not publicly known, we know that in 1964, for instance, forty-one people authored openly published scientific papers from the establishment.[9] [In 1966, forty scientific papers were published by staff of the MRE, according to a Parliamentary Answer.[54]] The MRE has a reputation for scientific excellence, and this could not have been gained behind closed doors. On the contrary, access to the MRE is relatively easy, and it opens its doors—or at least some of them—to around 2000 visitors every year.[1] Its policy is equally liberal towards the publication of research results. According to the Director—and a glance at the microbiological literature tends to confirm what he says—about 80 per cent of the work that goes on at the MRE is published in the open literature. Perhaps, in case there is any confusion about it, something should be said about the scientific nature of this unclassified work.

Perhaps the best known concerns the continuous cultivation of bacteria,[8] a technique if not actually pioneered at Porton then certainly followed up very quickly by workers there. The net result of this—and similar work, of course, in Czechoslovakia and the United States—was the ability to grow bacteria indefinitely at a constant rate under standard conditions and with constant composition. This technique has proved particularly valuable in industry for the preparation of vaccine material and for growing the fungi used in the production of antibiotics.

Another field of important work has concerned the pathogenicity of disease-causing organisms. Scientists at the MRE, for instance, identified a specific toxin liberated by the anthrax bacillus and later proved their ability to produce it *in vitro*. They also resolved it into three components.[10] Similarly, in work first reported in 1961, they found that the bacterium *Brucella abortus* which causes brucellosis, or Malta fever, has a predeliction for foetal tissue.[11] The MRE workers found that this was because such tissue contained erythritol which stimulated the bacterial growth.

A substantial number of papers have also been published by workers at the MRE on the subject of the survival of bacterial species, particularly in aerosol form. In 1966 a single issue of the *Journal of General Microbiology* carried four articles by MRE scientists.[12, 12a] One dealt with the nutritional requirements of the plague bacillus and related species, two were on the survival of bacterial aerosols and the factors affecting it, and the last was on the survival of bacteria in suspension. Though the very fact that these papers were published at all virtually proves they are not representative of the growth, storage, and dispersal of British biological plague bombs, they do show that there is more than one way of interpreting the nature of the research effort at Porton. Officially, of course, all work there is either concerned with defence or is so basic that it has no military implications at all. Equally, and several workers at the MRE have admitted this, there is no clear dividing-line between offence and defence in these matters. Even to study defence requires that scientists learn how to produce samples of various weapons so that different defensive measures can be evaluated. The production of these samples may provide information useful to a nation which wishes to produce sample weapons on a larger scale—and perhaps one should recall that Porton has very few secrets, if any, from similar establishments in Australia, Canada, and the United States.

Is there, then, any concrete evidence that any of the work carried out at Porton, other than that done during World War II, has been done for offensive purposes? Early in World War II Defence officials sprayed anthrax on the island of Gruinard off the north-west coast of Scotland.[13, 14, 15] This was clearly a field trial of a biological weapon and one of the few that has ever been openly recorded. But the aim of the exercise, according to the present Director of the MRE,[1] was to establish whether or not biological warfare was at that time feasible. Dr Gordon Smith, Director of MRE, has said that it was then that several officials really began to believe that biological warfare was practically possible.[1] The experiment, incidentally, also demonstrated one of the great drawbacks of biological warfare in that the island that was sprayed in the 1940's is still contaminated and, according to Dr Gordon Smith, is likely to remain so for another hundred years. There is no evidence that this experiment, however, was the first step in the production of biological agents for use in war. We know of no other fields trials until the 1950's, when inanimate particles were sprayed from aircraft in the Bahamas area in 1954.[16, 17] However, for chemical weapons, which do not necessarily require field testing over large areas, we are aware of several field trials. Thus Porton Technical Paper No 239 of 1951 is entitled "The Lethality to Rats of GB and GE from HE/Chem. Weapons in the Field",[18] while No 424 of 1954 is entitled "The Production of Casualties in Monkeys with GB Vapour".[19] These two papers are not openly published. But again it could be easily argued that the trials were to test various defensive measures.

Detailed discussion of the exact balance of offence and defence in exercises of this kind is somewhat futile until such time as the officials concerned can be persuaded to reveal more about them. The overwhelming evidence at the present time is that both units are concerned primarily with defence and that a relatively small proportion of their work, possibly inevitably, may also have offensive implications. Neither is there any evidence of the manufacture of any weapons at Porton. We know, of course, that the equipment for the manufacture of the raw material for biological warheads is available at the MRE at Porton. Indeed, during the Asian 'flu epidemic of 1957, the MRE produced more than 600,000 doses of 'flu vaccine.[8] This means they could equally well produce 600,000 doses of a biological warfare agent. In that sense, the existence of the MRE must be reassuring to officials concerned with BW policy. For although Britain has both signed and ratified the Geneva Protocol[20] forbidding the use of chemical and biological weapons in war, the Protocol does not preclude retaliation in kind. While Britain has never shown any indication that she intends to break the Geneva Protocol, officials must have considered the possibility that a potential enemy might do so first. If they did, and it was decided to retaliate in kind, the MRE at Porton would probably provide the necessary biological material.

Chemical Weapons

If this seems obvious the situation with regard to chemical weapons is much less so. We do know that Britain possessed chemical weapons, but never used them, throughout World War II. After the War they were mostly disposed of, about 100,000 tons in all, some off the west coast of Ireland[21] and some in the Bay of Biscay.[22] The last load was sunk in September 1948,[21] under the direction of the Ministry of Transport. Captured German stocks were for the most part also sunk, tens of thousands of tabun shells, for instance, were sunk in the Baltic.[23] Captured German gas bombs were still being sunk in 1957, by then in the Atlantic.[24]

Have any chemical weapons been manufactured since then? Except for various riot-control agents, there is no evidence of this. There was a pilot plant built for the manufacture of DFP, Britain's rather weaker version of the German nerve gases, at Sutton Oak, in Lancashire,[25] which began operating in 1945, but has since been resited at Nancekuke, Cornwall. In fact, we know of next to no evidence of the manufacture of chemical weapons nor of any arrangements with industry for such manufacture if it should be required.* Such arrangements existed before the last War and indeed were widely proclaimed. However, in view of the similarity of the nerve gases to some of the modern insecticides, there is no doubt that the chemical industry could go over to nerve gas manufacture without much difficulty.

Optimistically, one is tempted to conclude that Britain has no operational stocks of chemical weapons, but the psychology of the situation is obviously so delicate that no official is ever going to confirm or deny such a suggestion, whichever way the truth lies.

Britain's Defence Potential

On the other hand, there is absolutely no doubt of Britain's determination to defend herself against chemical and biological attack. We are not only carrying out an expensive research and development programme into the best ways of achieving this, but we have, for instance, some several million post-World War II gas-masks already stocked for civilian use.[26] Furthermore, chemical

* But *see* p. 114. *Ed.*

defence equipment is now standard for troops in specific areas, particularly the British Army of the Rhine. Every soldier in areas where chemical warfare is thought likely is now issued with the S6 respirator and with three auto-injectors loaded with atropine for the treatment of nerve gas poisoning. In addition, British soldiers involved in chemical warfare would have chemically sensitive pads sewn on their battledresses, which would respond by colour changes if liquid chemical became splashed on to them. Soldiers are also issued with specially impregnated pads with which to wipe off any chemical that comes into contact with skin. The chemical and biological suit that was developed at Porton is now being made available to soldiers in special areas, and a residual vapour detector —a device to tell when the atmosphere is free from contamination— is being made available to section leaders, *i.e.* the leaders of every ten men.

Much of this equipment will also double as protection against biological weapons, but a pack of broad spectrum antibiotics would also be issued to soldiers for use as a 'blanket cure' should they become involved in a biological attack.[26] One can only hope that the scientists who recommended this particular policy have since looked closely at recent figures on infective drug resistance.

From information such as this, and from some knowledge of the research activities at Porton, it would be tempting to conclude that Britain is genuinely concerned only with defence against chemical and biological weapons.

Future policy

There is, however, one area in which there is still room for doubt. That area concerns the exploitation of discoveries made at Porton during the various research programmes. The normal way of exploiting inventions and discoveries is through the medium of patents, but when one examines those in which the British Defence authorities have had a hand, a number of dubious points emerge.

Most of the Ministry of Defence patents which have been published have an obvious usefulness in industry, sometimes of great significance. These patents are justifiably exploited to their full commercial worth. They include those for British Anti-Lewisite[28] for the treatment of metal poisoning, artificial breathing-machines,[29] cascade impactors[30, 31] for studying air pollution, the spinning-top atomizer[32] for producing accurately dimensioned particulate sprays, an improved process for making dialkyl phosphorohalidates,[33] (essential raw materials in the production of many insecticides), and

H

plague vaccines.[34] Most of these have been exploited through the conventional channel for doing so, the National Research Development Corporation (NRDC). Indeed, one of the purposes of the NRDC is just that, to exploit commercially discoveries made in Government laboratories.

The decision as to whether the Ministry or the NRDC should handle a Government patent application rests with the Ministry, although the NRDC's advice is being increasingly sought. In general, the Ministry will retain those patent applications in a field in which it can operate better than the NRDC, for example a field in which only its contractees are likely to need patent protection. Thus, the Ministry has retained the title in the patent[6] on the riot-control agent CS and in that on a novel process for making the nerve gas sarin.[25] Occasions do arise when a patent application is assigned to the NRDC who then finds that there is no normal commercial outlet for it, in which case it may well be assigned back to the Ministry, perhaps for future use.

But there are occasions when this process of assignment and re-assignment looks odd, particularly if it is so timed that the patent is published in the name of the NRDC. It might almost be said that this process was intended solely to conceal the Ministry's connection with the patent, particularly if the patent goes on to live its full life. There are two particularly pertinent instances of this. One such patent[36] discloses a method of forming carbon-phosphorus bonds by way of what is now called the 'Perrin-Kinnear complex' after its discoverers at Porton. This patent was subject to security measures during its early years, and was kept in force for its full term. It describes an extremely simple method of making nerve-gas intermediates. The second patent[37] discloses a continuous process for making methylphosphonothionate esters, compounds which are possible intermediates in V-agent manufacture.

In view of the continued payment of annual taxes on these patents, and of the convoluted history of their proprietorship, it is reasonable to assume that the Ministry thinks them important. It is not in the least improbable that the Ministry is licensing their inventions, profitably, to other nations or to industry. But there is little further evidence to support this, apart from the existence of overseas equivalents to some of the patents concerned.[38, 39]

The position over the exploitation of Porton discoveries under international exchange agreements is much clearer. In 1960 the Ministry of Defence confirmed[40, 41] a newspaper report[42] that information had been supplied to the United States under such an arrangement, and that that information formed the basis of a process for making a nerve gas which was about to go into large-scale production, at the Newport nerve-gas plant. It was not disclosed which nerve gas it was, but since the Americans had then a very satisfactory process of their own for manufacturing sarin or GB, the assumption is that it was their other now-standardized nerve gas, the V-agent VK. If this is so it may be that the information passed included that disclosed in the last patent referred to.[37]

Conclusions

There appears to be no evidence directly available that the United Kingdom is producing lethal offensive chemical weapons or even that she has stockpiles of them. The patent literature, however, leaves room for doubt about a number of connected issues. There is very little doubt that the United Kingdom has in the recent past supplied know-how to the United States of direct relevance to the manufacture of at least one nerve gas which is being stockpiled there. And, finally, the presence of a number of patents in the literature suggests that the United Kingdom is in a position to sell toxic weapons, or at least components of them, to other countries. We know this is done for some of the lachrymatory agents; it is also possible that it could be done for some of the lethal agents.

It is interesting to compare the British Government's security classification of chemical defence work with that of the Americans. Until recently the British attitude was almost invariably to keep it secret. Even the official history of the World War II weapons development programme makes practically no mention of chemical warfare equipment, beyond admitting that "it absorbed a great deal of energy and many notable developments occurred."[43] The Americans on the other hand follow a very erratic course. There are times when it has seemed that their classification system has broken down. On several occasions the Department of Commerce have published in one of their information journals abstracts of still classified reports.[44] On another occasion they published through unclassified channels an index[45] to an entire range of classified reports published over a period of a year.

During General Creasy's great public relations campaign[42, 46] to get both the public and Congress to accept the idea of toxic warfare, a great quantity of material was declassified, some of it describing still classified British work. As the campaign backfired, the declassification programme slowed down until the present time, when the U.S. Department of Defense is possibly more cagey than our own Ministry. In several instances, declassified reports[47, 48] which had been made available in our scientific libraries were recalled to the United States, never to be seen again.

The same sort of thing happened immediately after World War II. Thus in 1946, reports of the interrogation of German chemical warfare workers were published,[49] only to be quickly recalled. Similar Japanese reports remained published however. On the British side, the German reports remain classified, but the Japanese ones were released a short time ago.[50]

The final point that should be made concerns the reason why the two units at Porton have remained steadfastly classified since World War II. The hope that they might become civilian establishments has been raised several times[51, 52, 53] since then, and indeed a number of scientists have left Porton simply because they were under the impression that the units would be declassified and they then realized that this was not going to happen. Why not? From what has been described of the work there very little if any would be out of place in any major civilian chemical or microbiological research centre. Why, then, does such a move not take place? Our guess is that the Ministry of Defence wishes to continue having its cake and eating it. Under the present arrangement it can maintain a front of having only defence interests with an immediate option of diverting its efforts, via Porton, into totally different channels. It is difficult to see what other reason there could be for not declassifying the establishments and thus allaying the largely unnecessary suspicion which still lingers round them.

ADDENDUM

Since the Conference, further information about the activities at Porton Down has become available, partly as a result of the publicity following the Conference itself, partly as a result of the publication of the evidence of the House of Commons Select Committee on Science and Technology, which has been examining the role of Britain's Defence Research Establishments. The Select Committee visited Porton on May 6th 1968 and heard evidence from Mr G. N. Gadsby and Dr C. E. Gordon Smith, Directors respectively of the CDEE and the MRE. Part of the information given in these hearings was published in "The Observer", May 26th 1968, and was subsequently judged to be a breach of Parliamentary Privilege. The full report of the Committee was, however, eventually published on July 8th 1968, although certain sections of the evidence were omitted, apparently on security grounds. According to "The Observer", July 28th 1968, the Ministry of Defence originally wanted to leave out rather more of the evidence, but changed its mind both in view of the prior "Observer" leak and the adverse publicity which Porton was receiving. What follows is a summary drawn from this evidence, the replies to a number of Parliamentary Questions and related news stories (see, e.g. "The Times", June 1st 1968).

—Editor.

Cost, facilities and policy

Of the two Establishments at Porton, the CDEE costs £1,600,000 annually and employs some seventy scientists and engineers (including medical doctors). The MRE costs £900,000 a year and houses forty-eight scientific officers and seventy-six experimental officers (an item, presumably relating to medical doctors, was censored from the Minutes here). Some of this cost, to both Establishments, is recovered in sales to other government Departments, and also commercially, by way of patents let through the National Research Development Corporation.

Porton is advised by a group of external scientists, drawn partly from the universities; the current list of twenty-two (1968) includes: Professors N. K. Adam, F.R.S., F. Bergel, F.R.S., E. Boyland, J. I. G. Cadogan, N. B. Chapman, R. C. Cookson, D. H. Everett, R. B. Fisher, D. J. E. Ingram, C. A. Keele, P. L. Krohn, F.R.S., G. J. Kynch, W. V. Mayneord, F.R.S., M. D. Milne, P. R. Owen, A. E. Ritchie, H. N. Rydon, J. B. Speakman, R. H. S. Thompson, S. Tolansky, F.R.S., M. Weatherall, A. Wilson, and Dr R. D. Keynes, F.R.S.

As well as these external advisers, Porton has attached to it a number of Service officers—thirteen altogether on the establishment of the CDEE, from Army, Navy, and Air Force, whose function is to specify Service requirements in detail; amongst these officers are medical doctors. There is also a member of the U.S. Standardisation Office, U.K., permanently located at Porton, a standing reminder of the existence of the Quadripartite Agreement between the U.S., U.K., Australia, and Canada on information-sharing. Another reminder was, incidentally, provided recently when a paper jointly authored by two workers at the MRE and one at Fort Detrick on gene transfer between two strains of *Pasteurella Pseudotuberculosis* (a relative of the plague bacillus) appeared in the *Journal of General Microbiology*. Other versions of this Quadripartite Agreement, both tripartite and bilateral, exist with other NATO countries.

Despite these links, the Directors of both CDEE and MRE have categorically stated that the work of their Establishments is entirely defensive, and that stockpiles and retaliatory capacity, should Britain be attacked, are both lacking. Porton's responsibility, according to the Director of CDEE, is confined to providing defensive techniques for the Forces; Dr Gordon Smith extends his definition of the defensive role of MRE to the civilian population as well. So far as secrecy is concerned, MRE publishes, according to its Director, some 80 to 90 per cent of the work done, but "it is an extremely difficult figure to calculate with any degree of accuracy." To a question as to whether the actual output from MRE, if what was published amounted to some 80 to 90 per cent was not somewhat meagre, the Director replied: "I think our publication record is quite good. I think it could be improved if some members of staff who are rather slow at writing papers would hurry up with them . . . it is our practice to try and offer a substantial piece of work before we publish it." No figures are available for the proportion of CDEE's work which is published, but it was generally agreed to be considerably less than that of MRE.

Nonetheless, secrecy at Porton has become a matter of considerable public concern. The Select Committee asked whether Porton held 'open days' and was told that its directors had asked to hold them but that permission had not been granted. Even before the Minutes had been published, though, it was announced in Parliament that open days at Porton would be instituted. A later amplification by Mr John Morris, Minister of Defence for Equipment, made it clear that the first open day was to be for MRE only and that attendance would be by invitation to "representatives of universities, learned societies, research associations, local authorities, industry, the press" and "a number of organisations likely to be interested in the work of the establishment." There appears to be no intention of extending the open day to the work of CDEE as well.

Porton and the Universities

In addition to its external advisers, Porton has another type of link with the universities. This consists of a series of collaborative projects with individual members of university staffs and of specific research contracts. An example of the type of collaborative project is that which resulted in a joint publication by two workers at St Thomas's Hospital and the Director of MRE in *The British Medical Journal (January 29th* 1966) which contains a description of research in which a series of patients suffering from terminal cancers were experimentally infected with live Langat virus—which causes encephalitis, though is normally not infective in humans—and which for various reasons the authors hoped might serve to alleviate some of the effects of the cancers (which were mainly leukaemic); the research findings were negative, however; all the patients subsequently died.

So far as the research contracts go, the CDEE has twenty-seven, including those with Birbeck College, London, University College of Wales, Oxford, Oxford College of Technology, Birmingham, King's College, London, Welsh College of Advanced Technology, Institute of Neurology, Middlesex Hospital Medical School, University of Liverpool, Chelsea College of Advanced Technology, Queen's University, Belfast, Portsmouth College of Technology, University of Edinburgh, University of Southampton, University of Sheffield, St Mary's Hospital Medical School, University of Exeter, University of Kent, and University of St Andrews.

Exact details of many of these contracts are not available, but a summary is provided in the Table. Examples include a contract to Professor Henry Rydon, Exeter, (who is also on the Advisory Board and previously worked at Porton) to study the isolation, purification, and structure of the plant toxin ricin—rather analogous to botulinus and tetanus toxins, though much less powerful; to Dr Mary Whittaker, Kings College London, for work on acetylcholinesterase enzymes (those whose activity is blocked by the nerve gases); to Dr B. Jacques, Portsmouth College of Technology, on the synthesis of 4-hydroxyl, 1, 2, 3, 4 tetra-hydroisoquinolines (substances with related structures are known to be hallucinogens); and to Professor Harry Smith, Birmingham, on the fractionation of compounds of microbial origin important in the pathogenesis of infectious diseases.

None of these contracts appears to be for a very large amount of money, and most appear to be administered so as to allow a fair degree of freedom to the recipients; that is, they are not specifically classified. Indeed Professor Rydon has laid down as the criteria under which he would accept any external contracts coming into his department (at a Teach-In on CBW held at Exeter University on June 11th 1968) that the work must be of relevance to the interests of the Department and must have no restrictions on the right to publish. Such criteria are certainly wholly admirable; nonetheless it must be noted that what the Ministry of Defence means by unclassified is given in a Parliamentary answer by the then Under-Secretary of State for Defence on February 26th 1968:

When arranging a research contract the Ministry of Defence agrees with the university who is to supervise the work, but the Ministry does not normally have a voice in deciding who should carry it out. The results of research for defence are, in accordance with general scientific practice, published freely *provided there are no overriding considerations of national interest, including security*. Universities undertake to consult the Department before publication. Over the past two years, no university has declined to undertake a research contract offered to it. [Our italics].

One must also assume, that however the recipients of the Porton contracts read the significance of their work, those who awarded them the contracts in the first instance must have felt that the work was in some way related to Porton's prime mission; it certainly has no brief to function as a charitable foundation, awarding money for projects irrelevant to its interests.

Nancekuke and the CS controversy

Apart from Porton, other 'in-house' developmental work on chemical warfare is carried out at the Porton outstation of Nancekuke (Portreath) in Cornwall, where pilot-plant facilities for the manufacture of chemical agents exist. Two substances at least are known to be manufactured there, the nerve gas VX, currently made in test quantities only, and the harassing agent CS (see Chapter 1). CS is manufactured in quantities of around four to six tons a year. Some at least of this is transported to the factory of Schermuly Ltd. (a subsidiary of the Charterhouse group), near Dorking in Surrey; here the CS canisters are made and filled, CS is exported to about sixty foreign countries at a price of 35 shillings per pound. In addition, it is supplied to thirty-six of the eighty police forces in England and Wales, as well as to some in Scotland. Police instructions as to the use of the CS is that it is "only to deal with armed criminals or violently insane persons in buildings from which they cannot be dislodged without danger of loss of life, or as a means of self-defence in a desperate situation, and that in no circumstances should they be used to assist in the control of disturbances". (Mr Buchan, Under-Secretary of State for Scotland.) If the evidence of Dr Kahn (Chapter 7) is taken into account, though, it is clear that the use of CS in the type of confined space envisaged in this instruction to police might not be without its hazards. Taking the figure quoted by Porton for the L Ct_{50} of CS, one might expect that the explosion of one Porton CS grenade in the average-sized suburban living room would result in the build-up of a dose lethal to half the exposed population within twenty minutes—(assuming the CS powder remained dispersed in the air) doubtless less if those exposed were at all unhealthy, or included young children (see also the discussion of the toxicity of CS in *Science Journal,* August 1968).

It is certain, though, that the CS used in Vietnam is not of British manufacture. Nor is the gas used during May 1968 by the Paris police, which, code-named CB, the French version of CS, is apparently produced in that country. British-made CS is apparently not exported either to France or the USA. It may be noted in passing that the French CB grenade, according to an analysis made in May 1968 by Dr Kahn, holds a charge of no more than 1–2 grams of CS. The Porton-patented canister described in the preceding chapter contains 30–40 grams, whilst the Mighty Mite used in Vietnam may contain 80 pounds (that is, 35,500 grams). Nonetheless, even though in Paris the gas was used on the open streets, several casualties from the use of CN and CS have been reported from Paris, including allegations of partial or total blindness and at least one death. It is likely that most of these were CN casualties, but it must be emphasized that a proper medical evaluation of this data is not currently available in England. But additional evidence as to the potential hazards of these agents, and also the American combined agent, containing mainly CN, and known as Mace has come from a study made at the University of Michigan, and reported in the *New Scientist* (June 20th 1968), has made clear that the spread of their use should not go unquestioned.

Table 9   CBW Research Contracts let to British Universities*

CHEMICAL DEFENCE EXPERIMENTAL ESTABLISHMENT

Nature of Research	Location
Research on Fluorohydrocarbons	University of Birmingham
The isolation purification and structure determination of physiologically active peptides	University of Exeter
The Development of Ultra Microbiochemical Techniques to explore the mode of action of drugs	University of Liverpool
Synthesis of Components of Pharmacological or Therapeutic interest	University of Manchester I. of S. and T.
A study of the processes concerned with the metabolism of drugs and toxic substances	St Mary's Hospital Medical School
Determination of the Structure of Pharmacologically Active compounds	University of Sheffield
Studies in the chemistry of organo-phosphorous compounds	University of St Andrews
Synthesis of 4 Hydroxy 1, 2, 3, 4 Tetrahydriosoquinolines	Portsmouth College of Technology
Histopathological Studies in Neurotoxicity Institute of Neurology	London University
Research on the optical properties of Aerosols	University College of South Wales
The Absorption and Removal of Hydrocyanic Acid Gas by Solids	University of Bristol
Metabolism and Toxicity of Highly Fluorinated Cyclohexames	University of Birmingham
Effect of prolonged inhibition of Cholinesterase in Animals	Middlesex Hospital Medical School
A combined behavioural electro-physiological and biochemical investigation of the central action of certain drugs	University of Birmingham
Investigation of the preparation and properties of fibrous absorptive carbons	University of Bristol
A Physico-chemical investigation of the reaction of Nucleophiles with unsaturated gases	King's College, London
An investigation of the ability of some biological systems to inactivate acetyl chlorine and of the mechanism of such inactivation	Chelsea College of Science and Technology
Genetica Factosa and the effect of infantile stimulation on the activity of the acetycholine—cholinesterase and other systems in the brain of the rat	University of Southampton
Nucleophilic Catalysis in Relation to the treatment of Organophosphate poisoning	University of Kent
Some aspects of the Biochemistry of the skin	Queen's University, Belfast
Factors influencing the gelation of liquids with special reference to organic liquids and gels without chemical cross-links	Welsh College of Advanced Technology
The effect of drugs on neuro-muscular transmissions and contractile force of mammalian skeletal muscle ...	University of Bristol
Studies relevant to the reactivation of Organo-phosphorus inhibited enzymes	University of St Andrews

MICROBIOLOGICAL RESEARCH ESTABLISHMENT

Nature of Research	Location
Investigation of Fluorocarbohydrates	University of Oxford
Diffusion controlled electrodes for use in biological systems	Birkbeck College, London University
Investigation of the use of Hydrated Calcium phosphate and related materials for the purification and fractionation of viruses and viral compounds	Oxford College of Technology
Fractionation of Compounds of Microbial Origin important in the pathogenesis of infectious diseases	University of Birmingham
Electrophoretic Behaviour of Bacteria	University of Liverpool

* Source Hansard, May 29th 1968

10. United States Elinor Langer

Recently research on the chemical and biological weapons establishment in the United States has made considerable progress. Research within the establishment has undoubtedly made progress as well, but that is beyond the control of the concerned scientists, campus activists, and reporters who are responsible for the upsurge in public attention to the CBW question. As a result of these labours we can begin our discussion on a somewhat more sophisticated level, and specifically by clearing the air of a number of points of official propaganda concerning CBW that, while not necessarily technically untrue, have a cumulatively misleading effect. Briefly, these official contentions are that the CBW programme is marginal; that it is inexpensive; that it is unsuccessful; and that it is defensive in nature.

The terms "marginal" and "inexpensive" are relative ones, applicable to the CBW programme only when compared with the nuclear weapons programme, the military space programme, or any of the other multi-billion-dollar American defense activities that involve the substantial acquisition of hardware. Because chemical and biological weapons development is by its nature less costly, comparative expenditures reveal nothing of the scope of the programme, the intent of its sponsors, or their degree of commitment to it. The scientific resources of the United States are so great that commitment of even a fraction of its energy holds promise of significant results. In other words, the CBW programme can be both marginal and capable of vast destruction.

Second, "unsuccessful". For many years certain sections of the U.S. Defense Department have made an effort to communicate the sense that the difficulties in developing CBW weapons, particularly biological weapons, were insurmountable. (The CBW enthusiasts, housed chiefly in the Chemical Corps, have always resented this and have tried to put their contrary view across, but have been somewhat restrained by security precautions in doing so.) The origins of this contention lie in part in public relations and in part in the genuine dilemmas encountered by the research programme in its early years, particularly during and after World War II. To be usable as weapons systems, biological organisms must possess a number of complex characteristics simultaneously. In the early post-war years it was not clear that the necessary combinations could be achieved, and there was honest debate over feasibility. There is still debate and much of it is still honest; however there is also an obvious tendency on the part of Government officials and researchers to use the earlier difficulties as a smoke-screen for the substantial progress that has been made. Men of enormous ability have been working prodigiously on these problems for a number of years. References in the open literature and interviews with those close to military developments leave little doubt that these workers have met with much success, particularly in understanding techniques of aerosol dissemination. In addition, references in military manuals strongly suggest that at least some biological weapons systems have become available. In the United States the answers to two key questions that would help establish the truth ("What is the current view of the feasibility of biological weapons?" and "Which biological agents have gone into the production stage?") are classified. Granted that classification can conceal failure as well as success and is frequently used in that fashion, the point is that we have no reason to assume failure.

Third, "defensive". With a few exceptions, such as development of detection and protective equipment, little CBW research can be accurately described as defensive—a word that may conceivably apply to the intentions of the policy-makers (*i.e.*, we are doing it because others are doing it) or to the occasion of CBW's use (*i.e.*, we don't mean to use it first). Because of the nature of chemical and biological weapons, research even in seemingly 'pure' areas, such as the development of vaccines, has at least equal implications for offensive and defensive use. This central point has in fact played a key role in early (and continuing) internecine fighting about the CBW programme. When the biological warfare programme was expanded around 1942 the Army Surgeon-General took the position that only the defensive aspects should be studied. The Chemical Corps argued successfully that offensive and defensive aspects could not be separated, and was awarded control of the entire programme. For years the disapproval of the Army Medical Corps of the CBW programme was so intense that they refused to station a medical team at Fort Detrick, the BW research centre. In recent years, however, opposition has waned, and the Army doctors have been represented at Detrick, though the medical unit appears to centre its attention on medical aspects of CBW research such as immunization and therapy. As one of the military's CBW manuals points out "CB defence is a prerequisite to an attack capability."[1]

Development of chemical and biological research

The current healthy state of the U.S. CBW research programme is intimately related to a larger trend in U.S. weapons policy, the swing away from the 'massive retaliation' doctrine that began in the late 1950's and reached its fruition under Kennedy in the New Frontier. Before that time the Army Chemical Corps was something of an orphan, a victim of the uproar against gas warfare that set in after World War I. The Corps believed in itself and went about touting statistics demonstrating that gas casualties in the War suffered less than other types of casualties (the statistics are still frequently recited), building up its constant theme that chemical and biological weapons are more "humane" than other forms of warfare. But the audience was small and made up mostly of the already committed. The Corps was given only crumbs of the military budget, usually around $35 million a year. There was another peak, during the build-up of Detrick at the time of World War II, but that concentration dissipated too in the demobilization after 1945. In 1959 the Corps invented and carried out an expansionist mission "Operation Blue Skies", designed to win public support for its latest enthusiasm, "incapacitating" weapons, particularly psychochemicals. It was that campaign, endorsed by potent interest groups such as the American Chemical Society, that dovetailed with the decision of the Kennedy administration to acquire a weapons arsenal more versatile than the nuclear stockpile. CBW budgets began to rise, along with the budgets for a variety of other non-nuclear armaments which seemed to offer more flexibility in fighting limited wars. Between 1961 and 1964 the CBW budget (Research and Development) nearly tripled, rising from $57 million to about $158 million. The bulk of R & D money is spent by the Army, although the Navy and Air Force in recent years have also undertaken CBW research. In 1961 about another $136 million was spent (by the three services) for procurement; procurement figures for more recent years are not available. In addition to the funds for R & D and procurement, there is a large standing capital investment in CBW. How large it is impossible to say as the figures are tucked away under various camouflaged titles in the military budget. However, according to its own advertisement, Fort Detrick alone, the centre of U.S. biological warfare research, occupies 1300 acres of land (near Frederick, Maryland), has a building complex valued at $75,000,000, "one of the world's largest animal farms", and "facilities for conducting research with pathogenic organisms that are among the best in the world".

Civil involvement

For a variety of reasons the military has found it necessary and desirable to contract out a substantial portion (perhaps as much as half, or more) of its CBW research and development to universities, research corporations, and private industry. The reasons are interesting and reveal something about the climate in which work in CBW is performed. The Chemical Corps has a public relations problem even within the Pentagon. Defense Department employees, who have attended high-level Pentagon briefings on a whole range of U.S. weapons systems, report that seasoned generals and admirals who can calmly devote whole mornings (or whole careers) to the business of nuclear destruction become queasy and indignant when it is the Chemical Corps' turn at the blackboards. The reluctance of competent researchers to submit to the conditions of work on military-controlled bases has posed considerable problems of recruitment for 'in-house' research. In addition, there has been considerable interest on the part of industry in getting a share of the work. Reluctance to work on a military base is not the same thing as scruples about the substance of the research, and the contracting-out operation until recently ran into scant opposition. In a sense it has permitted university and other private researchers to have what they might well consider the best of two worlds: military money and private prerogatives.

An item-by-item count of who is doing what has been built up over the last few years, and part is shown in Table 10. But the conclusion may be briefly summarized: virtually any topic we could think of that would facilitate the development of usable weapons systems is under study in the United States. Labour is rationally divided, with basic scientific research being performed chiefly at universities; research on the means of delivery by industry, particularly the aero-space industry; and a variety of functions of both sorts by the non-profit organizations. It appears that at least fifty universities, perhaps twenty-five companies, and about a dozen research institutes are now holding or have recently held CBW contracts. The work ranges in scope from the million-dollar research on weapons-dissemination at the University of Pennsylvania to individual medical research contracts of perhaps $10,000 a year; it ranges in apparent lethality from the study of the "supersonic delivery of dry biological agents" (Litton Industries) to investigation of the "chemical and physical principles applicable to BW detection" (The University of Buffalo). The list of co-operators includes not only universities, non-profit organizations, and industry, but some of the most prestigious organizations of American science, including the National Academy of Sciences, which runs a fellowship programme, and the American Society for Microbiology which has for years provided Fort Detrick with advisory services. The U.S. Public Heath Service maintains close liaison with Fort Detrick, and receives a few hundred thousand dollars a year for its efforts. A number of foreign university researchers have also accepted contracts and grants stemming from the CBW research programme.

Defense establishment

Notwithstanding all the outside assistance, the internal capacity of the Government remains substantial. Fort Detrick, with a staff of 120 Ph.D.'s, 110 M.S.'s,* 320 B.S.'s,* 34 veterinarians, and 14 physicians, is the principal CBW station with a major research function. Only about 15 per cent of the research findings are published through conventional scientific channels. Detrick is particularly proud of the three or four occasions when, in co-operation with other scientific societies, it organized research symposia (the principal topic: airborne infection). Another of these occasions—a joint symposium with the American Institute of Biological Sciences in celebration of Detrick's 25th birthday—has recently taken place and—a symptom of changing tempers—was boycotted by a large percentage of the intended participants. But most of the research done at Detrick becomes part of a secret literature managed by the Defense Department and available to other Government agencies or contractors only on a 'need to know' basis.

Fort Detrick, in addition to its research activities, is involved in process development, small scale production, and design and operation of pilot plants. Closely related to Detrick is the Dugway Proving Ground which employs about 900 people (and occupies an area in Utah almost as large as the county of Hampshire). Dugway is the principal station for field assessment and testing of

* The American M.S. and B.S. degrees are similar to the British M.Sc. and B.Sc. *Ed.*

chemical and biological munitions. According to Pentagon officials there are no large-scale trials of chemical and biological agents on human subjects. Limited testing is done at Detrick using volunteers—Seventh Day Adventists who serve in the Armed Forces only as non-combatants—and experiments have from time to time been performed on prisoners. But the military evidently believes that the value of testing is outweighed by the dangers of contamination and limits its trials to animals or to non-pathogenic simulants of active biological warfare agents. Sometimes testing on animals is inadvertent, as with the accidental slaughter of 6000 sheep during recent tests of a new nozzle for dissemination of nerve gas at Dugway (the sheep were grazing on ranch lands 30 miles away). It is worth noting that the Pentagon insists—contrary to opinions voiced by some in the conference—that these trials would form an adequate basis on which to test deployment of chemical and biological weapons.

Biological munitions are produced at Pine Bluff Arsenal, a 15,000 acre installation outside Pine Bluff, Arkansas, which employs about 1400 people. Pine Bluff also produces toxic chemical munitions and riot-control munitions. Its activities range from manufacturing the agents to filling and assembling the weapons. Research and development on chemical weapons and some production and assembly take place in a number of components of the Edgewood Arsenal, in Edgewood, Maryland. A variety of chemical munitions, including nerve gas, mustard gas, 'incapacitants', and anti-crop weapons are produced at the Rocky Mountain arsenal in Denver. The U.S. also operates a major manufacturing plant—at an estimated annual cost of $3·5 million—in Newport, Indiana, where the nerve gas, sarin (see Chapter 1) is produced and loaded into rockets, land mines, and artillery shells. The plant is managed by the Food Machinery Corporation, has 300 employees, and is reported to have been operating twenty-four hours daily since 1960. Additional chemicals were manufactured during the middle 1950's at a plant in Muscle Shoals, Alabama, now closed. Training of officers and troops in the use of chemical and biological weapons takes place at the U.S. Army Chemical Centre and School at Fort McClellan, Alabama; related activities in the Air Force occur at Eglin Air Force Base, in Florida.

Most of the procurement of the chemical defoliants and herbicides in use in Vietnam is done on a commercial basis.

In the summer of 1967 the Pentagon announced the award of $57·7 million to the following chemical companies to purchase defoliants for Vietnam: Dow, Diamond Alkali, Uniroyal, Thompson Chemical, Hercules, Monsanto, Ansul, and Thomas Hayward. About another dozen companies also sell chemicals, including various tear gases, to the Government.

Chemical weapons are produced in forms fit for the requirements of all military services. They are available in a variety of manifestations from artillery shells to the Sergeant missile, which has a range of 100 miles, the Honest John and Little John rockets, and chemical land mines. They are also available as bombs for delivery by conventional military aircraft. Detailed information on delivery systems for biological agents is classified, but the unclassified manuals suggest that they are available as warheads for missile systems (for large area attacks), as cluster bombs, and as spray tanks and dispensers mounted on aircraft.

The justification—the protesters

Recent protests in the United States have called forth a variety of defences from those in CBW and related research and development. Some representative samples: "We are an electric utility and our contract with the Federal Government covers the supplying of electric services for the Dugway Proving Ground. That is as far as our relationship with the Dugway Proving Ground goes and what the power is used for is beyond our knowledge." E. A. Hunter, Vice-President, Utah Power and Light Company.[2]

"Government contracts represent a big part of our research efforts—it's a way of life." H. Ridgely Warfield, director of John Hopkins Institute for Co-operative Research, recipient of over $1 million in contracts for "studies of actual or potential injuries or illnesses, studies on diseases of potential BW significance, and evaluation of certain clinical and immunological responses to certain toxoids and vaccines."[3]

"In no way do we feel that our firm is being 'morally compromised' by handling CBW work for the Pentagon. We feel we have an obligation to respond to Pentagon requests for assistance." R. L. Carnahan, vice-president, Travelers Research Center, a major recipient of contracts involving study of factors affecting dissemination of chemical and biological weapons, and author of a study of public reaction to CBW use.[3] A similar response was made by Dow Chemical Company following protests over its manufacture of napalm. Dow issued a statement which read in part: "Dow accepted this contract because we feel that simple good citizenship required that we supply our Government and our military with those goods they need when we have the technology and capability and have been chosen by the Government as a supplier."

"No war was ever fought with the intent to be kind. Each weapon as it is used to kill makes man quite as dead, his family quite as bereaved. As a weapon is effective, so it will be used, and the resources of the entire nation will be utilized by the Government on request, or by requisition, to produce those weapons deemed by the Military to be most effective in concluding the war . . . Scientists make their peculiar contribution to man's welfare. At times it is used well. At times, inventions for survival in one time of history become agents for genuine human betterment and even become powerful agents to impress on man his need to abrogate force. But other men than scientists also direct the course of civilization. If you spend your powers assaulting one aspect of a problem which cannot be solved by that aspect, you waste your powers. By your reasoning, nearly every facet of American life should be halted, from the production of breakfast food to air transport, since almost all contribute to the prosecution of this war which no one wants. Stop the war with adequate international action or accept the reality that man is still primitive, and that a man or a woman or a child is as dead from mortar fire or shrapnel or a simple rifle." Melvin Calvin, Nobel prize winner, professor of chemistry and molecular biology, University of California, Berkeley, member, Board of Directors, Dow Chemical, manufacturers of napalm. (Calvin's letter appeared in the campus paper, Daily Californian, after a graduate student had challenged him to state his views on the manufacture of napalm and its use in Vietnam.)

"I submit that there is almost no major corporation that is not contributing in some way to the Vietnam war regardless of the points of view of its executive". Thomas Watson, President, IBM. (Letter to Brown University campus paper criticizing students there who attacked Dow Chemical.)

In general, university protesters over CBW and related war research have divided into three groups—a 'left' or radical minority willing directly to confront the issues of the moral use of research results for war; a 'rightist' or conservative minority (usually in the engineering sections) fearful of the damaging consequences to themselves of ending military contracts on any grounds; and a liberal 'centre' willing to oust the research but chiefly on the libertarian or educational grounds that faculty members must not interfere with one another's interests. The Dow argument (the Government needs us) is also heard with regard to university and CBW, though less frequently.

A number of universities have attempted, in the wake of unfavourable publicity, to divest themselves of their CBW research projects (the University of Pennsylvania) or of all university-sponsored military or secret research (Cornell, the University of Michigan). In each case, divestiture has provoked considerable tumult, and efforts have been made to find grounds for cancellation not involving moral censure. Instead, dialogue has focussed on the issues of 'publishability' and 'relevance of the research to the university's teaching mission'. The contrary argument, made by— among others—University of Pennsylvania President, Gaylord Harnwell, is that by tradition American universities guarantee their faculties 'academic freedom' to research whatever questions they choose; the administration's job is to insulate the faculty from changing political winds.

Policy

U.S. policy regarding CBW see-saws between two poles—the declaration of no first use by President Roosevelt in 1943 and the refusal of the Pentagon and State Department to endorse a similarly worded declaration in 1960. What about Vietnam? So far, *known* U.S. operations have been confined to spraying the jungle and NLF food crops, and to the use of theoretically non-lethal gases, albeit not necessarily in a non-lethal fashion. (The use of BZ has been alleged, but to my knowledge not proven. The same is true of alleged experimental use of other chemicals in underground tunnels, etc.) [But *see* Chapter 7.] According to a recent report by the Midwest Research Institute (commissioned by the Pentagon in response to scientists' protests), enough herbicide was used in 1967 to 'treat' 965,000 acres, although because many areas were treated more than once, the total acreage defoliated was less. Its conclusion, briefly, is that the possibilities of long-term adverse effects are minimal and that the spraying may even be beneficial in some instances. Is this chemical and biological warfare? U.S. officials repeatedly say it is not: others insist that it is. But perhaps the importance of the question is overrated. Surely the important thing is not to name these activities, but to understand what they, along with the other barbarities, are doing to that country. The question in the use of herbicides, as Jean Mayer has pointed out (Chapter 6) is the ethics of starvation, not the ethics of the means of destroying crops. The issue in Vietnam is not the vehicle of destruction but the destruction itself.

I think that this raises an important question: Why are we spend-

I

ing so much time on CBW? I have had to think about this a great deal myself in the course of my own work and have come to reject most of the conventional answers. I do not believe that CBW is less moral than other means of war, or even that it is necessarily a more unpleasant way to die. I do not accept the argument that the tenuous restraints on CBW which have been followed up until now indicate that man is capable of 'civilizing' warfare; I believe that the United States—as well as other countries—would use any means of war that they believed, overall, would advance their interests.

I believe that CBW is a violation of international law, but I believe that 'resettlement' of villagers in Vietnam is a violation of equal proportion, and that law is as unlikely to restrain one as the other. I agree with those who say that CBW is a perversion of science, but I believe that with Hiroshima and other developments science had already demonstrated sufficient perversion and CBW does not appear unique.

I think those who argue that CBW should be watched because it is of special utility in the counter-revolutionary wars the United States and other imperial powers will undoubtedly be fighting have so far done no more than assert their point. Finally, I think that to confine talk about the risks of 'escalation' in Vietnam or elsewhere to chemical and biological weapons at a time when escalation is taking other equally dangerous paths is academic.

Why then bother about CBW? I think there are a few main reasons, although perhaps they will seem rather ethnocentric ones. First, I think that many people believe that some or all of the arguments above are true, including people who, for a variety of reasons, are unwilling to engage in direct anti-war activity or to oppose the government's policies overtly. This is true, for instance, of the scientists' coalition in the United States as well as of a number of university-based protesters. As a result CBW has become a good tactic for dissidents; it is a vulnerable point in the military-industrial complex. A related reason is that it exposes how some of America's structural and civil liberties, such as 'academic freedom', are inadequate to guarantee an ethical scholarly climate.

Concern about CBW may, in consequence, help to promote serious university reform. The same may be true in Britain and in a number of continental countries that co-operate with the U.S. defense-research effort. A final reason is that CBW is small enough and manageable enough for outsiders to come to grips with the problem as a whole, and reform seems possible; it weighs less heavily than the tangled mass of the Vietnam war, on the one hand, or the arcane mysteries of nuclear defense, on the other. Progress in opposing CBW seems possible. But the fact is that we could abolish CBW altogether without making the world much safer or our universities more wholesome. At the risk of sounding trite, CBW is only a symptom. Perhaps these are not good words for a CBW conference. But it is important to remember that CBW is only a battle; it is not the war.

TABLE 10 U.S. university involvement in CBW research, 1961-68*

SELECTED EXCERPTS

University	Department	Researcher	Project
Boston	Chemistry	Dr. Mason	**CW agents**
California (Berkeley)	Chemistry	Dr. Rapoport	**Lethal and incapacitating agents**
California (Los Angeles)		Dr. Taylor	**Medical aspects of CW**
Connecticut	Pharmacology		**Synthetic products of psychedelics**
Illinois (Urbana)		Dr. Finger	**Crop and food destruction agents**
Illinois Institute of Technology		Dr. Ehrlich	**Improved biological aerosols**
Indiana		Dr. Rudsell	**More effective toxic compounds**
Johns Hopkins			**Disease of potential BW significants**
Maryland		Dr. Woodward	**Vulnerability of man to BW**
Massachusetts		Dr. Kunsberger	**Emetics as possible incapacitating agents**
Oklahoma			**BW in remote conflict areas**
Pennsylvania		Drs. DuBois, Koelle, Haugoard	**Applied research on CBW systems including evaluation of defoliants in Vietnam**
Virginia Medical College		Dr. Hoff	**New lethal and incapacitating agents**
Washington State		Dr. Hendrix	**Anti-crop warfare**

This list is selected from a directory of 57 universities, institutes all having U.S. Department of Defense contracts: the total of all D.o.D. contracts to U.S. universities amounted to $ 380 million in 1966. Other colleges etc. include:—Brooklyn, Buffalo, California Medical Schools, Chicago, Clarkson, Columbia, Cornell, Delaware, George Peabody, George Washington, Georgia, Hahneman, Iowa, Kansas, Maryland, MIT, Michigan, Minnesota, New York, N. Carolina, Ohio, Oregon, Pittsburgh, Rutgers, St. Louis, Stanford, Tennessee, Texas, Utah, Washington, Western Reserve, William and Mary, Wisconsin, Yale.

* Data compiled from details published by Michael Klare, *Viet Report*, January, 1968.

11. Soviet Union   D. E. Viney

This chapter seeks only to assemble a few salient facts publicly known about the potential for chemical and biological warfare of the Soviet Union and the Government's apparent attitude towards it; and to add a minimum of what seems to the author reasonable speculation.

Potential

Soviet spokesmen have, since World War II, repeatedly forecast that future world conflicts are bound to involve the use of both chemical and biological weapons (if only because the 'aggressor' would initiate it), and as the Soviet Union is patently capable of producing many kinds, it would be surprising if she had not proceeded from intensive research to the stockpiling of whatever agents she had decided to rely upon. This further step would of course not necessarily follow if the Soviet Union came to regard a conflict between CBW-capable powers as unlikely, or if she abandoned faith in the efficiency of deterrence, or the legitimacy of retaliation, in the CBW field; there is no sign of her adopting these positions. There is no reason to think she would stockpile newly discovered agents of dubious value; one can be less sure that she would destroy old stocks of agents which, for her, had been outdated by more sophisticated ones, but might again prove useful in special circumstances or be made available to friendly nations with different military requirements.

It is well known that the Russians acquired a headstart in the business of nerve gases at the end of World War II by overrunning a German plant manufacturing the least toxic of the nerve gases then known, tabun, and seizing a stock of some 12,000 tons of it. In view of their subsequent interest in organo-phosphorus compounds generally, it would be surprising if they had not kept at least level with the West in perfecting the manufacture of more toxic ones, and of both more and less volatile agents than tabun. Perry

Robinson (Chapter 1)[1] mentions that the Russians were, surprisingly, the first (in 1960) to publish percutaneous toxicity figures for the V-agents.

Among the less advanced agents, the same chapter mentions evidence that the Russians stockpiled what might be called the 'lethal-irritant' dichloroformoxime, in World War II, as well as adapting for field use hydrogen cyanide (which in the West has often been dismissed as a possible weapon because of its volatility).

Around 1960 U.S. sources, in the course of a campaign to make CBW more acceptable, published statements claiming that some 15 per cent of all ballistic warheads on the Warsaw Pact front were chemical ones—an estimate neither confirmed nor denied by official quarters in any other country (nor, incidentally, attacked as provocative by Soviet spokesmen). Some Warsaw Pact exercises have certainly been conducted on the assumption that chemical weapons would be employed, alone or in conjunction with nuclear attack. The use of chemical warheads with tactical ballistic systems such as the SCUD missile (range up to 150 miles) or the FROG free-flight rocket (range of later versions up to 30 miles) would represent a formidable capability, each missile, assuming a warhead filled with nerve gas, being able to produce a high proportion of fatalities over an area of 1 sq.km. or more among target personnel, unless they were provided with the most advanced protective clothing and were wearing it at the time of attack.

American writers have spoken of Soviet preparedness for delivery of chemical agents by such other means as normal artillery shells and aircraft bombs. They have also mentioned spray-tanks for dissemination from aircraft,[2] and though it might be thought unlikely that much faith would be placed on aircraft flying at vulnerably low altitudes and speeds in a European theatre of conflict, their military utility could be higher elsewhere; it is in any case known (*see* Chapter 1) that the Russians adapted hydrogen cyanide for dispersal by just such means.

Nothing is known, on the other hand, of any Soviet success in developing feasible incapacitating agents. As for biological agents, intensive research can be assumed if only for the same reason as with other advanced countries, *i.e.*, the need to produce vaccines. It is widely reported that the Soviets have field-tested mild pathogens, and they obviously have ample territory for the purpose. Soviet research into the possibilities of mass vaccination from the air must have suggested military applications. However, the crucial facts require no detailed evidence; the Soviets are clearly in a position to embark on large-scale manufacture of biological agents if ever they decide to; and equally, there is no reason to assume that they have formulated a military requirement of this kind, or ever will. The felt need for a deterrent, *i.e.*, retaliatory, capability does not mean a felt need for the means of replying to every agent with the same agent, or even to every whole class of agents with the same class.

As for Soviet defensive equipment against chemical or biological weapon attack, it was said in 1964[2] to include a very advanced gas-mask, adequate qualities of protective clothing against chemical agents, detection and identification equipment similar to the West's, but no automatic warning systems. Civil defence preparedness is actively promoted by paramilitary and youth organizations through which perhaps half the population have at some time received thorough classroom training in defensive techniques. Underground shelters with air-filtration exist in major population centres, though their capacity is no doubt just as inadequate in terms of general war contingencies as in any other country.

Military doctrine

Doctrine can best be inferred from deployment, so that the following remarks apply only to the Soviet Warsaw Pact front, and only to chemical weapons.

Until a few years ago it may well be that chemical warheads were seen by Russians partly as a substitute for tactical nuclear warheads, which were harder to develop than the more powerful nuclear warheads used on long-range missiles, and so were not available in sufficient quantities to counter the known American capabilities. Assuming however that there is now some balance on the tactical nuclear level, a lethal chemical weapon capability would still make sense in these roles: (i) tactically, to destroy personnel without destroying installations and communications to one's own detriment, and without rendering large areas inaccessible to one's own side for such long periods as would nuclear weapons; (ii) to furnish a military option above the conventional level, but still short of nuclear escalation; and (iii) to deter chemical weapon attack by an opponent.

Of these three roles, the first two only remain attractive as between nuclear opponents on the assumption (by no means certain) that the use of advanced chemical weapons would avert nuclear escalation and not simply precipitate it. But the third, deterrent, role would still remain valid, and even the existence of large, deployed stockpiles on the Soviet side would be consistent with a Soviet view that deterrence was their primary role, but that the capability must remain a large one in case deterrence failed. Although a distinction can be made of course between use of a chemical weapon capability to deter *any* attack and to deter a chemical weapon attack, this does not invalidate the foregoing argument.

Exaggerated inferences can be drawn from the statements of Soviet military men, who are after all just as liable—sometimes more—to inject political and empire-making considerations into their analyses as those of other nations. Marshall Zhukov's 1956 *obiter dictum* before a Party Congress that "a future war, should it be unleashed, will be characterized by the massive use of . . . means of mass destruction such as atomic, thermo-nuclear, chemical, and bacteriological weapons" cannot seriously be used in 1968 to argue an active Soviet interest in possessing an offensive capability in all parts of the spectrum. Marshall Sokolovsky says more soberly in the 1963 edition of *Soviet Military Strategy* that in a future war "one must expect the aggressor to use chemical and bacteriological weapons in conjunction with nuclear ones". A prefatory note by the publishers of *Bacteriological Weapons and How to Defend Against Them*[3] even more cagily says that "future war is considered by the aggressive circles of the USA to be a total war in which means of mass destruction will be widely used". This booklet is recommended for use by "agitators, propagandists, lecturers and teachers" and is largely devoted to a description of epidemic diseases and means of controlling them. It is possible, then, that instruction based on such books is seen primarily as a means of inculcating general hygienic practices and knowledge, with the anti-Western implications as a propaganda bonus. It is interesting, however, that this particular book does not repeat the charges lavishly made by Russians and Chinese alike at the time of the Korean War, that the Americans had actually used biological weapons—in particular insect-borne agents—at that time. Its historical review jumps from alleged Japanese activities during World War II to the use of defoliants and anti-crop compounds in Vietnam.

Arms-control doctrine

The USSR is one of the fifty or so countries which have signed the Geneva Protocol of 1925 binding them not to use "asphyxiating poisonous or other gases", nor "analogous liquids, materials or devices", nor "bacteriological methods of warfare" against fellow-signatories. Like Britain and many others, the Soviets put in a reservation releasing them from these restrictions if they found themselves at enmity with a country "whose forces, or the forces of whose allies" failed to respect the Protocol. Strictly, then, the USSR is not inhibited by the Protocol vis-à-vis the U.S. (as a non-signatory), nor would she be against British forces allied to U.S. forces in a conflict in which the United States was not respecting the Protocol. Of course, the United States may be held to have a virtual 'no first use' policy regarding CBW; and some jurists argue that the Geneva Protocol, though contractual in form, has entered into the body of international customary law (*see* Chapter 12) through long (if not universal) observances, so that it is binding among non-signatories as much as signatories. Possibly some Soviet jurists would take this view, and the tendency in Soviet legal writing is certainly to take the Protocol seriously and grant it some efficacy as a factor which, alongside mutual deterrence, prevented chemical agents from being used in World War II.

These considerations do however draw attention to the greatest East-West bone of contention in regard to CBW, *i.e.*, whether non-lethal chemical agents are in fact banned under the Geneva Protocol. It is outside the scope of this chapter to mention the many arguments that have been adduced on each side. Suffice it to point out that though the Soviet authorities have used tear gas for riot-control just as Western states have done, it by no means follows that they, or we, must logically condone the use of the same agents in wartime against enemy forces. The last major international debate on CBW was that in the U.N. at the end of 1966, where the Hungarians and various African delegates made most of the anti-American running; the Soviet delegates do not appear to have spoken at all. (The debate ended with a general appeal for all countries to adhere strictly to the Protocol, but cast little light on the points at issue.) The Soviet Union is meanwhile on record with its 1962 plan for General and Comprehensive Disarmament (GCD) which proposes complete abolition of both chemical and biological weapons, during the second of three 3-year disarmament stages; against this, the corresponding Western blueprint advocates study of the special difficulties of chemical and biological arms-control in Stage I, a halving of stockpiles in Stage II, and elimination of the rest and of manufacturing facilities in Stage III. The Soviet plan makes no mention of inspection difficulties, nor of discrimination problems, and by analogy with the Soviet stand over inspection in other fields one must assume that at present they would not contemplate giving alien inspectors the right to do anything but observe the actual destruction of agreed quantities of agents. It seems a long time, too, since those inter-war disarmament negotiations when the Soviets proposed that factory committees in each country should ensure the non-production of prohibited weapons.

It must be feared in any case that implementation of the GCD plans is not a thought uppermost in the minds of negotiators of any major power today, so doggedly do the obstacles seem to have grown instead of shrinking. Meanwhile the Soviets are probably happy to stand pat on the Protocol as they see it, plus their known capability in those CBW fields which they consider effective. In regard to the contentious non-lethal agents, they may feel themselves to be in somewhat of a public relations quandary. As occasional users of riot-control agents they could not approve of any statements appearing to condemn these as intrinsically inhumane. On the other hand they probably do not foresee any great military need for these or other non-lethal agents on their own side (expecting to be on the guerrilla, not counter-guerrilla, side of limited wars) and can hardly oppose any criticism of the Americans in Vietnam. It is therefore not likely at present that the Russians will be eager partners in any efforts to secure a redefinition of terms as a means of strengthening the Protocol. And even where lethal agents are used in clear violation of the Protocol, as in the Yemen, political considerations will put a severe brake on Soviet reactions. It is not suggested that those seeking ways of constraining CBW, and especially of constraining the spread of CBW capabilities, should give up: simply that they should bear the political background in mind.

DISCUSSION

Two major issues were raised in this discussion. First, the nature of the quadripartite and tri-partite agreements between Britain Canada, Australia and the United States were questioned by Professor Wall, who quoted an interview given by Dr Pennie, Deputy Chairman of the Canadian Defence Research Council to a Canadian magazine.[1] This interview gave two important items of information.

One was a fairly detailed description of the Suffield Proving Ground north of Medicine Hat in Alberta, Canada. It consists of a set of closed laboratories and also a thousand square mile tract of land which is used specifically, according to Dr Pennie, for studying the spread of organisms. Equipment from all parties to the agreement was tested there. Asked how the pact works, Dr Pennie replied: "There are regular meetings of scientific staff engaged in this particular line of work in all three countries, and there is free disclosure of information in all these areas. We also attempt to divide the work between laboratories whether they be in Britain, the United States or here (Canada) wherever the work suits. You can understand that you need specialized facilities for this type of work. There are facilities in Canada which don't exist in Britain; there are some in Britain which do not exist in the United States so it makes good sense and sound logic to try and divide up the work."

Professor Wall went on to point out that the existence of an agreement of this kind places equal responsibility on all four members of this quadripartite pact.

The second major theme concerned the issue of secrecy: should work at Porton continue to be secret? If it was exclusively defensive in character, why could it not be declassified?

The general arguments in favour of secrecy were indicated by Dr Viney and Professor Meselson who pointed out that there were two sorts of secrecy: conspicuous and clandestine. The former variety could lead to opinions in other defence establishments that there was something worth investigating. The very knowledge of the existence of secret research is a powerful deterrent to one's enemies. But the clandestine sort also has considerable advantages —there is less danger of spying and political control is easier.

Countering the move to declassify secret research at Porton, Dr Viney pointed out that if one disclosed all the facts about a genuinely defensive capability, then the research becomes undermined because the potential enemy knows what one is equipped to defend oneself against. Further, revealing all that is known about CBW would amount to a proliferation of dangerous knowledge. Whilst this does not mean that secrecy must be eternal in a world of sovereign states, there are sound, peace-loving reasons for maintaining secrecy until such time as it can be assumed that all countries have given up offensive intentions.

Finally, Professor Meselson showed that, from the point of view of a British Minister of Defence, Porton probably offered an extremely high return on investment. In exchange for a small expenditure at Porton and the maintenance of the quadripartite agreements, he had access to the results of the much larger programme of the United States. For this reason alone, the Ministry would probably fight quite hard to maintain secrecy.

After some theorizing as to the actual percentage of secret work carried out at Porton, the Conference heard the arguments in favour of declassification. Mr T. Dalyell (Member of Parliament for W. Lothian) suggested that many of the scientists at Porton might prefer to work in the open in order to achieve healthier relations with university scientists. Dr Sidel felt that the chances of the development of offensive weapons by any power would be much reduced in a world where a policy of complete openness was pursued. Dr Rose pointed out that throughout the history of science, secrecy or no secrecy, there are many instances of simultaneous discovery. For example, it is now abundantly clear that the Soviet Union would have developed its own atomic weapons within a very short space of time irrespective of the leakage of secrets that occurred in the 1940s and early 1950s. An exactly comparable situation applies today to CBW—the South Africans are surely capable of making many of the weapons, whilst one can be reasonably confident of the ability of the universities and chemical industry in Western Germany to be sure that they require very little help from Porton's publications. In fact, one could say that the synthesis of the chemical agents described by Perry Robinson are within the scope of any reasonably competent organic chemist. As far as biological agents are concerned, the central problem is that of mass production and this should be within the capabilities of any drug house with a pilot plant.

Mrs Galston attempted to deal with Dr Viney's concern that scientific information should not fall into the wrong hands by pointing out that in our present world every hand at this point and for this type of weapon is the 'wrong hand'.

PART FOUR
LEGAL ASPECTS OF CBW

12. Legal Aspects   I. Brownlie

General features of the law

The first and major characteristic of the law of war is its paradoxical nature. The United Kingdom *Manual of Military Law*[1] states that the development of the law has been determined by three principles:

> First, the principle that a belligerent is justified in applying compulsion and force of any kind, to the extent necessary for the realisation of the purpose of war, that is, the complete submission of the enemy at the earliest possible moment with the least possible expenditure of men, resources and money; secondly, the principle of humanity, according to which kinds and degrees of violence which are not necessary for the purpose of war are not permitted to a belligerent; and thirdly, the principle of chivalry, which demands a certain amount of fairness in offence and defence, and a certain amount of mutual respect between the opposing forces.

In spite of the element of paradox, the law has produced certain factors of discrimination in the means of carrying on war. The principal factors are, first, the prohibition of weapons which cause unnecessary suffering in proportion to their destructive effect, and, secondly, a distinction between combatants, whether regular or irregular, and non-combatants.

The law and the statesmen who influence its development utilize categories which may not seem very sophisticated or up to date. In many ways legal categories are bound to have rough edges partly because they set standards for a great variety of people most of whom are neither scientists nor lawyers. However, the legal categories have in general maintained a sufficiently close relationship with technical developments. The law has employed the category of chemical warfare since at least 1919, though the legal reference is usually the formula which prohibits "the use in war of asphyxiating, poisonous or other gases, and of all analogous liquids, materials or devices." The *Dictionary of U.S. Army Terms*, published in 1953, defines chemical warfare as "the tactics and technique of conducting warfare by use of toxic chemical agents." The weapons may be thought to include incendiary fuels[2] and smoke gases, but this is a matter of doubt. The indisputable content of the category is the list of anti-personnel gases; incapacitants, for example, hallucinatory drugs; choking gases, such as chlorine and phosgene; nerve gases, including sarin and tabun; gases which affect the oxygen supply in the blood; and blister gases including mustard gas and lewisite.

Since 1925 the legal materials have contained the category of "bacteriological methods of warfare". The modern technical concept of biological warfare includes bacteriological methods, but extends to a wider range of agents. The *Dictionary of U.S. Army Terms* defines biological warfare as "the employment of living organisms, toxic biological products, and chemical plant growth regulators to produce death or casualties in man, animals or plants; or defence against such action." The *U.S. Army Manual*, published in 1956, describes biological warfare as "the military use of living organisms or their toxic products to cause death, disability, or damage to man, his domestic animals or crops" and continues: "It includes the employment not only of bacteria but also of other micro-organisms and higher forms of life, such as insects and other pests . . . While certain chemical anti-crop compounds are not truly biological warfare agents, they are so considered as a matter of convenience." It seems to be a matter of historical accident that the use of gases has been regarded as chemical warfare while the use of bacteria and 'toxic biological products' is classified separately.

Other features of the law require brief notice. Much of the law consists of treaties, and in some connections states are concerned to point out that they are not a party to this or that treaty. Nevertheless, international law may develop rules of customary law which are evidenced by state practice in the form of protests, official warnings, manuals of military law, and various diplomatic materials. A treaty may by its terms provide evidence of the state of general international law in two ways: by containing statements purporting to be declaratory of existing law; and independently of the first method, by being accepted as a statement of the law even by non-parties. Finally, the modern principle is that the law of land warfare applies to international conflicts whether or not the parties characterize an armed conflict as a 'state of war'. An insurgency may constitute an armed conflict, and, although it will not be of an international character unless there is substantial foreign intervention against the lawful government, it is now generally accepted that the general principles of the humanitarian law of war apply to internal conflicts.

The prohibition of chemical warfare in customary international law

There is a great deal of evidence in support of the view that chemical warfare as a *genus* is prohibited by customary international law. The peace treaties of World War I and the Treaty of Berlin of August 25th, 1921, between the United States and Germany, contain provisions which prohibit the importation or manufacture by Germany of certain gases and other liquids and devices, and in doing so treat *as already prohibited* "the use of asphyxiating, poisonous and other gases and all analogous liquids and devices." In 1922 the Washington Treaty was concluded.[3] This contains a provision the substance of which was to be repeated in the Geneva Protocol of 1925. Article V prohibits "the use in war of asphyxiating, poisonous or other gases, and all analogous liquids materials or devices." The United States ratified the Treaty on June 9th, 1925,[4] but it failed to come into force because of the absence of French ratification. The French failure to ratify, it may be noticed, had nothing to do with the reference to chemical warfare, but flowed from the limitations on submarines in the Treaty.

The Geneva Protocol signed on June 17th, 1925

The Protocol is the most important instrument concerning prohibited weapons. It provides as follows:

> . . . the undersigned Plenipotentiaries, in the name of their respective Governments:
> Whereas the use in war of asphyxiating, poisonous or other gases, and all analogous liquids, materials or devices, has been justly condemned by the general opinion of the civilised world; and
> Whereas the prohibition of such use has been declared in Treaties to which the majority of the Powers of the World are Parties; and
> To the end that this prohibition shall be universally accepted as a part of International Law, binding alike the conscience and the practice of nations;
> Declare:
> That the High Contracting Parties, so far as they are not already Parties to Treaties prohibiting such use, accept this

K

prohibition, agree to extend this prohibition to the use of bacteriological methods of warfare and agree to be bound as between themselves according to the terms of this declaration.

International lawyers of great authority have held that insofar as the instrument relates to chemical weapons it is declaratory and affirmative of the customary law at the time.[5] Forty-nine states signed the Protocol, which came into force in 1928. In 1944 there were forty-four parties by ratification or accession. Since then another fourteen states have become parties, including India, Pakistan, Cuba, and a number of African States. China's accession of 1929 has been recognized by the People's Republic of China. The United Kingdom, France, the USSR, and a number of other states are parties subject to a condition of reciprocity.[6] The United States did not become a party to the Protocol, but the Protocol has acquired considerable prestige and is referred to as evidence of the general law.[7] Thus in the *Shimoda* case[8] a Japanese court concerned, *inter alia,* with the legality of the atomic attacks on Hiroshima and Nagasaki, referred to the Protocol as a source of relevant rules although neither the United States nor Japan were parties to it.

The United States and CBW

The position of the United States obviously calls for further examination since its non-participation in the Geneva Protocol is a companion to that country's scientific and military resources and proven readiness to prepare and resort to chemical warfare and related techniques.

The failure to ratify the Protocol did not stem from any decisive negative stand on its subject matter but from a desire to avoid an omnibus prohibition. However, since World War II the United States policy has been more equivocal. The *U.S. Army Field Manual*[9] expressly states that "the United States is not a party to any treaty, now in force, that prohibits or restricts the use in warfare of toxic or non-toxic gases . . . or of bacteriological warfare".

American official sources have in fact adopted a fairly clear view on these matters on a number of occasions in the past. In 1932, on the basis of proposals by President Hoover, the General Commission of the Disarmament Conference adopted a resolution which condemned the use of gas, bacteriological, and incendiary warfare as methods of warfare. A study by the U.S. Naval War College in 1935[10] concluded that "the use of poisonous gases and those that cause unnecessary suffering is in general prohibited; the use of smoke-screens and of tear gas has not been included in the category of prohibited acts, but the use of bacteriological warfare has been prohibited". Of interest is the robust statement of President Roosevelt which is printed in the *Department of State Bulletin* dated June 12th, 1943.[11] This statement includes the following passages:

> From time to time since the present war began there have been reports that one or more of the Axis powers were seriously contemplating use of poisonous or noxious gases or other inhumane devices of warfare.
> I have been loath to believe that any nation, even our present enemies, could or would be willing to loose upon mankind such terrible and inhumane weapons. However, evidence that the Axis powers are making significant preparations indicative of such an intention is being reported. . . . Use of such weapons has been outlawed by the general opinion of civilised mankind. This country has not used them, and I hope that we never will be compelled to use them. I state categorically that we shall under no circumstances resort to the use of such weapons unless they are first used by our enemies.

In a debate in the United Nations General Assembly on October 16th, 1952, Dean Acheson, then United States Secretary of State, declared:[12] "We will not commit aggression with chemical weapons or bacteriological weapons, which we have been falsely and slanderously accused of using."

The American position would seem to be far from consistent, and in the case of chemical weapons the *U.S. Army Field Manual* ignores the evidence for the existence of a customary rule prohibiting use. In any case the American position, in so far as it appears to deny the existence of prohibitions, relates to non-prohibition of chemical and biological weapons as a class, *tout court*. Thus it is subject to various specific rules as to methods of conducting war in general. I shall enlarge on this aspect of the matter later on.

The 1966 Resolution of the United Nations General Assembly

On December 5th, 1966, the General Assembly of the United Nations adopted the following resolution:[13]

The General Assembly

Guided by the principles of the Charter of the United Nations and of international law:

Considering that weapons of mass destruction constitute a

danger to all mankind and are incompatible with the accepted norms of civilisation.

Affirming that the strict observance of the rules of international law on the conduct of warfare is in the interest of maintaining these standards for civilisation;

Recalling that the Geneva Protocol for the Prohibition of the Use in War of Asphyxiating, Poisonous or Other Gases, and of Bacteriological Methods of Warfare, of 17 June 1925, has been signed and adopted and is recognised by many States.

Noting that the Conference of the Eighteen-Nation Committee on Disarmament has the task of seeking an agreement on the cessation of the development and production of chemical and bacteriological weapons and other weapons of mass destruction, and on the elimination of all such weapons from national arsenals, as called for in the draft proposals on general and complete disarmament now before the Conference.

1. *Calls for* strict observance by all States of the principles and objectives of the Protocol . . . signed at Geneva on 17 June 1925, and condemns all action contrary to those objectives;

2. *Invites* all States to accede to the Geneva Protocol of 17 June 1925.

The resolutions of the General Assembly are normally not binding as such on member states, but resolutions on legal questions provide clear evidence of the state of the law, since the resolutions represent the deliberate and collective view of those states giving affirmative votes. This resolution is expressly concerned with legal issues and was adopted by 101 votes. No state voted against, but three—Cuba, France, and Gabon—abstained.

The significant features of the resolution are as follows. First, it assumes that the Geneva Protocol today constitutes general international law and no longer a mere contract for actual parties to it. Secondly, this assumption extends both to chemical and bacteriological warfare. Thirdly, the prohibition seems to be of these types of warfare *tout court* because the weapons concerned are weapons of mass destruction. On this third point it might be argued that the reference to weapons of mass destruction cuts down the effect of the resolution because not all chemical or bacteriological weapons are necessarily of this type. However, the intention of the resolution is clearly to deal with these weapons as types; hence the focus on, and emphatic reference to, the Geneva Protocol. In general the resolution clearly militates against the former apparent reservations in the position of the United States. The United States took part in the process of amending the original proposal and voted for the resulting text.

The question of conditional legality

The materials examined so far relate primarily to the issue of prohibition unconditionally of the classes of chemical and bacteriological weapons. It is important to tackle the problems from a different point of view for a number of reasons: the United States might renew its stand against prohibition *tout court*; the observer, and especially the non-lawyer, may feel that the alternative to categorical prohibition is that CBW is *lawful* without qualification. This cannot be so on any view of the legal position.

Insofar as particular chemical and biological weapons have indiscriminate effects, or cause unnecessary suffering, they can only have conditional legality. The *U.S. Army Manual* necessarily adopts the principle of conditional legality, since any more permissive principle would be utterly untenable. Paragraph 36 of the *Manual* thus provides:

The use of weapons which employ fire, such as tracer ammunition, flame throwers, or napalm, and other incendiary agents, against targets requiring their use is not violative of international law. They should not, however, be employed in such a way as to cause unnecessary suffering to individuals.

Although the *U.S. Army Manual* is equivocal in dealing with both chemical and bacteriological weapons, the general implication is that in its regime a conditional legality exists as in the case of fire weapons.

The position of conditional legality must be given some elaboration. It is an uncontestable principle of customary law that it is forbidden to use arms, projectiles, or material calculated to cause unnecessary suffering.[14] Moreover, numerous rules of customary law, repeated and developed in the Geneva Conventions of 1949, would be inevitably broken if weapons are used which produce extensive, indiscriminate, and possibly unknown and uncontrollable results. Two Conventions in particular are involved here: the Geneva Convention for the Amelioration of the Condition of the Wounded and Sick in Armed Forces in the Field,[15] and the Geneva Convention Relative to the Protection of Civilian Persons in Time of War.[16] The indiscriminate character of certain types, at least, of chemical and biological techniques needs stressing. Moreover, the elements of persistence and consequential action may aggravate the problem.

Assessment of the legal position

It is not very useful to examine the various forms of special pleading to be found in some of the literature in favour of freedom of action and choice of weapons. The fact is that the vast majority of writers in various languages take the firm view that both chemical and bacteriological weapons are prohibited and that the Geneva Protocol now represents general or customary international law.[17] The current United Kingdom *Manual of Military Law* contains a careful codification of *The Law of War on Land* prepared with the assistance of Sir Hersch Lauterpacht, later the British judge on the International Court of Justice. Paragraph 111 of *The Law of War on Land* provides that "the use of poison and poisoned weapons, asphyxiating, poisonous or other gases, and of all analogous liquids, materials or devices, and bacteriological methods of warfare are forbidden." This view of the law receives recent and very substantial reinforcement from the General Assembly resolution of 1966. In the debate on that resolution the United States reacted to charges relating to the conduct of the war in Vietnam by saying that the only gases it had used were irritant gas, tear gas of the type normally used in riot control.

The United States' position is interesting because it does not lay stress on permissiveness, but pleads that an exception exists to the overall prohibition. The exception does create some difficulty. In all probability the definition in the Protocol was intended to be comprehensive for the *genus* of substances with which it dealt. In November 1930, the United Kingdom presented a memorandum to the Preparatory Committee of the Disarmament Conference which stated that the Protocol definition included non-toxic gases and notably irritant gases.[18] On the other hand, if the *genus* concerned is confined to those weapons which cause unnecessary suffering tear gas may not be included as such, and everything will depend on the type and the way it is used. It may be noticed that the U.S. Naval War College Study of 1935 states that the prohibition does not include smoke-screens and tear gas.

A more serious threat to the legal regime comes from the doctrine of reprisal. Several parties to the Geneva Protocol, including the United Kingdom and the USSR, made a reservation of reciprocity, and the customary law contains the principle that reprisals may be employed in reaction to a prior violation of the law committed by the enemy. However, the doctrine of reprisals is limited in that a reprisal must not be in excess of the degree of violation committed by the enemy and reprisals directed against wounded and sick prisoners-of-war and civilians, protected under the Geneva Convention of 1949, are unlawful and constitute war crimes. A further consideration is the possible effect of the strong terms of the General Assembly resolution: the consequences may be that the rules in the Protocol are now *jus cogens* and not subject to the doctrine of reprisals and also that reservations on the same theme are void.[19]

Some other relevant legal principles

The use on a substantial scale of weapons which cause indiscriminate harm to combatants and non-combatants and which in any case cause unnecessary suffering will involve the commission of crimes against humanity. Crimes against humanity were declared to be crimes under international law in the Agreement on Military Trials of 1945,[20] which provided for the establishment of an International Military Tribunal at Nuremberg. The definition contained therein refers, *inter alia*, to "murder, extermination, enslavement, deportation or other inhuman acts committed against any civilian population." The Agreement on Military Trials had twenty-three parties, and a unanimous resolution of the United Nations General Assembly affirmed "the principles of international law recognized by the Charter of the Nuremberg Tribunal and the Judgment of the Tribunal."[21]

Depending on the effects of the particular weapon and the conditions in which it is used, to resort to chemical and, more especially, biological warfare might constitute a breach of the Genocide Convention.[22] However, the intention in such a case must be "to destroy, in whole or in part, a national, ethnic, racial, or religious group, *as such* . . ."[23] Finally, if large scale and reckless use of weapons and techniques produced effects which spread over frontiers the state using weapons in this way would be in breach of the duties toward neutral states which the customary law imposes on belligerents. Article 1 of the Hague Convention of 1907, concerning the rights and duties of neutrality, provides that "the territory of neutral Powers is inviolable."

Defoliation and crop destruction

The practice of aerial spraying for purposes of defoliation and crop destruction was clearly not foreseen by the various legal controls relating to the conduct of war. Moreover, the rationale behind the existing rules is the causing of indiscriminate and unnecessary suffering to people by direct means. Nevertheless, practices which must result in depriving peasant communities permanently of their food resources constitute a crime against humanity and if persisted in, when large-scale distress is manifest, would amount to genocide. Large-scale destruction of the fertility of a countryside is an operation which is probably more strikingly indiscriminate as between combatants and non-combatants than any technique other than resort to nuclear weapons. A 'scorched-earth' policy which is carried out in circumstances in which specific material resources are kept out of enemy hands and which is accompanied by a taking of responsibility for the subsistence of civilians from the area concerned is not necessarily illegal. Of course, the normal scorched-earth technique is not aimed at the ecology of a region in any case. A further point is that pillage of captured places and unnecessary destruction of property are forbidden by rules of undisputed authority. Large-scale crop destruction must fall foul of these rules, more especially when it is carried out from the air.

Incendiary weapons

The classification of weapons has been a matter of conventional and historical association. Neither the legal definition nor, it seems fairly clear, the scientists include fuels and incendiary weapons in the category of chemical weapons. As Dr Sidel points out in his paper on napalm,[24] explosives and incendiary weapons are 'physical' weapons, producing their effects by blast and heat. As a class it is doubtful if such weapons are prohibited since they do not appear to fall within the terms of the Geneva Protocol.[25] Nevertheless, the normal rules of the law apply: napalm and similar weapons can be used lawfully only against military targets and "their use against personnel is contrary to the law in so far as it is calculated to cause unnecessary suffering."[26]

Control of armaments and disarmament

It is well known that, in spite of adherence to rules limiting or prohibiting the use of certain types of weapons, states may manufacture and/or, possess the weapons concerned. Disarmament is the better form of insurance therefore. Recent proposals for disarmament have shown particular concern for the prohibition of the production, possession and use of chemical and bacteriological weapons. This concern is perhaps an index of the growing role of such weapons in military preparations. In this connection it is worth recalling an existing treaty provision in Protocol III of 1954 to the Brussels Treaty of 1948.[27] Article One of the Protocol stipulates that the Federal Republic of Germany shall not manufacture in its territory atomic, biological, and chemical weapons. In Annex II the following definitions occur. A chemical weapon is defined as "any equipment or apparatus expressly designed to use, for military purposes, the asphyxiating, toxic, irritant, paralysant, growth-regulating, anti-lubricating or catalysing properties of any chemical substance." A biological weapon is defined as "any equipment or apparatus expressly designed for use, for military purposes, harmful insects or other living or dead organisms, or their toxic products."

Concluding remarks

It will suffice to make certain general points.

(i) If the Geneva Protocol is regarded as declaratory of the customary law only in respect of chemical warfare, then the distinction between chemical and bacteriological warfare may matter since the prohibition of the latter type may be less firm. The chemical-biological distinction is difficult to maintain in some ways at least. Thus the existence of non-biological poisons, the low molecular weight toxins, blurs the line with chemical warfare. However, the general practice of states and the evidence provided by the United Nations resolution of 1966 justifies the conclusion that both chemical and biological warfare are prohibited by general, *i.e.*, customary, international law.

(ii) The prohibition existing on the basis of the Geneva Protocol and the United Nations resolution is clearly not restricted to lethal gases. It almost certainly includes all anti-personnel gases.

(iii) Even if the Geneva Protocol was regarded as in some way defective, and even if it were to be denounced by some of the parties to it, it cannot be emphasized too strongly that the ordinary laws of warfare still apply. The layman, who knows about the Protocol but is ignorant of the law of war in general, is ready to assume that everything turns on the Protocol. The overriding principle, which applies to all weapons, is that weapons should not be used which are calculated to cause unnecessary suffering or are inevitably indiscriminate as between combatants and others. These principles may be found in any statement of the law of land warfare, including the British *Manual of Military Law*, Part II.

DISCUSSION

Discussion of Dr Brownlie's paper ranged extensively over many of the issues he raised; two particular topics may perhaps be singled out, the legality of the U.S. use of chemical weapons and defoliants in Vietnam, and the general question of whether the activities of international lawyers, in building a legal framework in which war could be conducted, helped reduce its risk.

On the first point, the use of the weapons in Vietnam, Dr Brownlie reiterated that attempts to discriminate between lethal and non-lethal weapons failed; the definition of chemical weapons was concerned not so much with lethality but with the concept of "asphyxiating, noxious or causing unnecessary suffering".

Dr Galston asked what the position was regarding the use of food deprivation as a weapon, and if the deliberate destruction of food, either by the dumping of captured bags of rice or by the destruction of rice plants in the field, were challenged and the United States asked to supply a basis for its actions, what likely legal basis would be used.

In reply Dr Brownlie pointed out that there is no legal provision on scorched earth policy as such. The *British Manual,* for example, which is quite detailed, not only in its actual provisions but in the comments on provisions, where it suggests examples of the scope of particular provisions, says that the poisoning of wells is illegal but the diversion of watercourses is allowed.

It comes back to the general principle that one cannot use means of conducting a war which cause unnecessary and indiscriminate harm to the civilian population. It thus becomes a question of how this general principle is applied to the particular facts. And this is a problem no matter what area of war is discussed. If a war zone is declared and treated without the slightest attempt to sort things out, then it would be very difficult to find a legal basis to say that this behaviour came within the accepted rules. On the other hand if a given war zone, before declaring it a war zone, is claimed to be occupied by foreign forces and the civilians were behind the lines somewhere (where one has lines), then there are no legal risks at all; one just treats everything as an open target.

Mr M. Leitenberg pointed out that the *U.S. Field Manual* (USFM 27.10.1949 para. 24 and 1956 para. 40, 41) was very precise on this point. Thus it states that destruction of food crops and food supplies is prohibited unless it can be shown that these are for the use of enemy combatant personnel. The United States has said repeatedly (i) that intended victims of this campaign are male Viet

Cong combatant personnel who are in isolation from the community and (ii) that to make sure that there is no unnecessary suffering caused to civilians they are warned in advance and told where they can go. Now, while this may not be the case in practice, there remains a very interesting connection between the U.S. law of warfare and what the U.S. Government claims to be doing. But according to Donald Hornig, President Johnson's Science Advisor, the real purpose of the anti-crop programme has been directed at moving the population out of NLF-controlled areas into those controlled by the Saigon regime. This puts quite a different perspective on the programme and is borne out by a survey of defoliated areas. Crop destruction has been most marked not in the sparsely-occupied areas where the effect would be largely confined to the NLF guerillas but to the densely-populated, fertile Mekong Delta —the 'Rice Bowl of South East Asia'.

Thus, as Dr Brownlie concluded, it all depends on the evidence on the particular case concerned. In the Vietnamese case, the U.S. policy of declaring war zones and then treating everything in the zone as a free target might be quite good evidence on this particular point.

The second theme was raised by Professor Arnott, who asked whether Dr Brownlie felt that the body of international law relating to warfare produces any inhibitory effect at all on the behaviour of governments when it suits them otherwise. Those who were engaged in the early battles to contain nuclear weapons, claimed Professor Arnott, do not believe that the fact that they haven't been used is in any way due to any international agreements, test bans, or whatever, but because so much is known about these weapons that they are politically impossible; this is the sanction which prevents their use. The same would be true for CBW as well.

Dr Brownlie replied to this challenge that his answer could not be his opinion as a lawyer, because this was a matter of politics and sociology. There was a difference between talking about rules and their efficacy. If one brought a criminal lawyer into the discussion, he would talk about criminal law, but he would not have said the law is probably not worth talking about because only ten per cent of warehouse break-ins in London ever come to conviction. Rules of themselves could not dictate in matters of high policy, but could have some sort of moral imperative which affect governments in this sphere. The problem of enforcement is a complicated one— the rules themselves are never self-enforced—they cannot be, and the rules of warfare present more of a problem than there would be in some other areas of law. But one of the ways out is to remind governments publicly that they have in fact said these things and signed these treaties.

One of the problems is the sociological question of why law is observed at all. Governments are not individuals—they are like rather vast and complex corporations. Within a government one can have different views on crucial matters of international law. In times past the Admiralty has had one view and another sector has another view. In the United States, on some leading questions of international law the State Department has a different view from the Department of Justice—on sovereign immunity, for instance, immunity of foreign states and their agencies. So if one is talking about states, one must remember they are not individual beings. The problems are different from those of making internal laws. On the world scene there is a newer type of community, a definite sort of community consisting of 130 large corporations which can behave as very complex units. Thus despite its inadequacies, the codification of international law remains a powerful tool.

PART FIVE
ETHICAL PROBLEMS

13. Preventing CBW   (a) J. H. Humphrey

In discussing what might be done about the danger that chemical and biological weapons may become accepted as part of the normal armoury of nations, it will be more useful if we consider them from the point of view of those who regard it as their business to prepare for wars as well as from that of those who regard resort to war as an unnecessary and unacceptable way of settling differences between nations. So long as national governments, and those who maintain them in office, continue to prepare for war rather than repudiate it, arguments about whether one way of killing people or of putting them out of action is more beastly than another are liable to appear academic and to be ineffective.

While I accept that to take part in the development and use of chemical and biological weapons poses ethical problems for the scientists involved and that to take part in 'public health in reverse' is indeed directly contrary to a physician's role, the ethical problems seems to me to be personal and not essentially different from those which face à physicist or engineer working on ballistic missiles or a bomb sight. Further, I doubt whether to those at the receiving end an attack with chemical or biological weapons could be much more unpleasant than one with napalm or saturation bombing with anti-personnel missiles. Once the weapons are such that the person who uses them is not made aware of the direct consequences of his actions, and especially if he has been taught to regard his enemies as creatures whose lives are incomparably less important than his own, he can escape such emotions as pity, disgust, or horror which might make him hesitate to use the weapons except perhaps in the heat of battle. To me and, I suspect, to military planners it seems illogical to set chemical and biological weapons in a category apart from other modern weapons on grounds of beastliness alone. The question is, are there other grounds on which these weapons can be distinguished? I think there are.

The first and most important, as explained by Dr Brownlie, is that the people in all countries and the politicians in their public

pronouncements recognize such a distinction—even though it may
be illogical and based on an accident of propaganda and history.
The terms of the Geneva Protocol, publicly supported at the United
Nations in December 1966, by the representatives of all the major
powers including the United States and Japan, forbid the first use
of chemical and biological weapons in warfare, although they do
not forbid research on or possession of such weapons. Despite its
obscurities and the tenuousness of any guarantees of observance the
Geneva Protocol provides a statement of good intentions which it
has not been possible to achieve in respect of any other weapons.

The second is that investment in CBW, although by no means
inconsiderable, is still small compared with investment in conventional and nuclear weapons. At present, so far as one can tell, CBW
is regarded rather as a useful adjunct to the existing armoury,
although the situation might change if both wars and the nuclear
stalemate continue. Some of the advantages claimed for weapons
of this kind have been set out in General Rothschild's book
Tomorrow's Weapons, and include cheapness, minimal destruction
of property and fixed installations, flexibility (including the capacity
to reach persons protected against all but very powerful conventional weapons), and, in a strange way, humaneness, since the non-
lethal weapons may incapacitate the enemy sufficiently to destroy
his fighting power temporarily. Although lethal chemical and biological weapons could conceivably be used against more or less
specific targets, they are nevertheless essentially indiscriminate in
their action and are classified as weapons of mass destruction. The
status of non-lethal chemical and non-lethal biological weapons (if
the latter are under serious consideration) has been left blurred, and
it is arguable whether they should be defined as weapons of mass
destruction. These are the weapons which are put forward by their
protagonists as being humane. Since few people—at least in peace-
time—relish the idea of killing, the humaneness claimed for CBW
could lead to its being regarded as acceptable, despite the Geneva
Protocol. I find it hard to understand—and this doubt is confirmed
by the example of the use of non-lethal chemical weapons in
Vietnam—how non-lethal weapons can deter or defeat a determined
enemy, except when used as a means of making conventional
weapons more effective. This is a matter which requires careful
discussion and hard thinking.

The third difference is that much of the research which goes into
the development of chemical and biological weapons, or into
defence against them, is of a very similar nature to research which

would legitimately be pursued without any consideration of CBW. For example, the toxic properties of the organo-phosphorus insecticides need to be studied for the sake of the persons who make and use them; similarly important is work aimed to discover antidotes and to devise adequate protective clothing. The defoliants used in Vietnam are standard agricultural chemicals, and spraying them from aeroplanes to defoliate trees—rash though this may appear to ecologists—has already been done in Africa in attempts to clear the tsetse fly, vector of trypanosomiasis, from parts of the 'tsetse belt.' What sets apart work on chemical weapons is the deliberate and secret investigation of properties which increase their toxicity for man, the preparation and manufacture of devices for use in war, and the stockpiling of chemicals for this purpose. Similarly the development of biological weapons requires research into factors controlling the pathogenicity of microbes and their mode of dissemination; study of techniques for rapid detection and identification; large-scale culture methods; preparation of protective vaccines; and so on. Nearly all the research required could quite properly be undertaken as non-military projects in universities, medical research institutes, or enterprises engaged in the manufacture of vaccines. Even intensive investigations on uncommon and exotic highly virulent microbes could be entirely justifiable in a wholly peaceful world, both on scientific grounds and because of the possibility that some time, somewhere, such microbes might become disseminated and give rise to serious epidemics such as have repeatedly ravaged man and other animals in the past. As with chemical weapons, microbiological research and development become biological weapon research only insofar as techniques are devised for deliberately spreading pathogenic infective agents in war.

A fourth feature of chemical and biological weapons is that their manufacture does not require elaborate or highly specialized installations which would be difficult to conceal. Indeed the potential activity per unit weight of these weapons, especially of biological weapons, is so great that quite small factories or parts of factories could suffice to supply the military requirements. Apart from the need for precautions essential for the handling of highly dangerous materials nothing obvious need distinguish such factories from others making ordinary fine chemicals or, say, antibiotics or bacterial vaccines. Consequently, inspection and verification to ascertain whether the ingredients of such weapons were being made would present much greater difficulty than in the case, for example, of fissile material for nuclear weapons.

L

With these four general points in mind, it seems to me that there are a number of ways in which the further development of chemical and biological weapons might be halted and the danger of their further use in war diminished.* The first is by ensuring that the support publicly given to the Geneva Protocol by almost all the national delegations at the General Assembly of the United Nations in December, 1966, is strengthened and not eroded. This means that the issues involved must be clearly discussed and widely enough understood to put political pressure on the governments of those countries which have not ratified the Protocol to do so. Without minimizing the unpleasantness of CBW or the ethical objections to weapons of this kind, I think that the most valid reason for doing this is that the Geneva Protocol, if not a giant confidence trick, is a real beginning in that limitation of weapons which all countries in the United Nations have declared they wish to seek. Until the difficulties presented by inspection and verification have been got round it may be difficult to extend the Protocol to forbid research on or possession of chemical and biological weapons, although states could be encouraged to renounce these for themselves, as Austria has done.

But even if all countries had adhered to the Geneva Protocol allegations of infringement in times of tension or war might still be made, and would require rapid investigation, since the right of retaliation in kind would remain. There is need for a recognized organization prepared to do this. It might be the International Red Cross Organization, or perhaps the World Health Organization because of its accepted expertise in epidemiology and its non-partisan reputation.

All this would minimize the danger of the future use of CBW, but it would not prevent countries from researching on and preparing such weapons as a precautionary measure to permit retaliation. The next and more important goal is for all countries to renounce the use of CBW altogether. This would imply that no secret research, by government or industry, could be done on potential weapon agents, and that open research on them in scale and content must have a clearly non-military aim. Renunciation of CBW could be made soon—indeed it might become much more difficult later—because no country has yet made such a major in-

---

* Many of the issues mentioned here have been raised under the stimulus of discussions held under the auspices of the Pugwash Movement.

vestment in these weapons as to feel its security threatened by renouncing them as part of a general agreement. It would be a gesture of mutual confidence which could lead to other and more important steps towards disarmament in more sensitive areas.

Finally, what should be the future of the establishments which have been built up to study and prepare for national defence (and, to a greater or lesser degree, offence) in relation to CBW? It is important to consider this question, since on the one hand they are likely to have a powerful vested interest in their own continued existence, with the possibility of arguing for this at the top level, and on the other hand they represent a sword which could be changed, with a minimum of beating, into a magnificent ploughshare. I will consider our own establishments, the MRE and the CDEE at Porton Down. I will start with the assumption that their own public image of themselves is broadly correct. That is, that their function is to study potential offensive agents only in relation to devising means of defence against them; that the great bulk of the original scientific work done there is published; and that most of the scientists take jobs there not only to earn a reasonable salary, but because they are given excellent facilities to study scientifically interesting problems and because they have a genuine belief that their work is important for the military defence of the country. Furthermore, I know that they are willing to help other civilian institutions with advice and the provision of materials and facilities. Nevertheless, in accepting this image I think it necessary to make two reservations. The first is that the study of defensive measures may not be so innocent as it might appear if studies of offensive measures and discoveries relating to these are left to our American allies on a reciprocal basis. In the absence of other information it may be wiser to assume that the collaboration which began during World War II has not ended.

The existence of an agreement between Britain, Canada, Australia, and the United States, and of shared proving grounds for CBW research at Suffield, Alberta, and Innisfail, Queensland, are examples. It is important to know what are the general terms and duration of this quadripartite agreement. The second reservation is that the output of published work from Porton would appear somewhat meagre if it represented the total useful output from an ordinary research institute with a comparable staff and facilities, and this is bound to give the impression that more goes on there than is revealed. Despite these reservations, the fact remains that at Porton are collected teams much of whose work has a direct relation to the problems of civilian life, but has much less impact on these than it might do if the primary object of the establishments were not to undertake partly classified work for the Ministry of Defence.

I do not of course, know, what classified work goes on at Porton nor what is the purpose of keeping it secret. Let us suppose, hypothetically, that significant defensive advances have been made, such as the development of a very effective general purpose gas-mask or of a rapid and extremely sensitive method for detecting airborne microbes. Would the revelation of such developments diminish their defensive value? Or might not this actually be increased, by showing that it would be difficult for one country to steal a march on another in this field? The answers do not seem to me to be obviously 'yes' and 'no' respectively.

It would be unrealistic to expect that the Ministry of Defence could abolish its establishments at Porton out of hand, or even declassify all the past work which has been done there, unless other countries known to be interested in CBW such as the United States and the USSR were prepared to do likewise. However this does not mean that no initiative can be taken. Provided that our Government were not contemplating becoming engaged in a war within the next few years involving CBW—despite the Geneva Protocol—and especially if it were meanwhile prepared to make a real effort at the international level to reach agreement to renounce these weapons, I suggest that for a trial period of not less than five years all the future work carried out at Porton should be declared declassified. Because, I suspect, biological weapons are presently less important than chemical weapons it might be easier to declassify the MRE first. The CDEE might follow suit later, after allowing time to observe whether there was a favourable international reaction to the first initiative, and time to sort out possible complications about chemical weapons shared with our allies. Work on the defence of man and animals against highly virulent and pathogenic organisms or work on toxic chemicals could proceed much as at present and might well be more effective because collaboration with other workers would be easier and more natural. Of course the results would not be the exclusive property of the Ministry of Defence, but there would be nothing to prevent the armed forces from obtaining advice and making use of them as they wished. Even during the trial period I would like to see at least a part of MRE positively devoted to international collaboration, for example with the World Health Organization over problems of mutual interest (of which there are many) or with the

Food and Agriculture Organization over such projects as the large-scale production of micro-organisms as food additives for regions where dietary protein is inadequate. Similarly part of the Chemical Defence section might act as a Research Association for the by no means economically insignificant protective clothing industry (which at present has none). Collaboration of this sort would not only have the advantage of promoting goodwill but could help towards defraying the cost of keeping Porton going.

To make such a gesture would carry some risk, but it would be an act of leadership by this country which could produce quite disproportionate gains by helping to break the deadlock over disarmament. Furthermore, by making the gesture for an initial trial period, without disbanding the teams which have been built up, even the risk would be minimized.

(b) M. Meselson

Half a century has passed since the world's only major outbreak of poison gas warfare. Large-scale germ warfare has never been attempted. Gas and germ warfare are explicitly prohibited by international law in the Geneva Protocol of 1925. Considering the enormous scale of gas warfare in World War I, it is remarkable how well the Protocol has been respected. There have been only two instances of verified poison gas warfare since 1925—in Ethiopa, and in the Yemen. In Vietnam the United States has been employing a powerful but generally non-lethal anti-riot agent, maintaining that the Protocol does not forbid it.

When compared with the recent history of other forms of warfare the record shows that the governments and peoples of the world have come to practise and expect a degree of restraint against the use of chemical and biological weapons not found for any other class of weapons, except nuclear ones. The chief factor justifying that restraint is the same for both nuclear and CB warfare—apprehension that, once begun, it would open up an unfamiliar and highly unpredictable dimension of warfare that might lead to the extermination of very large numbers of troops and civilians, especially one's own.

Destructiveness of CBW

There is no doubt that existing nuclear weapons could destroy entire populations. Although the performance of chemical and biological weapons in any particular attack would be less predictable than that of nuclear weapons, they too have very great potential for mass killing. The most effective method of strategic CBW attack would presumably entail the production by bombers or missiles of a cloud of toxic or infectious material over or upwind from a target, to be inhaled or absorbed through the skin by persons in the attacked population. Although masks, protective suits, and special shelters can provide effective protection against known chemical and biological agents, the cloud would readily penetrate dwellings and other ordinary structures.

An attack by a single bomber, dispensing one of the more deadly nerve gases, could kill most unprotected persons within an area of at least five square miles, this being the size of the zone of high mortality caused by the Hiroshima and Nagasaki atomic bombs. Although nerve gases are among the most poisonous substances known to be suitable for military use, it may well be possible to devise weapons containing far more poisonous materials, perhaps toxins or related substances. Weapons based on such super-poisons might become as destructive to unprotected populations as thermo-nuclear weapons of equal size.

Poisonous as nerve gases are, virulent micro-organisms and viruses can be a million or more times more so, in terms of the amount that can cause incapacitation or death. Although many infectious agents are rapidly inactivated or lose their virulence when dispersed in the atmosphere, this obstacle to the development of biological weapons can probably be circumvented or overcome with sufficient research effort. If so, biological weapons could surpass thermo-nuclear bombs in terms of the area coverage possible for a weapon of specified size. However, even after very extensive research, the performance of biological weapons is likely to remain subject to great uncertainty. Their effects would depend in large measure on poorly understood and highly variable factors that determine man's resistance to infection. A biological attack intended to be highly lethal might actually kill very few persons, and, conversely, an attack expected only to cause temporary incapacitation could cause high mortality.

Although biological warfare agents might be chosen from among those that are not highly contagious under natural circumstances, this would not preclude the unexpected initiation of a widespread epidemic under the very unnatural conditions inherent in military use. Indeed, it is possible that bacteria or viruses disseminated in an aerosol cloud could subsequently emerge from the exposed population of humans, insects, birds, rodents, or other animals with increased persistence, contagiousness, and virulence to man. Large-scale operations in regions populated by many persons or animals would be more risky than small operations in desolate places, and viruses might be more hazardous than bacteria. However, we cannot evaluate the risks with any confidence in any of these situations. Therefore, the field testing of live biological weapons and especially the outbreak of actual biological warfare would constitute a menace to the entire human species.

The uncontrollability of CBW

A major uncertainty in predicting or controlling the course of CBW, once it is begun, would arise from the great variety of possible weapons and targets, from the incapacitating to the highly lethal and from the local battlefield to entire continents. Once begun at any level in earnest it would be very difficult to predict how far CBW might go. Distinctions and stopping places would be very difficult to define and to keep. The preparations and training required for one form of CBW would facilitate and therefore tempt escalation to larger scale and more deadly CBW operations. The breakdown of barriers to weapons once regarded as illegal and peculiarly uncivilized can inspire and encourage methods of warfare even more savage than those underway at the time.

The vulnerability of troops or civilians to CBW attack depends very much on the availability and effectiveness of protective facilities, the rigour of defensive training and discipline, and the performance of early-warning systems. All of this may act to place an unusually high premium on surprise or clandestine attack and on the use of novel or unexpected agents or means of dissemination. Once the effect of surprise has worn off and defensive precautions have been instituted, CB warfare might continue on a large scale but with relatively inconclusive effects until new weapons are introduced or until conventions against the attack of previously inviolate targets are transgressed.

The myth of humane CBW

It is well known that some chemicals such as tear gas are able to incapacitate a man for a short time with little risk of killing. Some people have concluded from this that the introduction of non-lethal chemicals and even of biological weapons thought to be non-lethal might actually make war more humane. The argument has shown considerable appeal both for thoughtless zealots who wish to advance the practice of CBW in any form and also for persons who genuinely hope to make war less savage. Although it is true that some chemical warfare agents are relatively non-lethal in themselves, it seems to me almost certain that their use would definitely not make wars on the whole less savage and would in fact risk making them much more so.

It is naïve to expect that in a real war non-lethal agents would be used by themselves. Once introduced into a combat area, the pressure would be very great to utilize them in any manner that increased the overall effectiveness of general military operations. Non-lethal chemical weapons would be used to increase the effectiveness of lethal ones. Tear gas can reduce the accuracy of enemy rifle fire, allowing one's own forces to approach more closely, increasing the accuracy and intensity of their counterfire. It can be used to force men out of protective cover and into the line of fire or the path of bomb and shell fragments. Under the desperate pressures of a war fought with artillery, bombs, napalm, and other lethal weapons, it is only reasonable to expect that "non-lethal" weapons once introduced will come to be used in order to kill. This has happened in Vietnam where the U.S. forces have spread riot gas over large areas to force persons from protective cover to face attack by fragmentation bombs. It happened in World War I when both sides used tear gas and other non-lethal chemicals in grenades and artillery shells to facilitate conventional infantry and artillery operations. This is not to say that non-lethal weapons would necessarily make war any more savage than it already is. However, it seems unrealistic to expect that they would make it any less so.

In any case, if tear gas or similar agents should prove at all effective when first used both sides would introduce protective devices and tactics, making subsequent use of such agents much less effective. Thus, except perhaps when they are first introduced, non-lethal chemical weapons are unlikely to have much effect except to set the stage for more deadly CBW operations.

The conduct of non-lethal CBW can greatly facilitate preparations and training for the use of lethal chemical and biological agents. When combatants learn to protect themselves against the effects of mild or 'conventional' agents the temptation will be strong and the means will be at hand to experiment with more deadly ones. During the first year of World War I both sides used tear gas and other harassing agents until the Germans introduced lethal chlorine gas. Following that, both sides tested a large number of poison gases seeking to find ones that would be decisive in battle. The first attack with poison gas had a devastating effect. The Allied front was broken, and 5000 of the 15,000 gas casualties died. However, even though more effective gases were introduced in great quantity by both sides, advances in defensive preparations prevented gas from being a decisive weapon in World War I. Advocates of "humane" gas warfare often point out that, at least toward the end of World War I, gas produced casualties with proportionately less mortality than did high-explosive weapons. However, this was not because commanders on both sides wished to fight without killing, but rather because the most effective gases then known caused more wounds than deaths. Modern nerve gases are vastly more lethal than the old World War I gases. Can anyone have much confidence that skin-penetrating nerve gas would not have been used in World War I had it become available in 1917? The difficulty of allowing the limited employment of gas without running the risk of bringing the whole chemical and biological arsenal into use has been concisely stated by T. C. Shelling in his book *Arms and Influence* (Yale University Press, 1966).

'Some gas' raises complicated questions of how much, where, under what circumstances; 'no gas' is simple and unambiguous. Gas only on military personnel; gas used only by defending forces; gas only when carried by projectile; no gas without warning—a variety of limits is conceivable . . . But there is a simplicity to 'no gas' that makes it almost uniquely a focus for agreement when each side can only conjecture at what alternative rules the other side would propose and when failure at coordination on the first try may spoil the chances for acquiescence in any limits at all.

These principles appear to have been understood by the leaders of both sides in World War II, during which neither lethal nor non-lethal gases were employed. At the outbreak of the War, both sides exchanged assurances that they would observe the Geneva Protocol of 1925. Later, in 1943, President Roosevelt declared:

Use of such weapons has been outlawed by the general opinion of civilized mankind. This country has not used them and I hope that we never will be compelled to use them. I state categorically that we shall under no circumstances resort to the use of such weapons unless they are first used by our enemies.

Although many rules of war were violated in that conflict, it is fortunate for all sides that the rule against gas was observed. Germany had secretly developed and produced a large quantity of nerve gas. Although the Allies had no weapon of comparable deadliness, they could have produced vast quantities rather soon after becoming aware of its existence. Since the previous restraints against anti-city warfare had already broken down, the introduction of nerve gas in the midst of World War II would almost certainly have caused a death toll vastly greater than it was.

Chemical and biological weapons by their very nature are suited to the attack of large areas; their natural targets are people rather than military equipment; important military personnel can be equipped and trained to use protective devices far more easily than can civilians. For all of these reasons, civilians are the most natural and most vulnerable targets for CBW attack. If the barriers against CBW are broken down, civilians are likely to become its main victims.

Chemical and biological weapons and minor powers

The development and initial production of a new weapon usually requires much greater sophistication and effort than is needed to reproduce a weapon already possessed by another. The accessibility of chemical and biological weapons to smaller powers will depend very much on the CBW programmes of great powers and, for a limited time, on measures to keep the results of those programmes secret. With chemical and biological weapons as with other weapons, great powers will probably lead the way unless they deliberately refrain from doing so.

The chemical compositions of several nerve gases are published in the open literature, and detailed manufacturing procedures could be specified by competent chemists and chemical engineers. Although no thorough cost-analysis has been published, it would appear that a considerable number of smaller nations could produce and integrate nerve gas weapons into their artillery and air forces without great economic strain. Commercial transport aircraft could be modified without great difficulty to drop or spray the gas. No small power is definitely known to produce nerve gas or to have been supplied with it by another, although there have been newspaper reports that Egypt has used a nerve gas on a small scale in the Yemen conflict.

The acquisition of nerve-gas weapons would greatly increase the destructive potential of a small nation's military forces, but it might also greatly reduce its overall security by provoking its neighbours to arm themselves similarly. This they might do by producing the gas themselves or by demanding it from their great power allies. If nerve gas warfare should ever break out between two small states, the population of one or both could be largely annihilated within a short space of time, and the intense feelings provoked around the world might well ignite a much larger conflict.

The attempt to develop biological weapons of reasonably assured characteristics would require a costly and technically sophisticated effort and an elaborate testing programme. Indeed, only use in war itself would provide the kind of information that responsible military men would require before placing much reliance on a radically new type of weapon. It seems unlikely that a small power would attempt the development of biological weapons except perhaps as a deterrent threat. However, this would be an extremely risky posture for a small power unless large powers had already legitimized the possession and threatening display or use of biological weapons.

Why single out CBW for special prohibitions?

As long as wars continue to be fought with high explosive weapons and napalm, what sense does it make to maintain special constraints on CBW? The question is understandable, but it seems to me that some substantial answers are contained in the remarks above. We realize that special rules are required for nuclear weapons. The distinction between conventional weapons and nuclear ones of any size is a real one, and the importance of maintaining it is generally understood. Chemical and biological weapons share with nuclear ones the attribute of potentially overwhelming destructiveness. Biological weapons could pose a threat to the entire human species. Both chemical and biological weapons place a high premium on clandestine and surprise attack, thus lessening stability. Once developed, chemical and biological weapons can be exceedingly cheap, relatively easy to produce, and quick to proliferate. They would threaten civilians especially. Their use would violate the oldest major arms control treaty still in force.

Finally, there are moral arguments, although each person must evaluate them for himself. It is widely held that the use of chemical and biological weapons would be cowardly and inhuman. Perhaps this is because their use could make mass killing and subjugation technically easier than it already is. Some have said that poison-gas warfare would be more humane than other forms of lethal combat. Perhaps so. But it may also be more acceptable to the onlooker and to those who might consider themselves responsible. Is it not partly in order to relieve the conscience of society that many civilized countries perform legal executions by means that are considered humane? Indeed, it may be that men inwardly dread the eventual consequences to civilization of introducing methods for the killing or subjugation of large numbers of their fellows easily and 'humanely'.

Preventing the use of chemical and biological weapons

It is important for nations to understand that it is in their long-term interest to prevent the use of chemical and biological weapons. This principle could be understood better and more widely than it is today. Discussions and publications by private persons can help. Studies by competent national and international organizations could command wide attention and respect.

The United Nations might consider forming contingency plans for the investigation of allegations concerning the use of chemical and biological weapons. Some of the political difficulties standing in the way of such investigation might be eased if the machinery were partly set up in advance and if its purpose were to establish whether or not chemical and biological weapons had been used rather than to identify the user. It might be agreed that the request of the alleged victim would be sufficient to initiate an investigation. If this were not acceptable it might be required, instead, that all combatants in a given conflict agree to the holding of any inspection. At least this would place the aggressor in the position of having to oppose an investigation.

Some nations or areas might declare themselves to be free of chemical and biological weapons. The Austrian State Treaty prohibits that country from developing or possessing such weapons. West Germany has given assurances to its allies in the Western European Union that it will not produce chemical and biological weapons, and the Union's Arms Control Agency conducts periodic inspections throughout its European territory to provide assurance that no member is producing these weapons. Obviously, there would be many problems and choices involved in setting up CBW-free areas. However, the possibility should be carefully investigated. A start in this direction has been made by the Pugwash Biological Warfare Study Group which has conducted experimental inspections for the non-production of biological weapons in NATO, Warsaw Pact, and unaligned countries.

As in most arms-control matters, the decisions lie mainly with the super powers, although the initiative may be taken in part by

other nations. Nevertheless, it is vital that the super-powers understand that the use of chemical and biological weapons anywhere
in the world would constitute a threat to their interests. Possessing
nuclear weapons, they do not need chemical and biological weapons
as a major deterrent.

There may be a certain symmetry in the view that biological
weapons are needed to deter the possible use of such weapons by
an enemy. However, in the nuclear environment, the proposition is
devoid of logic. The super-powers have no need for biological
weapons, and by producing and displaying them they would only
make trouble for themselves in the future.

The Geneva Protocol provides a relatively clear and unique
standard to guide both the practice and the expectations of member nations. The Protocol has been ratified by all major powers
except Japan and, ironically, the nation which proposed it at Geneva
—the United States. Many of the states organized since World War
II, including the People's Republic of China and both Republics of
Germany, have ratified the Protocol or have agreed to be bound
by the ratification of their predecessors. Less than two years ago,
in December, 1966, the General Assembly of the United Nations
passed without opposition a resolution calling for strict observance
of the Geneva Protocol and appealing for universal accession to it.
The United States and Japan voted in support of the General
Assembly resolution along with 99 other states. It is important to
secure the actual ratification of Japan, the United States, and other
nations that have not yet ratified the Protocol. Means should be
found to make clear that viruses as well as bacteria and non-lethal
as well as lethal chemical and biological weapons are meant to be
included under its prohibition. But great care must be exercised to
make sure that attempts to further clarify the scope of the Protocol
do not result in weakening its universal authority.

14. Medical Ethics   V. W. Sidel

Discussion of the role of the physician in relation to biological warfare is complex and difficult. One must consider not only the ethical implications of the various roles which the physician may be called upon to play directly in relation to such weapons, but one must also be concerned in more general terms with the roles of the military and civilian physician.*

It is first of all important to make clear that it is not simply a straw man that is being attacked—that is, it must be made explicit that biological weapons are being developed and produced[4] and that physicians are being asked to contribute to their development. Examples of physician participation are clear. Professor Rosebury wrote of his experiences: "At Detrick a certain delicacy concentrated most of the physicians into principally or primarily defensive operations; the modifiers *principally or primarily* [italics in the original] are needed because military operations can never be exclusively defensive."[1] An editorial in *Military Surgeon*, apparently commenting on nations other than the United States, says: "In certain positions, a military surgeon or civilian doctor might be assigned to jobs other than healing. He is perhaps required to perform or to participate in scientific investigations, the purposes of which are not new remedies for the sick, but more and more power-

* I am indebted to many people in the development of these ideas. Dr Theodor Rosebury, a microbiologist who directed research at Camp Detrick during World War II, has since repeatedly warned of the dangers of biological weapons and has discussed their ethical implications.[1] My colleagues in Physicians for Social Responsibility in Boston, especially Drs Robert Goldwyn, Bernard Lown, Peter Reich, and David Savitz, have contributed greatly to the discussions of these problems. Many of the ideas presented here have been drawn from papers written in collaboration with Dr Goldwyn: one was published in 1966 in the *New England Journal of Medicine*[2] and one will be included in a book on medical ethics to be published later in 1968 in the United States by Little, Brown, & Co.[3]

ful atomic, bacterial and chemical weapons of aggression."[5] At Fort Detrick, the major biological warfare research establishment in the United States, there are currently employed 14 M.D.'s, 120 Ph.D.'s, and hundreds of other scientists and technicians.[4] It is very likely that other physicians are associated with the many secret research projects in academic institutions which are listed in Chapter 10.

Before turning to the specific roles of the military and the civilian physician, the argument that it is unethical for a physician to participate in the development, production, or use of biological weapons must be briefly reviewed.

(1) The dangers to both civilian and military population of biological weapons have already been discussed. In summary, the dangers that have relevance to medical ethics are:

(a) They are likely to be used against non-combatants. Major General Thomas J. Hartford stated in a signed editorial in *Military Medicine*:

> It appears that . . . (biological weapons) would be used primarily for strategic rather than tactical purposes. It would be an excellent means of producing non-effectiveness without causing damage to material things. Thus it is possible that the civilian and not the military population might be the prime target. If an enemy were attacking the New York–New Jersey coastal area he would be more interested in producing disability in the millions of industrial workers than in the few thousand military personnel stationed in the target area. . . .[6]

(b) They are unpredictable. Beyond the immediate consequences there may be ecological, medical, and social results impossible to foresee. A biological agent introduced into a susceptible population may cause disease or mortality on a scale not visualized by the attacker. An example is the measles virus which, although usually relatively benign, can cause a large number of deaths under certain conditions—for example, in an unprotected population such as the Fiji Islanders, of whom 20 to 25 per cent died from measles or its consequences in 1875, or in a population weakened by war such as the women and children in Boer concentration camps in 1900.[7] In contrast to other weapons, biological agents may make the human being not only a victim but also a propagator. An example in another species occurred in May, 1952, in the Department of Eure et Loire in France. One or two rabbits were inoculated with myxomatosis virus; by the end of 1953 the disease had spread through 26 departments in France, and through Holland, Belgium, Germany, and Switzerland, killing between 60 and 90 per cent of the rabbit population.[8]

(c) They are truly 'public health in reverse'.[9] They are designed to undo much of the work that physicians and other medical workers have done to eliminate and control infectious disease. They are, therefore, clearly genocidal, and furthermore may be genocidal in the sense of damaging vast groups of the human race rather than a single people.

(2) There are specific passages in widely respected medical oaths which appear to argue against participation by medical doctors in such research. For example, the Hippocratic oath states: ". . . I will use treatment to help the sick according to my ability and judgment, but never with a view to injury and wrong-doing. Neither will I administer a poison to anybody when asked to do so, nor will I suggest such a course. . . ."[10] The Oath of Geneva, a modernization of the Hippocratic Oath, formulated by the World Medical Association in 1948, states: ". . . I will not permit considerations of religion, nationality, race, party, politics, or social standing to intervene between my duty and my patient; . . . even under threat I will not use my medical knowledge contrary to the laws of humanity."[11] Even more specifically, the Code of Ethics in Wartime of the World Medical Association states: ". . . It is deemed unethical for doctors to weaken the physical and mental strength of a human being without therapeutic justification and to employ scientific knowledge to imperil health or destroy life."[12]

(3) These professional oaths codify a body of professional conduct which has served through the centuries to make the physician better able to perform his healing role. Any member of the profession who weakens the ethical standards of the profession by taking part in activities which contribute to disease, disability, or untimely death only weaken the professional status, and therefore the healing potential, of all physicians.

Turning first to the role of the military physician, the entire role of the physician in the armed forces is an ambiguous one. One role for the military physician was eloquently stated in 1965 by Sir Theodore Fox, former editor of *The Lancet*: "A nation's lawyers must execute its laws even when this means the execution of a human being; a nation's soldiers must kill whomsoever their leader commands; but the doctor—perhaps because of his religious origins —is excused such destruction. Even in war, he may be permitted to believe in human brotherhood—to treat all men without political or racial or religious distinction."[13] And many physicians have indeed distinguished themselves in war by devoted and sometimes heroic service to both friend and foe.

But there is another side to the physician's participation in war or in the preparation for war. *Field Manual 8–10* of the U.S. Army states clearly that "the Army Medical service is a supporting service of the combat elements of the Army primarily concerned with the maintenance of the health and fighting efficiency of the troops." Its mission, the Manual continues, is to "conserve manpower . . . (for) early return to duty" and to "contribute directly to the military effort by providing adequate medical treatment and rapid orderly evacuation for the sick and wounded".[14] Dr Morris Fishbein, the former Executive Secretary of the American Medical Association, presents this side of the military physician's role even more strongly: "Military philosophers say there could never be wars if there were no doctors. No doubt they are right. The anguish and destruction of the human body in war with modern weapons would be impossible to contemplate without the healing ministrations . . . that modern medicine provides."[15]

Within this overall conflict of the healing and the combat-promoting roles of the military physician, there are a number of individual conflicts. Attempts have been made to resolve some of these dilemmas by formal codes of conduct. The best known of these are the Geneva Conventions of 1949 which stipulate that medical personnel are to be considered non-combatants; they are, if captured, to be returned to their own forces as soon as possible; and, in return for this special status, they are forbidden to use arms except to defend themselves and their patients.[16] It is clear that these Conventions perform a useful military function; the special non-combatant status of medical personnel enables them better to carry out their healing role. It would appear to be in the self-interest of the combatants to preserve the clear non-combatant role of the physician.

An example, not directly related to CBW, of the types of ethical problem which can arise is provided by the recent court-martial of Howard W. Levy, M.D., Captain in the Army of the United States. Although other issues were involved, one of the major charges on which Levy was convicted and sentenced to three years hard labour was his refusal to obey an order to train Special Forces troops in specialized techniques. This refusal was based in part on Levy's belief that such men, functioning in the dual capacities of combat soldiers and "medical personnel", would break down the distinction between combatant and non-combatant necessary to effective application of the Geneva Conventions; in training them, he felt, he would produce a net increase in disease, disability, and death. He

M

also believed that such poorly-trained, unsupervised men might do more medical harm than good and that, since their primary duty was as combat soldiers rather than medical personnel, they might be required to abandon sick and wounded patients or otherwise behave in a manner contrary to medical ethics and/or the Geneva Conventions. Whether Levy was right or wrong in these views is not relevant to our discussion here; what is relevant is that as a military physician he was ordered to do something he felt he could not ethically do as a physician and, upon refusing to do so, he was court-martialled and convicted. The defence that the order was contrary to Levy's view of his medical ethical responsibilities was held irrelevant and was not permitted as a defence at his trial.[17, 18]

The result of the Levy trial forces a re-evaluation of the role of the military physician. Until his conviction it may have been possible for the military physician to hold the view that he was still the arbiter of his own medical ethics; that he might do those things which contributed to health and were therefore ethical, and that he might refuse to do those things which he felt to be professionally unethical. Since the result of the Levy trial, if allowed to stand, suggests that the American military physician is no longer free to make such ethical decisions once he has entered the military service, the American physician may have no choice at all except to refuse to enter military service. This line of reasoning forces us to return to a paragraph written in 1938 by Professor John Ryle, Regius Professor of Physics at the University of Cambridge:

> It is an arresting, if at present a fantastic thought, that the medical profession which is more international than any other, could, if well co-ordinated, of its own initiative put a stop to war, or at least increase its uncertainties, and hamper its aims considerably so as to give pause to the most bellicose of Governments. It is everywhere a recognized and humane principle that prevention should be preferred to cure. By withholding service from the armed forces before and during war, by declining to examine and inoculate recruits, by refusing sanitary advice and the training and command of ambulances, clearing-stations, medical transport, and hospitals, the doctors could so cripple the efficiency of the staff and aggravate the difficulties of campaign and so damage the morale of the troops that war would become almost unthinkable. Action of this kind would also produce a profound effect on the popular imagination. In such refusal of service (if such refusal were decided upon in the last resort) there would be no inhumanity comparable with the inhumanity which medicine at present sanctions and prolongs. But let the dream pass and fantasy make room for facts.[19]

It would be ironic indeed if the court-martial of Captain Levy should be one of the events which would turn Professor Ryle's fantasy into fact.

The problem of the civilian physician, whose need to be guided by medical ethics is uncomplicated by a concurrent need to obey military orders, is quite different. Again a model may be found in circumstances which were not directly related to CBW, the conduct of German physicians during World War II. Although only a relatively small number of German physicians actually took part in the infamous medical crimes for which the Nazi physicians were convicted at Nuremberg, hundreds of others knew of them. As a 1946 editorial in the journal of the American Medical Association put it:

> Perhaps most serious of all is the failure of German medical organizations and societies to express in any manner their disapproval of these widely known experiments. Physicians have a right to expect that men trained in the traditions of medicine would refuse to participate in any way in such acts of inhumanity and brutality. In some instances the defence has been offered that these experiments were conducted under the highest authority of the German state. That cannot possibly be considered in the slightest an extenuation of the failure of these physicians to act in accordance with the principles and traditions of their profession.[20]

Thus the responsibility of the physician is visualized as far broader than simply refusing to take part in an activity which he finds unethical. He must not only refuse himself to participate but he must actively "express his disapproval". Failure to do so represents complicity. One of the greatest dangers in regard to CBW may simply be the apathy toward this problem of most of the medical profession.

What guidelines should the physician use with regard to his or another physician's, participation in research, development, production, or use of CBW? There seems no doubt of the unethical nature of the physician's participation in development, production, or use of offensive weapons of any type; the fact that chemical or biological weapons are the ones with which the physicians may become engaged and the ones about which he has specialized knowledge gives him a special responsibility not only to refuse to work on but also actively to protest against the development, production, or use of such weapons.

But what about research and development of defensive measures against chemical or biological agents? 'Defence' has often been given as justification for the work being done by physicians and scientists on such weapons. We have already noted that Dr Rosebury, who has participated in such research, feels that the distinction between offensive and defensive research is ethically and technically blurred. What guide-line should be used by the physician who wishes to work on defence against such or, a much more common problem, wishes to conduct research in fields which might in some unforeseeable way contribute to the development of weapons? It seems to me that the least ambiguous guide-line is that of free access of information. If the physician engages in research which is freely published, whether it be on micro-organisms in general or in defence against biological warfare in particular, he cannot be ethically faulted. It is when he engages in 'defensive' or 'pure' research in *secret* that he cannot be distinguished ethically from those who work on the development or production of weapons.

In summary, it seems to me that the ethical physician must continually ask himself whether what he is doing will lead to a net increase or decrease in disease, disability, and untimely death. For the military physician, it may at one time have been possible to consider his activities as producing a net benefit; I believe that, in the United States at least, recent events have made this view untenable, and the ethical physician may have to refuse to participate at all.

Finally, there appears to me to be no question that for the civilian physician ethical principles can best be protected by a refusal to participate in, and an active protest against, secret research in general and work on biological weapons in particular. As Rosebury has suggested: "Ethical principles are not a luxury; the essence of ethics—concern for the value of man—is indispensable for the survival of medicine as a profession and doubtless also for the survival of mankind as a species."[1]

DISCUSSION

Dr Sidel's paper on medical ethics raised isues that were discussed at length by the Conference.

Professor Mayer raised the point that he, like Dr Sidel, was a witness, in fact the opening defence witness, at the Levy trial. A feature of the court-martial was that the United States Army was abiding by the ordinary legal rules of having Captain Levy tried by a jury of his peers, but it considered that his peers were officers of similar rank, and the twelve officers who were sitting on the court-martial were, in fact, infantry officers. There was not a single medical officer on the jury. This is extremely significant because it means that the quality of a medical officer as a physician was not something which was considered relevant in his trial. The testimony on medical ethics, the history of the Geneva Conventions and their significance was, in effect, already discounted by the very choice of the court-martial. The American Medical Association and other medical bodies were extraordinarily indifferent to the fact that a physician could be tried on a question of medical ethics by people who were not themselves physicians and where physicians were not even represented. This suggests an abdication by the medical profession of its responsibility to look into possibilities of medical ethics being involved in a conflict with a civil power.

A second, still broader question raised by Dr Sidel is the need for a better definition of who in fact is a physician. Perhaps the definition of a physician is out of date if it implies that a physician is anybody who is a doctor of medicine or has an equivalent degree. Obviously the Hippocratic oath should apply to them in all situations including those in which they are in effect working on chemical warfare. If on the other hand the definition of a physician is one which involves only those people who are actively engaged in therapy a number of people who are doctors of medicine will not be covered, but at least in the United States many people who are in professions not usually considered as specifically medical, such as clinical psychologists, might well come under that classification. But many researchers on CBW would then be excluded from this ethical debate.

Mr M. Birnstingl was doubtful whether the moral responsibilities of the doctor could be restricted in this way. There is surely a danger of medicine allowing itself to become a tool of the current political ideology, when seen only in terms of the Hippocratic ethical tradition, without considering the wider issues. The Hippocratic tradition is concerned with the doctor's ethical and humanitarian role in relation to a single individual, his patient, and gives him no guidance as to his position regarding, for instance, the war in Vietnam. Modern warfare would be impossible without the cooperation of doctors, and they are able to take part without any violation of their ethics. They withdraw and wait while their fighting friends drop toxic gas or napalm, after which they may help the victims who survive. To a physician trained to prevent suffering, such a role may appear irrational, but it is sanctioned by medical ethics, through its apparent humanitarian function. But the wider situation has been well described by Dr Howard Levy as "Kill, Kill. Cure, Cure." and this is the situation which the doctor's presence supports. A doctor may need to do this kind of thing, but he cannot shelter behind his humanitarian role. He is always an accomplice to the wider act, and it is his relation to this which he must consider.

When civilian populations are being annihilated and other norms of human conduct disregarded a doctor must decide whether he can continue to subjugate medicine to such a policy. Professor Mayer has pointed out elsewhere that Howard Levy's stand was not solely a matter of medical ethics, although the circumstances of his trial may have forced him into making his defence on these narrow grounds. But Levy was also concerned with moral questions extending far outside his professional code, namely the submission that no doctor has a right to allow himself to be used in what he believes to be a genocidal war. And its corollary, an attempt to prevent medicine from being subjugated to a political purpose and becoming just a cog in a wheel of bad and degraded ideology.

Finally, that the doctor's dilemma was also the scientist's was stressed by Professor Burhop, who pointed out that in practice questions of the social responsibility of scientists could not be separated from assessments of political and moral factors. It was difficult to adopt simple-minded criteria applicable in all circumstances. During World War II he, like other scientific colleagues who had earlier been active in the movement against war and fascism, saw no contradiction in working on the development of the first nuclear weapon. It seemed clear that the development of a nuclear weapon by German scientists was entirely feasible and that, possessing such a weapon, Hitler would have had no compunction about holding the whole world to ransom in order to achieve his aims.

Similarly, today, it should not be difficult for an American scientist, mindful of his social responsibilities, to decide that to give freely of his knowledge and talents to assist his Government to subjugate the people of Vietnam, whether by the development of CBW or by the improvement of napalm or anti-personnel weapons, was evil and reprehensible.

Unfortunately, the situations one usually has to face are less clear-cut. For example, what attitude should a university adopt toward the question of accepting funds from defence agencies for open peace-time research in basic science? Perhaps the question of whether the research is open or secret could provide a useful criteria. Scientists should not participate in secret work, whether in university or government institutions. Secrecy is far more important for the development of new offensive than defensive weapons.

15. Scientific Responsibility   C. F. Powell

By way of an introduction to this theme, I want to comment in general terms on the place and responsibility of scientists in our present situation. I have no technical competence in CBW but I believe that this issue and the problems raised in the earlier chapters should be seen as only a part of the general problem of avoiding a catastrophe for our whole civilization. What is involved here is not only the future of humanity but also matters of great importance for the future of science itself—for its moral standing and effectiveness. It is possible, even if we avoid a general war, for scientific research to decline, and this research is our indispensable instrument for overcoming the grim prospect of widespread hunger in the next twenty years to which Bernal has quite recently again directed our urgent attention.

We were brought up in a situation in which science enjoyed immense respect and prestige. I believe this derived from the aims and methods which characterized the development of science under the stimulus of the Baconian philosophy and the work of those in Europe who thought like him—Leonardo, Galileo, Descartes. The new method was to replace the appeal to ancient authorities by reliance upon the observation of nature and by acting upon it, by experiment. And the new aim was to be the improvement of the human condition. It was Bacon's passionate conviction that the discovery of printing, the compass needle, and gunpowder gave only a faint intimation of what was becoming possible for mankind if the search for fruitful knowledge were pursued in a systematic and organized way.

Contrary to those who sometimes assert that Bacon was naïvely optimistic about the advantages which would follow from the progress of discovery, he well understood that the advancement of knowledge could be put to good or evil purpose: speaking of the fruits of mechanical invention he said: "Out of that same fountain come instruments of lust and instruments of death. For, not to speak of the arts of procurers, the most subtle poisons, as well as cannon and other instruments of destruction are the fruits of mechanical invention, and well we know how far in cruelty they do exceed the Minotaur himself". There could hardly be a better passage with which to illustrate the theme of this book.

Bacon was also clear about a point that is of great contemporary importance; that the advancement of knowledge was not to be judged only on the basis of its immediate utility. In the fable of Atalanta he makes the point very clearly. Atalanta lost the race because she stooped down to pick up the golden apple. She is typical of that short-sighted mechanical ingenuity which fails to see that the true aim is the widening of our basic understanding, so that useful applications may flow "not singly, but in knots and clusters".

It is unnecessary for me to stress the immense success of the developments which Bacon foreshadowed. The whole material basis of our civilization has been transformed, and surely it is a process to which there is no limit. This is not always firmly understood. It is easy to acknowledge that our whole society has been transformed by the advancement of science without really understanding that, if we don't destroy ourselves, the whole world in a hundred years' time will be as different from the present as our own times are from the world of 1800. Of course material prosperity is not the only thing for securing a happy life. But it certainly shouldn't be underrated. At least in the developed countries, technology has immensely improved the human condition; the most severe critics would hardly deny that the three-fold increase in the expectation of life in the United Kingdom is a good thing. What could be more important than an increase in good health or of the life-span?

But our powers have now reached the point where we are presented with the familiar dilemma where we have on the one hand the possibility of an indefinite extension of human well-being and, on the other, the growing danger of a fearful catastrophe. A number of clear responsibilities rest upon scientists in this situation, and one of the bright features of our time is the growing disposition of scientists to assume them.

The first is that they should take an active part in public affairs, especially in fields where they have special technical competence. At least in some scientific circles this idea has not, in the past, always been welcome. I can remember eminent colleagues of mine, less than twenty years ago, most vigorously asserting, and taking some pleasure in doing so, that their work had no relevance to practical affairs. Of course, we have to make a clear distinction between the manifold aims which animate scientists in their work and why great public resources should be applied to their support. It is very dangerous to take too narrow a view here in formulating public policy. It is possible for a scientist to be passionately interested in his work and to be quite indifferent to the practical consequences which flow from it. But his indifference is not a reason for not supporting him if his work contributes to the advancement of science, or to the intellectual quality of the work and teaching of the institute in which he is employed, or to practical benefits in the short or the long term, or to all of these ends.

But the idea still persists in some circles that fundamental science merely provides a pleasant diversion, an agreeable life, for scientists, without any real advantage to society. An engineer from one of our great steel companies recently asserted to me, for example, that fundamental science had never contributed anything substantial to the advancement of industry. He was somewhat taken aback when I asked him if he attached any importance for industry to the discovery of electricity. Of course this was rather an extreme example, but we can find undercurrents in the same direction in many places.

Even among scientists scholastic attitudes still linger on, in the sense that there is an indifference to the practical advantages flowing from scientific discovery, and this indifference ought to be corrected by the close involvement of scientists in everything touching the consequences of their work. But the advantage of their involvement in public affairs does not depend only on their technical competence. They are the representatives of severe disciplines. They are used to challenging the basic premises of their subject, and it is not only in science that this process is of fundamental importance for the formulation of wise policies leading to successful action. It is easy for us to laugh at the flat-earth theories of the Middle Ages and to fall into the same kind of error in relation to the imaginative leap required to resolve the profound problems which we face in our sciences and our societies.

It is in the nature of the human condition that we find it difficult to escape from the limitation of our commonly accepted premises. We establish principles which are valid for the particular range of experience with which we are familiar in our local situation in history, in time, and in environment. And their success in allowing us to take successful action in our particular circumstances encourages us to assume for them a universal, eternal validity, until painful experience overthrows our pride. This process of rejecting cherished assumptions in the face of a wider experience, although often painful, is familiar to scientists, and they can help with the resolution of some of the great problems of public affairs to which, with their expertise, they seriously apply themselves, through the critical and creative approach to problems which science encourages.

It is in such issues that it seems to me scientists have the responsibility to speak out, not least in order to ensure the continuing prestige of their calling. I remember a discussion with Joliot* in which he pointed out that it is an illusion to think that in order to influence people and opinion it is sufficient for a man to tell the truth as he sees it. An element of art is involved here. One can be so far ahead of one's audience as to be out of sight, so that one becomes isolated and ineffective. But to give any kind of leadership in the formation of opinion one has to be ahead and not dragging behind the march of events. And surely our standing is increased when through the march of events the soundness of the position we have taken early is demonstrated.

I have said that the public involvement of scientists is essential for the maintenance of the morale of science. Scientists too would be flat-earthists if they thought that they could count automatically upon the continuing esteem they have enjoyed in the past while doing nothing in the face of the fearful possibilities which have arisen as the result of their work. In this connection they ought to be deeply concerned with the attitudes of young people, for example, in Western countries. What do they see? They may know of the aspirations of the founders of modern science, but what is the present reality? They see not only the fearful perversions of modern science that we have been discussing, but they may reasonably be anxious that the balance between the good and the evil seems to be rapidly changing. Of all our resources on a world scale, about 70 parts in 1000 are devoted to armaments—and much of it today to scientifically based armaments; and 3 parts in 1000 to fundamental science.

They see that, by contrast with the immense resources going into armaments, relatively little is going into the developing countries, most of it ill-considered and therefore ineffective—and quite insufficient in the prevailing political situations in these states to enable them to take any serious steps to ensure the economic and social emancipation of their people. In this situation, the appraisal of science by the young people is such that they begin to prefer what they tend to regard as more innocent and less exacting occupations.

* The French physicist; one of the fathers of atomic science. *Ed.*

The sciences in our time are exacting disciplines and make great demands on young people. With our increasing penetration into nature, the language of science and its basic conceptions and ideas become more and more remote from those of our ordinary lives. Young people welcome challenges to their creative powers; they are prepared to submit to severe disciplines if they believe in their validity and moral standing, but they are not prepared to meet the personal sacrifices involved if they suspect the ends to which their work leads, or if they regard them as evil. I am anxious in that these considerations seems to me to have a bearing on the fact that in the United Kingdom the number of young people entering science is, in a growing population, beginning to decline; and this is at a time when science and its even wider applications is our indispensable resource for the resolution of the profound problems with which we are faced.

Of course, scientists have other responsibilities too, but I have tried to indicate some of the crucial ones. I may add perhaps the important battle for the recognition of the proper role of science, for the increase in its standing. The fact is that it is still true that science in our country is almost outside the common culture. In the organs of government there are many people who are entirely innocent of any acquaintance with science. In a scientific age it is almost impossible to understand fully the role and significance of fundamental science, its potentialities and the problems involved in its proper sustenance and application if one has acquaintance with it only at second-hand. It is for this reason that scientists must become more involved in government, must contribute more effectively to the popularization of science, must help to ensure that our whole culture becomes more and more infused with all that is best in science.

In conclusion, let me add, that throughout his working life, in all these issues Bernal, in whose honour this conference has been held, has been one of our great champions. Without him, not only would this meeting never have taken place, but the whole level of our discussions would have been much poorer, and our possibilities of solving our problems much less. We are all deeply in his debt.

16. Some Conclusions   Steven Rose

The implications of CBW spread far beyond the issues of lethality versus non-lethality, or even legality versus non-legality. Firstly, any examination of CBW inevitably involves one in a study of its use in what has become the greatest political issue of our day—the war in Vietnam. Most of those who attended the Conference—as indeed most people throughout the world—had strong, though often divergent, views on this issue. That chemical weapons have been used in Vietnam is unquestioned. The scale of this use is outlined by Dr Kahn and Professor Galston in Chapters 5 and 7, and the profound effects on the population by Professor Mayer in Chapter 6. It is perhaps now doubtful whether the use of the weapons has or will alter the course of this war. If it is the case that chemical and biological weapons are seen by the military as in some sense ideally suited to anti-revolutionary, anti-guerilla warfare, in that they are primarily directed against the population as a whole, events in Vietnam are far from demonstrating the success of this strategy. And in terms of scale, conventional weapons, such as napalm, fragmentation bombs, etc., have certainly done more damage to the civilian population than has the—still relatively limited—use of CS or the defoliants. None the less the two issues, CBW and Vietnam, have, for better or worse, become inextricably intertwined.

But CBW research will continue even when the American expeditionary force finally leaves Vietnam to reconstruct itself. The research and development of these weapons has achieved a powerful, perhaps irreversible, momentum. And in this onward course, many hitherto untouched institutions of scientific research have been swept along. Attempts, as Elinor Langer describes, to assess the extent of CBW research in the United States revealed that substantial areas of American university life have become permeated by secret research on CBW and related defence topics. This classified research is now proceeding on an unprecedented scale; a considerable proportion of America's scientific talent is becoming locked up in activities directly or indirectly of service to the U.S. Department of Defense.

Until recently it had been possible to regard this as a uniquely American problem, but at the beginning of 1968 a series of Parliamentary Questions revealed that in Britain, too, universities were undertaking a significant amount of classified research. No less than thirty-seven classified research projects were let to British universities by way of the Ministry of Technology in the latter half of 1967, and two directly by the Ministry of Defence. The exact fields of these research projects are not known at present, although most probably they are concerned with many topics other than CBW as well.

But these revelations, which have sprung directly out of concern by the scientific community about the extent of CBW research, also change, at least in part, the emphasis of the issues raised.

Classified research in the universities presents a new class of problems; the traditionally open teaching and researching activities of the university are seen to be in danger of becoming undermined, so that various fields of scientific research, ostensibly without military significance, are supported by military funds and shackled by the demands of secrecy and security. The need for secret research may be argued; the case against it being performed in the universities in peace-time, so distorting and warping their educative role, is overwhelming. Here is another theme with which, inevitably, an investigation into CBW becomes interlocked.

The problem of the potentially military significance of basic scientific research raises other issues, too, that need a more thorough investigation. At least since World War II, a substantial proportion of scientific research, in fields as diverse as linguistics and high-energy physics, has been supported by money from a variety of Defence budgets, both in Britain and the United States—and probably many other countries too. This research, unlike the classified research we have so far discussed, has been open and often without any apparent military significance. Yet the chapters by Dr Sidel and Professor Powell inevitably raise the question of how far one should continue to regard this money as manna from heaven. Does the source of such funds—and the fact that the donors perceive a military advantage in obtaining this knowledge, even if its military significance is obscure to the scientist actually performing the experiments—mean that, to adopt Dr Sidel's phrase, "the ethical scientist or physician should have no truck with them"? Such questions begin to open out from the confines of CBW itself to the very heart of any exploration of the role of scientific research in contemporary society.

To return to CBW again, the third major issue raised is that exemplified in Chapter 13 by Dr Humphrey and Professor Meselson, and expanded in the discussion of the work of Pugwash and SIPRI which have not been included in this published text, of how far it is possible, by techniques of agreed international inspection and control, to limit the development of new weapons systems and the arms race that these imply. The endeavours of the arms controllers have so far met with some partial success in the field of nuclear weapons—the test ban treaty and the non-proliferation agreement are examples. CBW presents unique problems in that the relatively low-grade technologies required for the fabrication of the weapons are within the capacity of many countries, not merely the handful with nuclear capability, but it also presents unique possibilities for the achievement of control, because of both the legal position on the use of the weapons, discussed by Dr Brownlie, and the relatively cautious attitude to their development so far taken by most of the important powers with the possible exception of the United States. And, as Professor Meselson pointed out, the time to control a weapon is before it has been developed and put into the military arsenals.

Here perhaps lies our hope. The enormous repugnance that CBW arouses in most people and its present limited—though future enormous and enormously dangerous—potential, would seem to make both the possibility of and the need for some action imperative. This, certainly, was the message of our conference. We believe that this presentation of the record of our proceedings, by alerting as many as possible to the issues involved, will help in this aim.

Biographical Notes

Martin Birstingel, M.S., F.R.C.S. is a surgeon at St. Bartholomew's Hospital and visited Vietnam for the International War Crimes Tribunal.

Ian Brownlie, M.A., D.PHIL. is Fellow of Wadham College, Oxford, University Lecturer in International Law, and a barrister of Gray's Inn. He is the author of *International Law and the Use of Force by States* (O.U.P., 1966) and *The Law Relating to Public Order* (Butterworth, 1968), and editor of the *British Year Book of International Law*.

Eric Burhop, F.R.S., M.SC., PH.D. is Professor of Physics at the University of London. He is the author of *The Challenge of Atomic Energy* (Lawrence & Wishart, 1951) and numerous publications on atomic and nuclear physics.

Robin Clarke is the editor of *Science Journal* (London) and the author of *We All Fall Down: the Prospect of Chemical and Biological Warfare* (Allen Lane, the Penguin Press, 1968).

Arthur Galston, PH.D., M.S., B.S. is Professor of Biology at Yale University, President of the Botanical Society of America, and National Science Foundation, Science Faculty Fellow at King's College, London, Department of Biophysics. He is the author of *Principles of Plant Physiology* (Freeman, 1952) and *Life of the Green Plant* (Prentice-Hall, 1964).

John Humphrey, F.R.S., M.D., B.A. has spent almost his entire career in medical research, mainly immunology. His interest in chemical and biological warfare dates from his association with the Cambridge Scientists' Anti-War Group before World War II.

C. R. B. Joyce, M.A., B.SC., PH.D. is Reader in Psychopharmacology in the University of London and Head of Pharmacology at the London Hospital Medical College.

M. F. Kahn is Professeur Agrégé de Médecine in the Faculté de Médecine de Paris and a Consultant Physician to the Paris Hospitals. He was a member of the Scientific Commission of the International Tribunal for War Crimes in Vietnam, and a member of the Diversification team of the Tribunal in the DRV and the NLF held areas of South Vietnam.

Elinor Langer, B.A. is a former staff member of *Science* magazine (Washington D.C.) and did graduate work at the Johns Hopkins University School for Advanced International Studies.

Patricia Lindop, B.SC., M.B., B.S., PH.D. is Reader in the Department of Radiobiology at the Medical College of St Bartholomew's Hospital, London. She is medically qualified and is doing research on the long-term effects of radiation.

Ivan Malek, M.U.DR., DR.SC. is a member of the Czechoslovak Academy of Science and Director of the Czech Biological Institute where he conducts research into antibiotics and the continuous cultivation of micro-organisms. He has been associated with peace movements for many years including Pugwash and the World Federation of Scientific Workers and was awarded the Lenin Peace Prize in 1967.

Jean Mayer, PH.D., D.SC., M.A. is Professor of Nutrition and lecturer on the History of Public Health at Harvard University and a Fellow of the American Academy of Arts and Science. He is the author of some 400 research papers, 20 popular papers, and two books.

M. Meselson, M.S., PH.D. is Professor of Biology at Harvard and a Fellow of the American Academy of Arts and Science. He is winner of the U.S. National Academy of Science Prize for Molecular Biology.

Martin Pollock, M.A., M.B., B.CHIR., F.R.S. is Professor of Biology at Edinburgh University in the Department of Molecular Biology. He is medically qualified and is especially concerned with public health, bacteriology, and epidiomology.

C. F. Powell, M.A., PH.D., F.R.S. is Melville Wills Professor of Physics in the University of Bristol. He was awarded the Nobel Prize for Physics in 1950 and the Lomonsov medal of the Soviet Academy of Science in 1968. He is President of the World Federation of Scientific Workers.

Lord Ritchie-Calder was Director of Plans of Political Warfare in the Foreign Office during World War II, was Science Editor of the London *News Chronicle* from 1945 to 1967 and was Professor of International Relations at Edinburgh University from 1961 to 1967. He is author of 28 books including *Man Against the Desert* (Allen & Unwin, 1958), *Man Against the Jungle* (Allen & Unwin, 1954), and *Commonsense about a Starving World* (Gollancz, 1962).

J. Perry Robinson, B.A.(OXON) read Chemistry at Oxford University and wrote his thesis on certain aspects of chemical warfare. He is training to be a patent agent and has recently worked at the Stockholm International Peace Research Institute.

Steven P. R. Rose, B.A., PH.D. is a research biochemist. He graduated at Cambridge, read a PH.D. in London and was previously Research Fellow at New College, Oxford before returning to London to work on problems connected with the biochemistry of memory and learning. He is the author of *The Chemistry of Life* (Penguin, 1966) as well as general science articles and research papers.

Victor Sidel, M.D. is Associate in Medicine at Harvard Medical School and Chief of the Community Medicine Unit at Massachussets General Hospital. He is a member of the Executive Committee of the U.S. Physicians for Social Responsibility and editor with Frank Ervin and Saul Aronon of *The Fallen Sky* (Hill and Wong, 1963).

Derik E. Viney, B.A., PH.D. was previously a member of the Arms Control and Disarmament Research Unit of the Foreign Office and currently researches and broadcasts on international affairs.

Patrick Wall, M.D. is a neurophysiologist and novelist. He is Professor of Anatomy at University College, London.

References

INTRODUCTION

1. Quoted by M. Leitenberg in *Scientist and Citizen* August, 1967.
2. See M. Gowring, *Britain and Atomic Energy* 1939-45, (Macmillan, 1964).

CHAPTER 1

1. US ARMY CHEMICAL CORPS BOARD, ASTIA Documents Nos. 108456—108459, 23 July, 1956.
2. KEELE, C. A.; ARMSTRONG, D.: *Substances producing pain and itch* (Arnold, London, 1964).
3. MONCRIEFF, R. W.: *The chemical senses*, (Leonard Hill, London, 3rd edn, 1967).
4. PENN, W. E.: "Riot control chemicals" Ordnance 50, 192-4, 1965.
5. HER MAJESTY'S PRINCIPAL SECRETARY OF STATE FOR THE WAR DEPARTMENT: "Improvements in apparatus for controlling riots" British Patent No. 967660, dated 14 Nov. 1960.
6. GUIGNARD, J. P.; MUHLETHALER, M.; OTRAMARE, M.; FOREL, A.: *Vietnam: documents on chemical and bacteriological warfare* (Dr Philip Harvey, London, 1967).
7. PRENTISS, A. M.: *Chemicals in War: a treatise on chemical warfare* New York (McGraw-Hill, 1937), p 144.
8. JACOBS, M. B.: *War gases: their identification and decontamination* New York (Interscience, 1942), p 24.
9. BROPHY, L. P.; MILES, W. D.; COCHRANE, R. C.: *The Chemical Warfare Service; from laboratory to field* (Department of the Army, Washington, D.C., 1959), p 133.
10. HALDANE, J. B. S.: "Callinicus; a defence of chemical warfare" (Kegan Paul, London, 1925), p 10.
11. CHEMICAL DEFENCE EXPERIMENTAL STATION, PORTON: "A note on the toxicity of Z" Porton Report No. 2351, 15 April, 1942.
12. EDGEWOOD ARSENAL: "Status summary on the relative values of AC, CK and CG as bomb fillings" Project Co-ordination Staff Report No. 1, 10 July, 1944.
13. OFFICE OF THE CHIEF CHEMICAL OFFICER, GHQ, AFPAC: "Intelligence report on Japanese Chemical Warfare", Vol. II, BIOS/JAP/PR/393, 1 March 1946, p 61.

14. McAdams, A. T. and Joffe, M. H.: "A toxico-pathological study of phosgene oxime" MLRR 381, July, 1955.
15. Chemical Defence Experimental Station, Porton: "Systemic effects following skin absorption of diphenylchloroarsine" Porton Report No 2347, 25 March, 1942.
16. Admiralty, War Office, Air Ministry: "Medical Manual of Chemical Warfare" (H.M.S.O., 4th edn, London, 1955), p 46.
17. Reference 9, pp 55–61.
18. Mills, A. F. and Harris, L. E.: "Heeresgasschutzschule I, Celle" CIOS File No. XXIV–49.
19. Wood, J. R.: "Chemical warfare—a chemical and toxicological review" American Journal of Public Health 34, 1946, pp 455–60.
20. Woodward, F. N.; Williams, A. H.; Brown, R.; Gasson, E.J.; McCombie, H.; Hamilton, A.; Moggridge, R. C. G. "New organic sulphur vesicants" Journal Chem. Soc. (1948), pp 35–47.
21. Vocci, F. J.; Punte, C. L.; Yevich, P. P.; et al: "The inhalation toxicity of sequimustard (Q) aerosol........" MLRR 403 (September, 1955).
22. Gates, M.; Renshaw, B.: "Fluorophosphates and other phosphorus-containing compounds" Summary Technical Report, Division 9 NRDC, (1946), Vol. 1, Ch. 9.
23. Trask, C. H.; Christensen, M. K.; Cresthull, P.; Oberst, F. W.; McNamara, B.: "An estimation of the percent military effectiveness of soldiers with various degrees of incapacitation from GB vapour in various tactical situations" CWLR 2294, (August 1959).
24. Forsvarets Forskningsanstalt: "BC-stridsmedel" FOA orienterar OM No. 2, 1964 (revised June 1967).
25. Heilbronn, E.; Tolagen, B.: "Toxogonin in sarin, soman and tabun poisoning" Biochem. Pharmacol. 14, pp 73–77.
26. Berry, W. K.; Davies, D. R.: "Factors influencing the rate of 'aging' of a series of alkyl methylphosphonyl-acetylcholinesterases" Biochem. J. 100, (1966), pp 572–6.
27. Whitt, F. R.: "Silver and silver-lined chemical plant" Industr. Chem. 39, (1963), pp 310–3.
28. US Strategic Bombing Survey (Oil and Chemicals Division): "Powder, explosives, special rocket & jet propellants, war gases and smoke acid" Ministerial Report No. 1, (5 November, 1945), Exhibit CH.
29. Creasy, W. M.: "By-products disposal" Armed Forces Chem. J. 9 (3) 38, (1955).
30. Dubinin, M. M.: "Potentialities of chemical warfare" Bulletin of Atomic Scientists. 16, (1967), pp 250–51.
31. Lindsey, D.: "Selective malfunctioning of the human machine" Military Medicine 125, (1960), pp 598–605.
32. Imperial Chemical Industries Limited: "New basic esters of thiophosphonic acids and salts thereof" British Patent No. 797603, dated 4 June 1956.
33. Farbenfabriken Bayer AG: "Phosphonic acid esters" British Patent No. 847550, dated 23 June 1958.

34. FARBENFABRIKEN BAYER AG: "Verfahren zur Herstellung von N-substituierten Aminocyanphosphinsäure-bzw. — thiophosphinsäureestern" German Patent No. 767511, filed 22 July 1937.
35. US SECRETARY OF THE ARMY: "Decontaminating solution" United States Patent No. 3079346, issued 26 February 1963.
36. GENERAL ANILINE AND FILM CORPORATION: "Interhalogen products of polyvinyl pyrrolidone" United States Patent No. 2754245, issued 10 July 1956.
37. PETERS, R. A.: "Development and theoretical significance of British Anti-Lewisite (BAL)" British Medical Bulletin 5, (1948), pp 313–19.
38. The Times, 11 November, 1938, p 11. (Parliament: House of Commons: 10 November, 1938).
39. HILL, W.: "Improvements in or relating to projectiles, hand grenades and other means used for the purpose of attack or defence in operations of war" British Patent No. 8422/1915.
40. PERRY ROBINSON, J.: "Chemical warfare" Science Journal 3, (April, 1967), pp 33–40.
41. MCNAMARA, B.: "Mechanisms of incapacitation" CWL SP3 (1958), pp 167–170.
42. Contract No. CML–4564 between Chemical Corps Procurement Agency and Shell Development Company, California.
43. US DEPARTMENT OF THE ARMY: "Military Chemistry and chemical agents" Technical Manual TM 3–215 (December 1963).
44. ABOOD, L. G.; BIEL, J. H.: "Anticholinergic psychotomimetic agents" Internat. Rev. Neurobiol. 4, (1963). pp 217–273.
45. K–9 TRAINING AGENCY: "Training and use of dogs for CW detection" Final report on Contract No. DA 18–108–CML–6607.
46. FLEISHER, J. H.; FAYTOL, A. B.: "Effects of . . . . EPN on the toxicity of . . . . GB" Fed. Proc. 20, (1961), p 434.
47. ROZENGART, V. I.; BALASHOVA, E. K.: "Mechanism of 'aging' of cholinesterase inhibited by organophosphorus compounds" Dokl. Acad. Nauk. SSR. 164, (1965), pp 937–40.
48. MCDERMOT, H. L.; FINKBEINER, A. J.; WILLS, W. J.; HEGGIE, R. M.: "The enhancement of penetration of an organophosphorus anticholinesterase through guinea-pig skin by dimethylsulphoxide" Canadian Journal of Physiology and Pharmacology 45, (1967), pp 299–303.
49. STANFORD RESEARCH INSTITUTE: "Method of encapsulation of aerosols by in situ polymerization" United States Patent No. 3219476, issued 23 November, 1965.
50. US SECRETARY OF THE ARMY: "Light high explosive bomb for dispersing toxic and insecticidal aerosols" United States Patent No. 3207071, issued 21 September, 1965.
51. SHIRK, W. F.; MIRSHAK, W. G.: "Improvements in the 155 mm chemical shell, M121E1" DR–TR:2–61, Picatinny Arsenal, (July 1961).
52. COMINGS, E. W.: "Thermal generator munitions" Summary Technical Report, Division 10 NRDC, (1946), Vol. 1, Ch. 30.

N*

53. "Study, design, fabrication and test of Sergeant chemical warhead" American Service Technical Information Agency Document No. 427855.
54. US ARMY CB ENGINEERING GROUP: "Value analysis (value engineering)" ENGS No. SR-1 (December 1961, revised March 1963).
55. US SECRETARY OF THE ARMY "Barometric munition" United States Patent No. 3170398, issued 23 February 1965.
56. BAAR, J.: "Army seeks poison gas missiles" Missiles & Rockets (16 May, 1960), pp 10-11.
57. DUGWAY PROVING GROUND, UTAH: "500-lb, 1000-lb, 2000-lb, and 4000-lb bombs filled with nonpersistent agents" DPGMR 18, (2 June, 1944).
58. LT-GEN. THE (12TH) EARL OF DUNDONALD: "My Army Life" (Arnold, London, 1926), p 330.
59. AMERICAN CHEMICAL SOCIETY, SPECIAL COMMITTEE ON CIVIL DEFENCE: "Relative effects of CBW weapons" Advances in Chemistry No. 26, (1960), p 3.

CHAPTER 2

1. OSMOND, H.: Ann. N.Y. Acad. Sci., Vol. 66 (1957), p 418.
2. SHULGIN, A. T.; BUNNELL, S.; SARGENT, T.: Nature, Vol. 189, (1961), p. 1011.
3. URDIN, E.; EFRON, D. H.: "Psychotropic Drugs and Related Compounds," Washington, D.C.: Superintendent of Documents (1967).
4. SAMULENSON, R. J.: Science, Vol. 158, (1967) p 1031.
5. KLEIN, D. F.: Amer. J. Psychiat, Vol. 121, (1965) p 911.
6. JOYCE, C. R. B.: "Prediction from Man to Animals" in Animal Behaviour and Drug Action edited by STEINBERG, H. et al. (Churchill, London, 1964).
7. US DEPARTMENT OF THE ARMY, NAVY AND AIR FORCE: "Employment of Chemical and Biological Agents" Field Training Manual FM 3-10 (1966) Washington, D.C.
8. GUIGNARD, J. P. et al: Vietnam: Documents on Chemical and Bacteriological Warfare. (Dr P. Harvey, London, 1967).
9. GEHER, W. F.: Science Vol. 158, (1967), p 265.
10. IRWIN, S. AND EGOZENE, J.: Science Vol. 157, (1967), p 313.
11. ROBINSON, J. P.: "Chemical Warfare" Science Journal Vol. 3 pp 33-40 (April 1967).
12. DOWNING, D. W.: "Psychometric compounds" in Psychopharmacological Agents, ed. GORDON, M., Vol. 1 (Academic Press, London, 1964).
13. GOODMAN, L. S. and GILMAN, A.: Pharmacological Basis of Therapeutics" (Macmillan, New York, 1965).
14. JOCOBSEN, E.: "Hallucinogens" in Psychopharmacology: Dimensions and Perspectives, ed. JOYCE, C. R. B. (Tavistock, London, 1968).
15. WEISS, A. J. et al: Science Vol. 136 (1962), p. 151.

16. HOFFER, A.; OSMOND, H.: *The Hallucinogens* (Academic Press, New York 1967).
17. SIDEL, V. W.; GOLDWYN, R. M.: "Chemical Weapons: what they are and what they do" *Scientist and Citizen*, Vol. 9 (1967), pp 141–48.

CHAPTER 3

1. REICH, PETER; SIDEL, VICTOR W.: "Napalm" *New England Journal of Medicine 277*, (July 13, 1967), pp 86–88.
2. FIESER, L. F. *et al*: "Napalm" *Indust. and Engin. Chem. 38* (1946), pp 768–73.
3. FIESER, L. F.: *The Scientific Method: A Personal Account of Unusual Projects in War and in Peace* (Reinhold, N.Y. 1964).
4. "Napalm-B to Use Huge Amount of Polystyrene" *Chemical and Engineering News 44*: 24, (1966).
5. HOLLINGSWORTH, E. W.: "Use of Thickened Gasoline in Warfare" *Armed Forces Chemical Journal* 4: (June 1951), pp 26–32.
6. KLEBER, B. E. AND BIRDSELL, D.: *The Chemical Warfare Service: Chemicals in Combat* (U.S. Army, Washington, D.C. 1966), p 534.
7. ROTHSCHILD, S. H.: *Tomorrow's Weapons* (McGraw-Hill, New York 1964), pp. 189–93.
8. SANBORN, F. J.: "Fire Protection Lessons of the Japanese Attacks" in *Fire and the Air War*, ed. H. Bond, (National Fire Protection Association, Boston 1946). pp. 169–74.
9. "Napalm" *Armed Forces Chemical Journal 7*: (July 1953), pp 8–14.
10. HARVEY, FRANK: *Air War—Vietnam*. (Bantam Books, Inc., New York, 1967).
11. U.S. DEPARTMENT OF DEFENCE: *Emergency War Survey*: U.S. Armed Forces issue of NATO Handbook prepared for use by the Medical Services of NATO Nations. (U.S. Government Printing Office, Washington, D.C. 1959), pp. 23–25.
12. *The Times*, London, December 11, 1967.

CHAPTER 4

1. HEDEN, CARL-GÖRAN: "Defences against Biological Warfare", prepared with assistance of the Royal Swedish Academy of Engineering Sciences as a working document for the Pugwash Study Group on Biological Warfare, Mariánské Lázně/Czechoslovakia, May 13–20, 1967.
2. LANGER, ELINOR: "Chemical and Biological Weapons: once over lightly on Capitol Hill" *Science*, 155; (1967), pp. 1073–74.
3. MÁLEK, IVAN and RAŠKA, KAREL: "Some Problems of Disarmament in the Field of Biological Warfare" in the Proceedings of the eleventh Pugwash Conference on Science and World Affairs "Current Problems of Disarmament and World Security," Dubrovnik/Yugoslavia, September 20–25, 1963, pp 194–98.
4. ROSEBURY, THEODOR: *Peace or Pestilence* (Whittlesey House, New York, 1949).

5. Report of the International Scientific Commission for the Investigation of the Facts Concerning Bacterial Warfare in Korea and China. (Peking, 1952).
6. Proceedings of the sixteenth Pugwash Conference on Science and World Affairs. "Disarmament and World Security, Especially in Europe", Sopot/Poland, September 11–16, 1966, pp. 88–106. London.
7. Report of the Meeting of the Pugwash Study Group on Biological Warfare, Stockholm, September 4–6, 1967.

CHAPTER 5

1. DONNELLY, DIXON, ASSISTANT SECRETARY DEPARTMENT OF STATE: Letter to plant physiologists, *Bioscience* Vol. 17, (January 1967), p 10.
2. GALSTON, ARTHUR W. *et al*: Letter to President Johnson, *Bioscience* Vol. 17, (January 1967), p 10
3. LEWIN, RALPH A.: Personal communication with the author.
4. UPI Release, *New Haven Register* (December 18, 1966), p 29.
5. LANGER, ELINOR: "Chemical and Biological Warfare (II): The Weapons and the Policies" Science 155:303. These numbers were supplied to *Science* in January 1967 by the Pentagon.
6. *New York Times*, September 10, 1966.
7. *National Observer*, February 28, 1966.
8. "Drafting a Weed Killer" *Business Week*, April 22, 1967.
9. *The Pesticide Review* (U.S. Department of Agriculture, Washington, D.C., October, 1966).
10. *St. Louis Post-Dispatch*, July 11, 1967.
11. "Military Assistance Command in Vietnam" Answers to questions posed by *Farm Chemicals*, published in that journal, June, 1966, p 53.
12. *The Merck Index of Chemicals and Drugs* 7th edn (Merck and Co., Rahway, N.J., 1960), p 184.
13. CHANSLER, J. F. and PIERCE, D. A.: *Journal of Economic Entomology* 59:1357 (1966).
14. *Newsletter*, Society for Social Responsibility in Science (December 1965).
15. *Baltimore Sun*, January 15, 1967.
16. BURG, S. P. and BURG, E. A.: "The interaction between auxin and theylene and its role in plant growth." *Proc. Nat. Acad. Sci.* (U.S.) 55: (1966), p 262–69.
17. *New York Times*, July 25, 1966.
18. U.S. DEPARTMENT OF COMMERCE: United States Overseas Mission Report on defoliants in the Bien Hoa area. A.D. 824314.
19. *National Geographic* Vol. 131 (1967), p 191.
20. GEBOTT, MICHAEL D. "Thin Layer Chromatographic Technique for the Detection of Chlorophenols in Water Samples," *Solutions* 6:1, (June 1967).
21. CROSBY, D. G. AND TUCKER, K. R.: "Toxicity of aquatic herbicides to *Daphnia magna*." Science 154, (1966), pp 289–90.

22. AUDUS, L. J.: *The physiology and biochemistry of herbicides* (*Academic Press*, London and New York, 1964).
23. HORTON, BOB, in *The Minneapolis Star*, Sept. 8, 1967.

CHAPTER 6

1. Senate Committee on Foreign Relations, Subcommittee on Disarmament, "CBR Warfare and its Disarmament Aspects" (Washington, D.C. 1960).
2. DONNELLY, DIXON, ASSISTANT SECRETARY DEPARTMENT OF STATE. Letter to Arthur Galston and other plant physiologists, September 28, 1966. Published in full in *Bioscience*, (January 1967), p 10.
3. LANGER, ELINOR: "Chemical and Biological Warfare (II): The Weapons and the Policies" *Science*, 155:303. These numbers were supplied to *Science* in January 1967, by the Pentagon.
4. "Republic of Vietnam, Nutrition Survey, October-December, 1959." A Report by the Inter-departmental Committee on Nutrition for National Defense, July, 1960.
5. COLLINS, J. L.; ERVIN, FRANK; LEVI, VICKI; SAVITZ, DAVID: "Medical Problems of South Vietnam" Physicians for Social Responsibility, Boston, January, 1967.
6. UNITED NATIONS COMMISSION FOR ASIA AND THE FAR EAST: "Multi-Purpose River Basin Development, Part 2B Water Resources Development in Burma, India, and Pakistan" (Bangkok, December 1956).
7. PAKISTAN MINISTRY OF HEALTH (in collaboration with the University of Dacca and the U.S. Nutrition Section, Office of International Research, National Institutes of Health). "Nutrition Survey of East Pakistan, March, 1962—January, 1964" (U.S. Department of Health, Education and Welfare, May 1966).
8. *Pakistan 1955–56* (Pakistan Publications, Karachi, 1956).
9. WEITZEL, FRANK H.: "Testimony before Hearings of the Subcommittee to Investigate Problems Connected with Refugees and Escapees of the Committee on the Judiciary, United States Senate, Eighty-Ninth Congress, July 13–September 30, 1965." (U.S. Government Printing Office, 1965).
10. *New York Times,* October 9, 1966.
11. ARNETT, PETER; FAAS, HORST: "American Claims of Progress in Vietnam Disputed" *St. Louis Post-Dispatch* (AP), July 3, 1967.
12. RUSK, HOWARD: "Refugee Crisis in Vietnam," *New York Times,* September 12, 1965.
13. *Statistical Yearbook, 1966,* (U.N., 18th Issue, New York, 1967), p 277.
14. FALTERMAYER, EDMUND K.: "South Vietnam's Economy" *Fortune* March 1966, p 228.
15. "Refugee Problems in South Vietnam," *op. cit.,* p 137.
16. *Ibid.,* p 366.
17. BALDICK, ROBERT: *The Siege of Paris* (Batsford, London, 1964).

18. KRANZBERG, MELVIN: *The Siege of Paris, 1870–1, A Political and Social History* (Cornell University Press, Ithaca, New York, 1962).
19. KEYES, ANCEL, et al: *The Biology of Human Starvation* Vol. 1 and 2 (University of Minnesota Press, Minneapolis, 1950).
20. SCHREINER, GEORGE A.: *The Iron Ration* (Harper and Bros., N.Y., 1918).
21. WERTH, ALEXANDER: *Russia at War* (E. P. Dutton and Co., N.Y., 1964).
22. ANTONOV, A. N.: "Children Born During the Siege of Leningrad," *J. Pediatrics*, 30:250–59, 1947, quoted by Keyes.
23. MOHR, CHARLES: "U.S. Spray Planes Destroy Rice in Viet Cong Territory" *New York Times*, December 21, 1965.
24. ABC Broadcast, July 2, 1967.
25. BERG, GEN. WILLIAM W.: Letter to Senator Jacob K. Javits, May 18, 1966.
26. WELLES, BENJAMIN: "Pentagon Backs Use of Chemicals," *New York Times*, September 21, 1966.
27. "Republic of Vietnam Nutrition Study," pp. 1, 62, 85.
28. "Refugee Problems in South Vietnam and Laos," p. 134. [This refers, of course, to only the rural areas under Saigon control.]
29. Quoted in *Blockade and Sea Power* M. Parmalee (T.Y. Crowell Co., New York, 1924).

CHAPTER 7

1. ROTHSCHILD, J. H.: *Tomorrow's Weapons*, (McGraw-Hill, New York, 1964).
2. PRENTISS, A. M.: *Chemicals in War* (McGraw-Hill, New York 1937).
3. *New York Times*, March 25, 1965.
4. *Time*, April 2, 1965.
5. FAAS, HORST; WHITE, EDWIN: Associated Press, 10th January, 1966.
6. AMETT, PETER: Associated Press, 12 January, 1966.
7. *New York Times*, January 13th 1966.
8. The pathological report based on studies of CS, performed in Professor Roussel's laboratory of industrial and environmental toxicity in Paris, was made available to conference participants, but is technical in nature and is not included in this text. It describes the lethal effects of Dr Kahn's sample on laboratory mice.
9. Dr J. P. Vigier, Senior Investigator, CNRS, member of IWCT.
10. SIDEL, V. and GOLDWYN, R.: *New England Journal of Medicine*, Vol. 277. (1967).
11. ROTHSCHILD, J. H.: "Chemical and Biological Warfare in Vietnam" *Science*, 167 (April 1967).
12. PUNTE, C. L. et al: *Toxicology and Applied Pharmacology* 4 (1962 pp 656–662.
13. —— *Archives of Environmental Health* 6 (1963), pp 366–374.

14. LACOMBE, A.; FARRIAUX, J. P.; FONTAINE, B.; MULLER, P.M.: *Revue de Pédiatrie* III (4) (1967), pp 207–13.

CHAPTER 9

1. BBC TV Programme, BBC–2, 25 April, 1967, *Horizon;* "The shape of war to come".
2. Ministry of Defence Press release, Ptn/AT 3001/2868/64. "The Chemical Defence Experimental Establishment, Ministry of Defence, Porton."
3. "New developments: CB protective garment" *Ordnance,* Vol. 51 (1966) p 304.
4. DAVIES, D. R.; GREEN, A. L.: "The chemotherapy of poisoning by organophosphate anticholinesterases." *Brit. J. Indust. Med,* Vol. 16 (1959), pp 128–34.
5. WAR OFFICE "Improvements in or relating to hypodermic injecttion apparatus" British Patent No. 915262, dated 29 January 1959.
6. —— "Improvements in apparatus for controlling riots" British Patent No. 967660, dated 14 November 1962.
7. BROPHY, L. P.; MILES, W. D.; COCHRANE, R. C.: "The Chemical Warfare Service: from laboratory to field" (Department of the Army, Washington, D.C. 1959).
8. SMITH, GORDON C. E.: "The Microbiological Research Establishment, Porton," *Chemistry & Industry* (1967), pp 33–46.
9. THE MICROBIOLOGICAL RESEARCH ESTABLISHMENT: "Abstracts of Published Work, 1964."
10. STANLEY, J. L.; SMITH, H.: "The three forms of anthrax toxin: their immunogenicity and lack of demonstrable enzymic activity" *J. gen. Microbiol.* Vol. 31 (1963), pp 329–37.
11. SMITH, H.; KEPPIE, J.; PEARCE, J. H.; FULLER, R.; WILLIAMS, A. E.: "Chemical basis of virulence of *Br. abortus.* I. Isolation of Br abortus from borine foetal tissue." *Brit. J. exp. Path.* Vol. 42 (1961), pp 631–37.
12. DIXON, B. "What are they up to at Porton Down?" *New Scientist* Vol. 32 (1966), pp 558–59.
13. *J. gen. Microbiol.* Vol. 45 (1966), p 2.
14. CLARKE, R: "The secret arms race", *Weekend Telegraph* 22 March, 1967.
15. *Times* 23 March, 1954, p 3 (Parliament, Commons, 22 March, 1954).
16. *Times,* 12 March, 1954, p 8 "Germ Warfare defence."
17. *Times,* 23 June, 1954, p 8. "Germ Warfare tests".
18. SNYDER, F. M.; CHADWICK, L. E.: "Lethality of G.F. and G.B. vapour to fruitflies, etc . . . ." MLRR 201, Edgewood Arsenal (July 1957).
19. CRESTHULL, P., CHRISTENSEN, M. K. and OBERST, F. W.: "Estimated speed of action of GB vapour for death and various degrees of incapacitation in man" CRDLR 3050, Edgewood Arsenal (January 1961).

200   CHEMICAL AND BIOLOGICAL WARFARE

20. "Protocol for the prohibition of the use in war of asphyxiating poisonous or other gases, and of bacteriological methods of warfare: Geneva, June 17, 1925." Cnd 3604 (Treaty series No. 24, 1930).
21. *Times* 7 September, 1945, p 2 "Poison-gas dumped in the sea."
22. *Times* 17 September 1948, p 2 "Disposal of Chemical ammunition."
23. *Times* 10 March, 1960, p 4 "Dangerous Cargo."
24. Hansard Vol. 620, Column 164 (31 March, 1960) (Written answer to questions).
25. ROBINSON, J. P.: "Chemical Warfare" *Science Journal,* Vol. 3, (April, 1967), pp 33–40.
26. CLARKE, R.: *We All Fall Down: the Prospect of Chemical and Biological Warfare* (Allen Lane, The Penguin Press, 1968).
27. ANDERSON, E. S.: "Transferable drug resistance" *Science Journal* Vol. 4 (April 1968), pp 71–76.
28. MINISTRY OF SUPPLY: "Improvements in or relating to the preparation of dithiol compounds" British Patent No. 579971, dated 15 April, 1943.
29. NATIONAL RESEARCH AND DEVELOPMENT COUNCIL: "Artificial breathing machine," British Patent No. 828731, dated 5 June, 1958.
30. ——"Improvements in apparatus for sampling porticulate clouds," British Patent No. 580705, dated 13 September, 1945.
31. ——"Improvements in or relating to air sampling apparatus", British Patent No. 1081881, dated 14 April, 1966.
32. MINISTRY OF SUPPLY: "Improvements in or relating to spray-producing and atomizing means" British Patent No. 629686, dated 31 July, 1948.
33. ——"A process for the preparation of esters of fluorophosphonic acids and chlorophosphonic esters," British Patent No. 601210, dated 12 February, 1948.
34. NATIONAL RESEARCH AND DEVELOPMENT COUNCIL: "Improvements in plague vaccines" British Patent No. 1020531, dated 2 March, 1962.
35. MINISTRY OF SUPPLY: "Improved process for the manufacture of organic phosphorus compounds" British Patent No. 810930, dated 4 March, 1955.
36. ——"Improvements in or relating to the production of organic phosphorus compounds" British Patent No. 707961, dated 20 May, 1949.
37. WAR OFFICE: "Improvements in the manufacture of dialkyl alkylphosphonothionates," British Patent No. 897698, dated 9 September, 1959.
38. MINISTRY OF SUPPLY: "Manufacture of monoalkyl alkylphosphoro-fluoridite" United States Patent No. 2957017, issued 18 October, 1960.
39. NATIONAL RESEARCH AND DEVELOPMENT COUNCIL: "Process for preparing dialkyl alkylphosphonothionates" United States Patent No. 3035081, issued 15 May 1962.

40. *Times,* 14 and 24 March, 1962, (parliamentary papers).
41. Hansard Vol. 620, Columns 1322–3 (30 March, 1960), (oral answers to questions).
42. *Times,* 8 March, 1960, p 12 "Pressure in U.S. for chemical weapons"
43. POSTAN, M. M., HAY, D., and SCOTT, J. D.: *Design and Development of Weapons* (H.M.S.O. 1964).
44. *e.g.,* JACKSON, J. B.: "Development of decontaminating solution DS–2" CWLR 2368.
45. Technical Abstracts Bulletin (ASTIA): Cumulative Index, January—December, 1961.
46. SCHNEIR, W.: "The Campaign to make chemical warfare respectable" *The Reporter* 1 October, 1959, pp 24–8.
47. *e.g.,* BOOZE-ALLEN APPLIED RESEARCH INC.: Quarterly Interim Report No. 16, 31 July, 1961 on Contract No. DA 18–064–Cml–206.
48. *e.g.,* ARMOUR RESEARCH FOUNDATION: "Aerosol studies with bacteriophage." Report for 25 January—8 February, 1960 on Contract No. DA 18–064–404–Cml–353.
49. *e.g.,* GORDON, K.: "Information on poison gas manufacture in Germany." Office of the Publication Board, PB report No. 12.
50. *e.g.,* "Intelligence report on Japanese chemical warfare, Vol. III" B.I.O.S./J.A.P./P.R./395 (1 March, 1946).
51. BUTLIN, K. R.: "Prospecting in industrial microbiology" *New Scientist* Vol. 13 (1962), pp. 804–6.
52. "The position of the Porton laboratory" *New Scientist,* 16 August, 1962.
53. Hansard Vol. 530, Column 19–20, 12 July, 1954, (oral answers to questions).
54. Hansard, Col 1026, 8 November, 1967, (oral answers to questions).

CHAPTER 10

1. *U.S. Field Manual:* 101–40, (1962), p 10.
2. LANGER, E.: *Science,* 155, 174–179 (1967).
3. Quoted by S. Hersch in *Chemical & Biological Warfare.* (Bobbs-Merrill, New York, 1968). MacGibbon & Kee, London, 1968.
4. LANGER, E. *Science,* 155, 299–305, (1967).

CHAPTER 11

1. ROBINSON, J. P.: "Chemical Warfare" *Science Journal* (April 1967). p 33–400.
2. ROTHSCHILD, J. H.: *Tomorrow's Weapons* (McGraw-Hill, New York, 1964).
3. ARKHANGELSKY *et al. Bacteriological Weapons and how to defend against them* (Moscow Military Publishing House, 1967).

CHAPTER 12

1. *The Law of War on Land* (H.M.S.O. 1958 edn, Part III).
2. See below—"Incendiary Weapons".
3. HUDSON, M. O.: *International Legislation* Vol. II (New York, 1931), p 794.
4. The date of ratification has some significance since it is close to the date of signature of the Geneva Protocol (see below). See also the resolution, supported by the United States, 3 May 1923, J. B. Scott, *The International Conferences of American States* (New York, 1931), p 290. This resolution made express reference to the provision of the Treaty of Washington.
5. See OPPENHEIM, L.: *International Law*, Vol. II, 7th edition, (London 1952), p 344; SCHWARZENBERGER, G.: *The Legality of Nuclear Weapons* (London 1952), p 38.
   Note also the Hague Declaration Respecting Asphyxiating Gases, signed 29th July, 1899; United Kingdom, *Manual of Military Law*, Part III (1958), p 199.
6. United Kingdom, *Manual of Military Law*, Part III (1958), p 216.
7. For other condemnations of chemical warfare see the Resolution of the General Commission of the Disarmament Conference, 23 July, 1932; Resolution of the League Council, 14 May, 1938; Resolution of the League Assembly, 30 September, 1938; Final Act of the Consultative Meeting of American Foreign Ministers of the American Republics, 23 September—3 October, 1939, item vi. See also Convention on the Limitation of Armaments of Central American States, 1923, article 5, M. O. Hudson, *International Legislation*, Vol. II, p 942.
8. International Law Reports, Vol. 32, p 626.
9. 1956 edition.
10. *International Law Situations*, U.S. Naval War College, 1935, p 106. See further HYDE C. C.: *International Law*, 2nd edn, Vol. III (Boston, 1945), paragraph 662A.
11. The statement is also printed in *International Law Documents*, U.S. Naval War College, 1942, p 85.
12. See *U.S. Department of State Bulletin*, Vol. 27 (1952) p 641.
13. *U.N. Monthly Chronicle*, December 1966, p 32; U.N. General Assembly, Off. Recs., 21st session, supplement No. 16 (A/6316), p 11.
14. For a standard account of the law see the United Kingdom *Manual of Military Law*, Part III, Chapters I and V.
15. *Ibid.*, p 224.
16. *Ibid.*, p 272.
17. For recent surveys of the law and literature see MEYROWITZ: *Annuaire francais de droit international*, 1964, p 81; O'BRIEN: in *Georgetown Law Journal*, Vol. 5 (1962) p 1; MORRIS GREENSPAN: *The Modern Law of Land Warfare* (University of California Press, 1959).
18. Parliamentary Paper, Misc. No. 17 (1930) Cmd. 3747.

19. On *jus cogens see* BROWNLIE, I.: *Principles of Public International Law* (O.U.P. 1966).
20. *Department of State Bulletin*, Vol. 12, p 222.
21. Resolution 95. See further SCHWELB: *British Year Book of International Law* (O.U.P. 1946), p 178.
22. See United Kingdom *Manual of Military Warfare, Part III*, p 217 and information in amendments to the *Manual*.
23. Writer's italics.
24. Cross-reference.
25. Though effects overlap, explosives and incendiary weapons are not classified together with Nuclear weapons. On nuclear weapons see BROWNLIE, in *International and Comparative Law Quarterly*, Vol. 14 (1965), p 437.
26. United Kingdom *Manual of Military Warfare* part III, paragraph 100, note 1. See also the *U.S. Army Field Manual*, paragraph 36, quoted above.
27. Protocol III on the Control of Armaments. Parties are Belgium, France, the Federal Republic of Germany, Italy, Luxembourg, the Netherlands, and the United Kingdom.

CHAPTER 14

1. ROSEBURY, THEODOR: "Medical Ethics and Biological Warfare" *Perspectives in Biology and Medicine* 6: 512–523, Summer, 1963.
2. SIDEL, VICTOR W. AND GOLDWYN, ROBERT M.: "Chemical and Biologic Weapons—A Primer" *New England Journal of Medicine* 274: 21–27 (6 January, 1966).
3. GOLDWYN, ROBERT M. AND SIDEL, VICTOR W.: "The Physician and War" in TORRAY, E. FULLER, ed. *Ethical Issues in Medicine: The Role of the Physician in Today's Society* Little, Brown & Co. Boston.
4. LANGER, ELINOR: "Chemical and Biological Warfare" in *Science* 155: 174–79, 299–305, 1967.
5. MAYER, C. F. (Editorial): "The Hippocratic Oath, The Pledge of Geneva, and ABC Warfare" in *Military Surgeon*: 369, (1952).
6. HARTFORD, J. T.: "Medical Defense Against Biological Weapons" in *Military Medicine* 128: 145, (1963).
7. BRINCKER, J. A. H.: "Historical, Epidemiological and Aetiological Study of Measles" *Proc. Roy. Soc. Med.* 31: 807–828, 1938.
8. CLARKE, R.: "Biological Warfare" in *Science Journal* (November, 1966).
9. U.S. DEPARTMENT OF HEALTH, EDUCATION AND WELFARE: *Effects of Biological Warfare Agents.* (U.S. Government Printing Office, Washington, D.C.,) July, 1959.
10. NOPAR, ROBERT E. "Plagues on Our Children: The Threat of Biological Warfare" in *Clinical Pediatrics* 6; 63–73 (February, 1967).
11. IRISH, D. P. AND McMURRAY, D. W.: "Professional Oaths and American Medical Colleges" *J. Chron. Dis.* 18: 275–289 (1965).

12. WORLD MEDICAL ASSOCIATION: *Code of Ethics in Wartime* (World Medical Association, New York, 1956).
13. FOX, THEODORE: "Purposes of Medicine" *Lancet II*: 801 (1965).
14. UNITED STATES ARMY: *Medical Service Theater of Operations, Field Manual FM8–10.* (Department of the Army, Washington, D.C., November, 1959). p 17.
15. FISHBEIN, M.: *Doctors at War* (E. P. Dalton, New York, 1945), p 3.
16. UNITED STATES ARMY: *Lectures of the Geneva Convention of 1949, 20–151.* (Department of The Army, Washington, D.C., April, 1958).
17. LANGER, ELINOR: "The Court-Martial of Captain Levy: Medical Ethics v. Military Law" in *Science* 156: 1346–50, 1967.
18. GLASSER, IRA: "Judgment at Fort Jackson: The Court-Martial of Captain Howard B. Levy" in *Law in Transition Quarterly III*: (September 1967), pp 123–56.
19. RYLE, JOHN A., Foreword in JOULES, H., ed.: *The Doctor's View of War* (George Allen and Unwin Ltd., 1939), pp 7–10.
20. Editorial: "Brutalities of Nazi Physicians" *J. Am. Med. Ass.*, 714, (1946).

Glossary

This short glossary defines those technical words and phrases that appear in the text but which are *not* defined there. Formulae of chemicals, or names of microbial organisms, which are referred to only *passim* are also not included.

Adamsite. Yellow irritating smoke containing arsenic.

Aerosol. Dispersion of fine droplets of a liquid in the atmosphere.

Anthrax. Malignant fever of sheep or cattle, or of humans infected by them; often fatal.

Antibody. Molecule produced as part of the body's natural defence against infection; it has the property of binding onto the surface of foreign particles or cells.

Asphyxia. Extreme condition resulting from oxygen lack and excess carbon dioxide in the bloodstream.

Atropine. Poisonous crystalline alkaloid which interferes with certain types of nervous stimulation. Under some conditions, in low concentrations, it can serve as an *antidote* to the anticholinesterase nerve gases.

Auxins. Plant hormones responsible for growth and leaf retention.

Avitaminosis. Debilitated condition caused by insufficient vitamin intake— often results from prolonged starvation or undernutrition.

Beri-Beri. Disease of the peripheral nerves due to lack of Vitamin B_1, common in tropical countries. The symptoms are body swelling and pain in the extremities.

Botulism, botulinus toxin. Fatal poisoning of the nervous system caused by the toxic product of a bacteria, clostidium botulinum.

Brucellosis. Bacterial infection which can cause abortion in animals and remittent fever in man.

Ecology. Study of the relationship between organisms and their environment.

ED_{50}. Dose of an agent (generally non-lethal) which is effective against half the population exposed.

Emetic. An agent which induces vomiting.

Enzyme. A biochemical substance (protein) which acts as a catalyst, changing the speed of a chemical reaction without itself being used up in the process.

In vitro. Biological term implying an experiment conducted in an artificial environment ("in glass", *i.e.*, a test tube).

Lachrymator. Substance which causes shedding of tears.

Laterization. An almost irreversible process whereby tropical soil exposed to the sun becomes converted to a hard, brick-like rock.

Lethal Dose. Dose of an agent sufficient to kill.

Lethal Dose$_{(50)}$ or LD$_{(50)}$. Dose of an agent which is lethal against half the population exposed.

Lewisite. Chemical warfare agent with blistering action.

Mg/metre^3. Measurement of the concentration of an agent as milligrams (thousandths of a gram) per cubic metre.

Mg/metre³/min. Measurement of the exposure to an agent; as exposure of a given number of minutes to a given concentration.

Necrosis. Death of a piece of tissue or an organ.

Neuritis. Inflammation of the nerve causing pain.

Non-pathogenic (of a micro-organism). Not causing disease.

Pathogenic (of a micro-organism). Causing disease or death.

Percutaneous. Effected through the skin.

Prophylaxis. Prevention of disease.

Psychotomimetic. Substance whose effects are similar to those of mental illness, *e.g.*, schizophrenia.

Psychotropic. Substance which acts upon the central nervous system causing effects on behaviour.

Pulmonary oedema. Swelling of the tissue of the lungs with results usually associated with bad circulation.

Pyrotechnic charge. A munition containing smoke-producing chemicals.

Sequellae. Abnormal condition resulting from previous disease.

Subcutaneous. Introduced below skin.

Tolerance. Phenomenon whereby with repetitive doses of a drug increasingly large concentrations are required to produce the same result.

Cross-tolerance. When doses of one drug produce tolerance to another.

Toxic. Acting as or having the effects of a poison.

Toxicity. Measure of the dose of a toxic agent required to produce a toxic effect.

Ugr. Microgram, *i.e.*, millionth of a gram.

Vector. An animal, insect, or other organism that carries and transmits a virus or other micro-organism.

Index